GRATITUDE, INJURY, AND REPAIR IN A PANDEMIC AGE

GRATITUDE, INJURY, AND REPAIR IN A PANDEMIC AGE

An Interreligious Dialogue

EDITED BY

MICHAEL REID TRICE AND

PATRICIA O'CONNELL KILLEN

GEORGETOWN UNIVERSITY PRESS / WASHINGTON, DC

Cataloging-in-Publication Data is on file with the Library of Congress.

ISBN 978-1-64712-479-3 (hardcover)
ISBN 978-1-64712-480-9 (paperback)
ISBN 978-1-64712-481-6 (ebook)

∞ This paper meets the requirements of ANSI/NISO Z39.48-1992 (Permanence of Paper).

26 25 9 8 7 6 5 4 3 2 First printing

Printed in the United States of America

Cover design by Jeremy John Parker
Interior design by Westchester

CONTENTS

Introduction 1
Michael Reid Trice and Patricia O'Connell Killen

1 Reflections on Gratitude, Injury, and Restoration in a Pandemic Age 5
Mona Siddiqui

2 Dislocating Gratitude: A Meditation from a Blasted Mountain 18
Patricia O'Connell Killen

3 "Grateful to the Proselyte": Jews among Gentiles in an Age of Injury 35
Nathanael Vette

4 Conflicting Civil Religions: Bellah, Lincoln, and the Alt-Right—Today's American Dilemma 52
James Spickard

5 On Not Letting a Pandemic Go to Waste: Theory for the Sick and Dying 76
Susan Abraham

6 Interdependence, Gratitude, and Justice: Hindu Perspectives 97
Anantanand Rambachan

7 Gratitude as a Revolutionary Act of Resistance 114
Edward Donalson III

8 Marked by 2020: Disorientation and Reorientation in a Pandemic Age 129
Jaisy A. Joseph

9 Trauma, Post-traumatic Growth, and Gratitude in the Time of the COVID-19 Pandemic 143
Kristi A. Lee

10 Traumatic Ontology: COVID-19—Epochal, Societal, and Personal Transformation 155
Douglas F. Peduti, SJ

11 Our Pandemic Age, Relationships, and Forgetting 173
Michael Reid Trice

List of Contributors 185

Index 189

INTRODUCTION

Michael Reid Trice and Patricia O'Connell Killen

In April 2021, a bit more than a year after the World Health Organization declared COVID-19 a global pandemic, thirteen scholars on two continents gathered—virtually, of course—to begin collaborative work on an interreligious study project hosted by the Center for Ecumenical and Interreligious Engagement (CEIE) at Seattle University that was titled "Gratitude to God, Sacred Texts, Injury and Restoration."[1] Originally conceived in the world before COVID, the project sought to understand what religious traditions say about the stability of divine-human relationships when life is painful in deeply personal and societal ways. Guiding questions included: What are the rituals for restoring the damaged divine-human relationship? If, through stages of life, stories of the divine provide succor and orientation in times of adversity, how is this true? And in what ways do sacred texts situate human experiences and expressions of gratitude in the face of an unjust or seemingly ambivalent cosmos? Scholar participants were tasked to consider these questions with, against, and within a sacred text of their choosing.

As expressed so powerfully in that April symposium's formal opening comments from Dr. Mona Siddiqui (whose work begins this collection), what we all had been living through and would continue to undergo throughout the two years of our collaboration made it impossible to pursue the project in its initially conceived form. Another interlocutor had joined us around our virtual table—the pandemic. We as scholars and human beings could not pretend otherwise. So as we incorporated the pandemic into our considerations, we realized the need to add a fourth term to our grappling, what Dr. Michael Trice identified as our "pandemic age," a concept he treats in the chapter that concludes this volume. During our conversations, "restoration" also became "repair." Given the scale of death and suffering and their uneven impact upon Black and Brown bodies—compounded by the murders of Ahmaud Arbery, Breonna Taylor, and George Floyd in the winter and spring of 2020—restoring what at one time was understood to be whole no longer seemed plausible (nor in many cases even desirable); repairing what was seriously broken might be.

Gratitude, Injury, and Repair in a Pandemic Age: An Interreligious Dialogue, then, is more than collected writings that grapple with these human experiences and their interrelationships. It explores these experiences and the theological, philosophical, psychological, ethical, and sociological links among them from the vantage of a chosen text. The chapters also display in real time how scholars, alone and together, think in a world upended by massive disruption, suffering, and death.

As singular offerings, the chapters that follow reveal the human being in the scholar; the reader experiences each author as self-aware of gratitude, injury, and repair in the pandemic age and, after sustained intrapersonal reflection, making interpretive choices including metaphors and theories to make meaning in a moment when life confronts us so clearly as partial, fragmented, and fragile. These were scholarly and existential moves on the part of the participants. Their work was never a purely theoretical exercise, and it required personal commitment at key points where any lesser response would diminish the reality of an illness that was perforating daily life, or otherwise would risk generalizing ongoing death, or would make any number of additional moral miscalculations. Scholars at moments struggled, within the limits of language, to explain their experience and their thinking, which renders the whole volume both a collective study on its topic and a volume worthy of a study on the collective will and creative act of scholarship during an enveloping global crisis of the magnitude of a pandemic.

As a collection, the chapters reflect a creative and determined spirit of discernment and a deep commitment to the experience of thinking and writing through a global emergency. The relationships among gratitude, injury, and repair across varied religious traditions constitute a complex theme, and it will be no surprise that the contributors' pieces express a range of understandings on each theme and their interrelationships and, on some points, reveal sharp tensions. Together, the chapters exemplify thinking with and through religious texts amid disruption and demonstrate the participants' flexibility and mutual discernment in conducting scholarly discourse under trying circumstances.

HOW TO READ THE CHAPTERS

Each chapter is a free-standing essay, so they need not be read serially. All grapple with gratitude, injury, and repair, and their interrelationship in a pandemic age; each chapter has its own distinct emphasis. The chapters do, however, have recognizable affinities of approach or a foregrounded concept. For convenience and accessibility, the chapters are ordered by these affinities. The first cluster—the chapters by Patricia O'Connell Killen, Nathanael Vette, James Spickard, and Susan Abraham—takes a diachronic approach to the project's overarching question and concepts. Working with quite different historical frameworks, each chapter tackles the topic by comparison with some prior natural, epidemiological, or political disruption to provide purchase on the relationship among the project's key concepts.

The second cluster—those chapters by Anantanand Rambachan, Edward Donalson III, and Jaisy A. Joseph—grapples with gratitude, injury, and repair in relation to racialized injustice, a reality of our age that the pandemic throws into stark relief in the United States and around the world. These chapters interrogate racialized injustice from unique local perspectives and racialized global contexts. The authors show how the pandemic discloses, conceals, aggravates, or gestures to a possible way forward in which society could try to repair or ameliorate a form of structural injustice.

The third cluster—the chapters by Kristi A. Lee and Douglas F. Peduti—provides concrete or practical interpretations of the pandemic, foregrounding trauma and multiple modes of recovery, repair, and coping. In these chapters, the injurious features of trauma remind the reader that a global pandemic does not conclude when an international agency, such as the World Health Organization, declares that a global viral pandemic has ended. The current mental health epidemic is painful evidence of this fact.

Finally, Michael Trice's conclusion to the volume develops the theme of a pandemic age and foregrounds an additional theme that runs like a deep current through many of the essays and captures the developmental task for all in this time—namely, spiritual forgetfulness and remembering.

NOTE ON THE CENTER FOR ECUMENICAL AND INTERRELIGIOUS ENGAGEMENT AT SEATTLE UNIVERSITY

The Center for Ecumenical and Interreligious Engagement is part of the Office of the Provost at Seattle University, one of twenty-seven Jesuit universities in the United States and 189 colleges and universities worldwide. The center's mission includes creating educational opportunities that respond to the challenges of our time and convening scholarly conversations and programs that exemplify excellence in the art of encounter and discovery at the heart of the Ignatian heritage.

Among initiatives it undertakes to enact this mission, the center regularly convenes groups of scholars across disciplines to study, to reflect, to deliberate and converse, and to provide responses to the significant issues and challenges of our time. These convenings follow an Ignatian way of proceeding.[2] The groups commit to two multiday meetings. At the first, participants respond to previously circulated brief concept or thought pieces. At a subsequent convening, participants respond to each other's draft papers, having both read and reflected on them before the meeting. This process aims for insightful, honest, sense making and discernment. It is grounded in the insights of Ignatius of Loyola, the founder of the Society of Jesus. All of the chapters of *Gratitude, Injury, and Repair in a Pandemic Age: An Interreligious Dialogue* are part of the CEIE Scholars Convenings on the topic as described.

For more information about the center and its initiatives, please go to www.seattleu.edu/ceie/ or contact its Director and Spehar-Halligan Professor, Dr. Michael Reid Trice, at tricem@seattleu.edu.

NOTES

1. Generous support from the Henry Luce Foundation made the project possible.
2. The term "Ignatian" comes from the name of the founder of the Society of Jesus (the Jesuits), Ignatius of Loyola, who established the society in 1539–40. Discernment is central to the Society of Jesus and to its educational work at all levels: teaching, scholarship, and administration.

CHAPTER 1

Reflections on Gratitude, Injury, and Restoration in a Pandemic Age

Mona Siddiqui

I am humbled to have been invited to write this reflection for the conference on Gratitude, Injury, and Restoration in a Pandemic Age. Since 2019 I have been researching gratitude from a theological, philosophical, and political perspective for a personal research project; however, I had not explored the meanings of injury and restoration as an intellectual endeavor. Yet as I began to give these concepts scholarly attention, I realized that so much of our personal lives and our lived experiences are exactly about these sentiments. Injury and restoration are relational concepts about how we salvage and sustain communication and goodness when harm has been done or trust has been broken. That which harms or degrades us is never easily forgotten. The search for restoration after any injury compels us to look inward, to reset our boundaries, and to reflect on what can be repaired and what remains irreparable.

In this reflective chapter, I refer to some of the writings of my colleagues who have thought about these themes deeply. Their beautifully written, thoughtful reflections from a diverse range of disciplines manage to encapsulate the challenges we face as we explore the varying dimensions of the conference's themes. Drawing on a range of events, I decided to divide my work into an overlapping structure with reflections on gratitude, injury, and restoration in the context of the ongoing pandemic alongside my own personal journey over the last two years.

At the time of our first online gathering in the spring of 2020, the world was dealing with the full measures of lockdown and social restrictions brought about by COVID-19. We were also just emerging from Easter, which is theologically a period of restoration, reconciliation, and hope. In a vibrant conversation in *The Christian Century* with William H. Willimon, the academic and pastor, Richard Lischer draws a parallel between Holy Saturday and the waiting associated with the coronavirus. He writes:

> Holy Saturday is no one's favorite religious holiday. It lacks the darkness and the drama of a dying Savior. Nor is it bathed in light to celebrate a risen Lord. Its color is a liminal gray. But it's where we are, all of us. It's the season that we are in. . . . In the world of the coronavirus, we are also waiting. But waiting for what? . . . In a time of contagion, our waiting does not appear to be enriched by hope. . . . Our waiting has an intransitive feel. "For what?" is hard to answer. For it to be over.[1]

Drawing on the Easter story in our conference, Jaisy Joseph said that "the full story recognizes the human condition caught between the agony of Good Friday and the glory of Easter Sunday—of life persisting through death, good amidst evil, and light in the darkness. From the lens of Holy Saturday, the possibility of gratitude after 2020 can only make sense within a narrative of persistence." For Jaisy, humankind must recognize and live with the disorientation of social injuries and traumas. In chapter 8, she uses the Gospel of John to explore the resurrection encounter of Thomas the Apostle with the crucified-and-risen Jesus. But even as we begin to reorient ourselves after any trauma, as with the experience of disorientation after 2020, the capacity to wound one another remains.

Over the last two years, much of the world has recognized that COVID-19 and its varying mutations continue to disrupt our lives. It has made me reflect on whether life can ever be restored to its former uninhibited freedoms, and if not, then what is it we are waiting, persevering, and indeed hoping for? When economic, psychological, ecological, and emotional concerns have become so intertwined as in the past year, how does one persevere with uncertainty? Uncertainty is no longer a philosophical concern, a struggle that for the stoics and epicureans of the classical world was a way to find the means of living well rather than to seek knowledge or wisdom for their own sake. Nor is it about the torments and the awkwardness of human existence that for Søren Kierkegaard ultimately meant taking a leap of faith into the arms of God. Today, uncertainty in our relationships, in our professional lives, in our health systems, and in our politics has created a marked level of anxiety. Uncertainty is also more than personal and societal distrust of our political and public institutions; rather, it points to a kind of fragmentation in society where our struggle to find meaning has become more acute.

This theme of uncertainty has historically been approached from a variety of angles and disciplines; however, much of the literature vacillates between a nostalgic sense of loss and the human struggle for a just and more healing vision of society. For many social and cultural theorists, there is a certain malaise of contemporary culture that, as Charles Taylor writes, "people experience as a loss or decline, even as our civilization 'develops.'"[2]

Against the rising uncertainties of our lives, living with the impact of COVID-19 has forced us to acknowledge the lack of human control and finitude. As certain as death is to human life, the human desire to control our surroundings and our destinies has not diminished. When lockdowns became a global phenomenon from March 2020 forward, we began living amid the first mass trauma event in several decades. Trauma here does not refer to a sudden event or a violent experience; it is more gradual and subtle. In a recent article for the BBC, Ed Prideaux writes:

> Trauma is a far subtler concept than many of us realise. It isn't just a word for something extremely stressful. It doesn't always come from short, sharp shocks like car accidents, terrorist attacks, or firefights. And, trauma isn't the same thing as post-traumatic stress disorder (PTSD). What trauma *is* about is events and their effect on the mind. But what separates it from something merely stressful is how we relate to these events on a deep level of belief.[3]

COVID-19 is an example of mass trauma with illness and bereavement everywhere, as well as the constant warning that our medical services may become overwhelmed. As Douglas Peduti writes, "In short, we are in a state of trauma from many trajectories." It is a trauma that has been universally shared, including by those who have never or will never catch the virus. It is also a trauma built on a paradox of the positive and the negative. People had more time to spend with their families, but anxieties increased. Many lost their jobs, even became destitute, while others managed to increase their savings. While people process trauma differently and respond to it with varying levels of resilience, trauma lingers in our lives. It lingers through the stories we tell of our experiences and the events we choose to remember.

I see gratitude as a response to human vulnerability and the vicissitudes of life. I see injury as a rupture, something that breaks in us and that always leaves its mark. A rupture, a break with the past whether voluntary or imposed, always demands a new beginning of sorts. COVID-19 has forced many of us to evaluate our future, and in that process, we have been obliged to rethink our past and present.

But rupture is not new. Many religious traditions understand rupture as a metaphor for all human earthly life. The most significant Qur'anic story signifying rupture is the expulsion of Adam and Eve from paradise. The Qur'anic equivalent of the Genesis story is a paradigm of the breaking out from innocence to disobedience, from desire to knowledge. Adam gives into Iblīs's seduction and temptation, thereby making his first act of freedom an act of ingratitude and human vulnerability. But this ingratitude goes deeper; it is a turning away, a repudiation of God and divine attention and care. Yet this dramatic entry of sin and disobedience into the world is a story of human struggle; it is a struggle from the fear of the unseen and Adam's longing for God to reestablish their former relationship of love and dialogue. Human beings remain God's creatures, seeking his mercy, but they are now creatures with a different purpose and a different future.

Restoration therefore is not a return but a moving forward. In March 2020, the United Kingdom was one of many countries in its first lockdown, and I, like millions of others, felt a little flat, deflated. Two of my children suddenly had to come home from university. My middle son, who had been planning his medical degree elective to the United States with his friends for the past eighteen months, had to cancel all travel plans, and even though not a day goes by when I am not grateful that we have all been well and got on with our lives, and enjoyed this extra family time, there is something slightly sorrowful about the moment that has now passed, about the moments that didn't deliver. At the time, with most long-distance travel limited or canceled, I declined all online speaking engagements; work-related meetings for the most part were tedious, nor did they seem real. I was blessed to have work, a regular income, and a family that remained healthy, but I experienced a growing restlessness. Against daily loss, the quotidian seemed small, and like many, I found solace in walking, in nature.

Perhaps it was a sense of being dislocated that added to people's social and emotional anxieties. The meaning and metaphor of dislocation have been poignantly analyzed by Patricia Killen in her essay on the fortieth anniversary of the eruption of one of the most active volcanoes in the Cascade Range of North America, Mount St. Helens, on May 18, 1980. She draws parallels between the effects of the volcanic eruption and the global pandemic, both of which can be seen as profoundly traumatic and disruptive events. While acknowledging that the eruption of Mount St. Helens falls in the category of natural disasters, the comparison aims to show "the human experience of gratitude amid cataclysm, . . . events that disturb and dislocate, crush and create." Killen probes the dynamics of gratitude during such events and ponders the possibility that dislocation is an integral element in the human experience of gratitude. Furthermore, both the COVID-19 pandemic and the eruption of Mount St. Helens are "boundary experiences" that for Killen confront us "with the reality that we need not exist and that we live in the face of death. Boundary experiences shine a spotlight on the fragility of human existence." The metaphor of boundary captures that in-between space that many of us have occupied because of COVID-19.

This fragility is not measured only by the tragic presence of disease and death but also by how many of us began to reassess our lives. Modern life has meant choice and freedom to move, to travel, but it has also tied us to the clock. Our working life is so often reflected in deadlines and commitments to our family, friends, and work colleagues. But under lockdown, with much of our lives spent indoors, with work-life boundaries blurred, time felt quite different. Despite the demands of domestic and professional work, there was a feeling of being suspended in time, waiting for the past to return or the future to start. This unease made me realize that time is also emotion, and at that point, I wasn't sure what to feel. We are creatures of routine whose lives are seemingly defined by being occupied, and when one is no longer busy in the same way, time and living seem distorted. Even though we humans aren't born with an innate sense of time, we learn to measure it as experiences and events, as memory and change, all of which fill our senses. When the rhythm changed, I stopped turning the pages of my diary. I don't know whether I was experiencing a trauma, but I was definitely feeling a sense of grief. I resisted acknowledging this because I did not want to be ungrateful. I had my family, my health, my job; as there had been no palpable loss, ingratitude seemed sinful.

When a family member's cancer recurred, I began to think more and more about those who were ill with terminal and other serious diseases and whose treatment had stopped because hospitals were prioritizing COVID-19 patients. Was it worse to die with COVID-19 than anything else, and how many lives would be lost simply through negligence or delay in treatment? COVID-19 dominated everything. It was portrayed as the worst illness and the loneliest illness. With vulnerability being synonymous with those in the older age category, so many other groups of people seemed invisible, or at least not on the daily news radar: those with physical and mental disabilities, children with learning and behavioral problems, young people who had only ever known freedom and were now struggling with levels of isolation, minority groups whose cultural norms meant the physical challenges of intergenerational households. But every now and again amid much grief, I would read something searing. A young journalist in the last stages of her breast cancer wrote of the necessity of finding joy amid the ever-present reminder of death: "Even in these depressing times try to find some part of the day that is worth relishing whether it is a moment of beauty half-glimpsed outside, the joy found in escaping into a different world on page or screen, or the pleasure of dressing up for yourself and no one else because it makes you feel fine. The worst thing that you can do is wish your life away thinking of what might have been."[4]

As the death toll from COVID-19 rose globally, so did our awareness of global inequalities. The media began to shed light on the desperate stories not only of people living in slums or extreme poverty but also of migrant workers who were left without work when societies went into lockdowns. Their helplessness in the face of COVID-19 was covered poignantly by the writer Arundhati Roy, who describes how many made the journey home in India:

> Many driven out by their employers and landlords, millions of impoverished, hungry, thirsty people, young and old, men, women, children, sick people, blind people, disabled people, with nowhere else to go, with no public transport in sight, began a long march home to their villages. They walked for days, towards Badaun, Agra, Azamgarh, Aligarh, Lucknow, Gorakhpur—hundreds of kilometres away. Some died on the way. Our towns and megacities began to extrude their working-class citizens like so much unwanted accrual. They knew they were going home potentially to slow starvation. Perhaps they even knew they could be carrying the virus with them, and would infect their families, their parents and grandparents back home, but they desperately needed a shred of familiarity, shelter and dignity, as well as food, if not love.[5]

The grim realization was that so many lives and stories would never be fully known and that so many deaths would not even be reflected in statistics.

As the months rolled by, weariness turned into acceptance. Then in the summer of 2020, at a time of such strange paradox, a small personal achievement came my way. I was awarded a grant from an American funder. On the one hand, projects and grants seemed almost an indulgence when daily news was full of grim statistics of illness and deaths, the months ahead remained uncertain, and no one knew how and when we would return to our workplaces. And yet I was also aware that having a future goal was important.

Some creative resilience is necessary both professionally and for our mental and emotional energy. I felt the curious privilege and flexibility of academic life even more when I visited a hair salon after the first lockdown ended. At the salon, the hair stylist, a bubbly and chatty young woman, spoke of her growing anxiety when lockdown began. She explained her frustration at not being able to see her clients in person: "My life is all about talking to other people as I make them feel good about themselves. When I couldn't do that any longer, I didn't know how to make myself feel good." As I walked out, I thought about the different ways we all work. As academics, most of us are trained and often happy to seek and work in solitude. But solitude can also be loneliness, and many people were struggling to cope on their own.

Around May 2020, I was writing the final section of my book on human struggle. The closing section of the last chapter looks at the long history of the Black struggle and in particular with the United States of America. African Americans, for all the progress made in winning civil rights, can still face injustice and discrimination at almost every level of society. Their particular injury assumed a new moral urgency with the death of forty-six-year-old George Floyd at the hands of a white police officer in Minneapolis, Minnesota, on May 25.[6] His gruesome death became the tipping point in the long history of police violence against members of the African American community. People were determined that his death wouldn't become yet another hashtag on social media. His killing would speak to the moral consciousness of the United States, a country that has built stunning monuments to human liberty but still struggles with the legacy of slavery.

The subsequent protests and vigils around the world mobilized greatly through the Black Lives Matter campaign, demanded accountability and justice. As the world witnessed scenes of cars on fire and shops being looted, there was endless discussion about physical destruction as criminal, even senseless, violence. But addressing the structural violence, a violence deeply embedded in the inequalities of societal institutions, was the much-needed conversation. Whether in housing, education, or employment, this discrimination is the violence that occurs daily against individuals, against their dignity and sense of self-worth. The struggle for racial equality is not just America's; it is the moral challenge in every society where skin color continues to divide communities. Breathing real freedom is an aspiration for many who live with systemic prejudice and violence; this long-standing injury is a chronic trauma but normalized as part of daily life. At the start of the subsequent trial of Derek Chauvin, the policeman who killed George Floyd, the Minneapolis clinical psychologist BraVada Garrett-Akinsanya said:

> For us as a Black community especially, we are so used to being traumatized, and we are so used to having microaggressive experiences that happen to us on a daily basis. So we are kind of normalizing trauma. I want people to know that they have the right to get support, and that right includes seeing people like psychotherapists or psychologists like me. In our community, talking about seeking help often translates into feeling like we're turning our back on our faith and that we should believe God to take us through everything, and we don't need psychologists or mental health providers to help us. People don't understand that mental health providers teach skills in looking at the world in a way that serves you and doesn't break you down.[7]

This normalization of aggression and injury against African Americans is analyzed in Edward Donalson's powerful exploration of the pervasive normality of injury that is based on racial prejudice and hate. In chapter 7 of this book, "Gratitude as a Revolutionary Act of Resistance", Donalson writes:

> Evil is perpetuated by ordinary citizens and agents of the state alike, in ways that refuse to be shocking because no matter how grotesque or bizarre, the injury has become commonplace.
>
> We watch police kneel on the necks of Black men while life drains from Black human bodies and these video clips circulate thousands of times an hour. It is a callousness that our genetic code embraces because we are descendants of people who sent postcards out with pictures of lynching. In this era of digital lynching, it is so common that any outcry against the mendacity of white supremacy is met with claims of reverse discrimination.

For Donalson, the striving "for freedom and personhood amidst an alien and racist surrounding culture uniquely prepares already injured and marginalized people for a robust conversation about resistance that is only made more complex and nuanced by the circumstances of a global health crisis." Adopting gratitude as an emotional, psychological, or spiritual lifestyle serves to militate against the feelings of insignificance that plague people for whom "self-determination is diminished by structural erasure. . . . Gratitude becomes a revolutionary act of resistance for marginalized people in that it is a vehicle for naming one's own truth." Whereas grief and lament have often been the partners of minoritized life, Donalson discusses, in Chapter 7, how gratitude uplifts the oppressed and "becomes a weapon to reclaim personhood."

Conversations on health inequality, yet another dimension of racial inequalities, have been magnified during these years of the pandemic. The tragic death of George Floyd became a catalyst and a movement, and while the moral imperative for change seemed ubiquitous, assessing what has actually changed on the ground remains difficult. For some in the medical profession, moral leadership lies with the state itself. In the United Kingdom, Chaand Nagpaul, the head of the British Medical Association (BMA), emphasized how the COVID-19 pandemic and the Black Lives Matter movement showed the importance of addressing health inequalities and racism in the United Kingdom and the National Health Service (NHS): "This is not just making a few small changes; this is about changing the entire system for the better. A change that will mean doctors in years to come will not face the same barriers as many others have and continue to face. The government has a moral imperative to address these inequalities and act now."

Sathish Jayagopal, a surgeon from the BMA's Salisbury division who proposed the motion, called for change after the death of George Floyd: "Racism is sometimes so common around us that we are accepting it as the norm. The boards of NHS trusts should reflect the ethnic make-up of the workforce of the organisations which they manage. This is not just about doing or saying something derogatory. It is also stereotyping, prejudgment, and bias that exists."[8]

While this hitherto muted public conversation became louder, I began to wonder whether it was also adding to the growing social anxiety. It seemed as if everything had gone from being quiet to very loud. Life, in all its beauty and brutality, still continued against the pandemic, but the voices of different peoples and communities held up a mirror to who we are as a society. Again, Arundhati Roy speaks of what might be new possibilities:

> Historically, pandemics have forced humans to break with the past and imagine their world anew. This one is no different. It is a portal, a gateway between one world and the next.
>
> We can choose to walk through it, dragging the carcasses of our prejudice and hatred, our avarice, our data banks and dead ideas, our dead rivers and smoky skies behind us. Or we can walk through lightly, with little luggage, ready to imagine another world. And ready to fight for it.[9]

For the first few weeks after March 2020, I had felt useless but saw around me thousands of others giving up their time to volunteer in all manner of ingenious and compassionate ways. People discovering new purpose, whether it was making more family time, helping in their neighborhoods, or raising money for good causes by taking on different challenges. Words attributed to Ralph Waldo Emerson come to mind: "The purpose of life is not to be happy. It is to be useful, to be honorable, to be compassionate, to have it make some difference that you have lived and lived well."[10] Throughout the last few months of 2022, what had gradually dawned on me was that we cannot let ourselves be overwhelmed by what we have lost. Hope is not just a feeling or a prayer; it is about living with renewed strength and purpose in the face of weariness and struggle. Gratitude in the simplest sense of the word allows us to feel joy in the expectation that there is much goodness in the present and will be in the future. Gratitude is a consciously nurturing attitude toward life.

I had continued with my walking throughout the summer. By the autumn of 2020, it was impossible not to pause every now and again during my walks and take in the beauty of the season with its array of red and yellow hues and the golden glow of the evening light. As the temperature fell, the burst of colors added a reddish warmth to the environment. Something about the rhythm of the changing seasons is comforting. Nature has its own purpose, and the autumnal joy and melancholy remind us to reset expectations in our lives. By this time, I was used to being at home and not unduly concerned about all the opportunities that had been deferred or canceled; they no longer mattered. It seemed to me that nothing was that important, not in a defeatist way but in the sense that every trauma, every life-changing period allows us to reevaluate what is important, what struggles really matter. Many of my professional colleagues had left their jobs and decided that it was time to do something different. Being at a certain age, the onset of the pandemic led several people to rethink their lives. The promise of a vaccine was also being heralded as our salvation, our way out.

I began to think of which aspects of my own relationships needed restoring, with restoration here meaning reaching out, forgiving others as well as forgiving oneself. It meant looking inward and acknowledging that hurt, betrayal, and grief all remind us that we love. As the former American monk and psychotherapist Thomas Moore has written, love is essentially about the need to care for the soul. Caring for the soul is a sacred art, and he writes, "suffering forces our attention toward places we would normally neglect." For Moore, caring for the soul is not a self-improvement project or even releasing oneself from the "troubles and pains of human existence." For the soul, "memory is more important than planning, art more compelling than reason, and love more fulfilling than understanding."[11] While Moore is careful to emphasize that he cannot explain precisely what soul is, nevertheless, caring for the soul demands that we remain concerned about the suffering around us as well as the aesthetics of our own lives.

By early November 2020, I was watching closely what was happening in the US elections. Fought against the devastation of a global pandemic that had already killed hundreds of thousands of people and had decimated jobs and industries, this election was described as the struggle for the soul of America. It gradually dawned on me that trust or the lack of it was a thread running through so much of 2020, and this itself had heightened the sense of trauma. President Joe Biden's victory as president-elect in November came with continued political and social division. Donald Trump's supporters challenged the election results for weeks afterward. Politics was becoming dangerous theatrics, and constant mistrust is hugely corrosive for society as well as our own mental and emotional well-being. A renewed trust and faith were needed.

In December 2020, the first COVID-19 vaccine had been granted regulatory approval in the United Kingdom, and with this news came new hope. In the weeks and months that followed, a full vaccination program rolled out across the United Kingdom and around the world. Millions were vaccinated in the following months, and a national confidence began to emerge. Despite the ups and downs of continued restrictions and the complexities surrounding data interpretation, vaccine skepticism was also rife. But the expectation was that as 2021 ended, the relative success of the vaccines would mean that the pandemic was in its demise. However, the detection of the Omicron variant of the virus and its rapid infection rate from November 2021 onward meant that COVID-19 continued to create social and financial disruption around the world.

We continue to live our lives between the uncertainties created by the virus and the hopes of a better future. As I reflect on the last few months of 2022, it seems to me that hope can only live among fear and grief, where it can't be neglected, only nurtured. And a society that lives on the right side of hope creates possibilities for new beginnings and the possibility of restoring and reviving the best of humanity. But hope is a process, a doing word, that is cultivated in small acts of generosity not only among families and friends but also between strangers. It shines through prophetic social and political milestones when we have the courage to reach and work for more just and empathetic societies. Broken relationships and resentments only heal through humility, trust, and courage. Hope is at the very least the first step toward this restoration.

Imagination and hope for a better world seem to inspire and drive many not only toward happiness in the present but also to change in the future.

Imagination is about seeing and understanding the world, an inherently moral activity. Through observation we become aware of our human freedom to think and act, of our relational existence, of a moral impulse to make things better. Without effort and change, things do not improve. As Bertrand Russell wrote, "It is not a finished Utopia that we ought to desire, but a world where imagination and hope are alive and active."[12]

We scholars in the liberal arts are a kind of artist because our job is to help others think and reimagine the world. We cannot simply dwell on destruction or grief; we must think past it and be a source of inspiration for others. Our work does not lie on the margins of society but is central to the development of thought and culture, of rebuilding society. The English historian Arnold Toynbee believed that civilizations are always confronted with challenges and that societies either flourish or flounder and ultimately fall based on whether a creative minority crafts the right responses to those challenges. Thus, whatever our individual concerns, our collective responsibility may well lie in being the prophetic voices that can show another way, a better way.

As Toni Morrison has expressed so eloquently about the need for artists in our moment of crisis: "'This is precisely the time when artists go to work.' . . . There is no time for despair, no place for self-pity, no need for silence, no room for fear. We speak, we write, we do language. That is how civilizations heal."[13]

NOTES

1. Richard Lischer, "The Coronavirus Pandemic Feels like an Unending Holy Saturday," *The Christian Century*, April 8, 2020, https://www.christiancentury.org/article/critical-essay/coronavirus-pandemic-feels-unending-holy-saturday.
2. Charles Taylor, *The Ethics of Authenticity* (Cambridge MA: Harvard University Press, 2018), 1.
3. Ed Prideaux, "How to Heal the 'Mass Trauma' of Covid-19," BBC, February 3, 2021, https://www.bbc.com/future/article/20210203-after-the-covid-19-pandemic-how-will-we-heal.
4. Sarah Hughes, "'Find a Part of Each Day to Relish': Coping with Cancer and Covid," *The Guardian*, November 15, 2020, https://www.theguardian.com/society/2020/nov/15/coping-with-cancer-and-covid-find-a-part-of-each-day-to-relish. Sarah Hughes died in April 2021.
5. Arundhati Roy, "The Pandemic Is a Portal," *Financial Times,* April 3, 2020, https://www.ft.com/content/10d8f5e8-74eb-11ea-95fe-fcd274e920ca.
6. "George Floyd: What Happened in the Final Moments of His Life," BBC News, July 16, 2020, https://www.bbc.co.uk/news/world-us-canada-52861726.

7. BraVada Garrett-Akinsanya, "The Trauma of George Floyd's Killing Has Been Renewed with Start of Chauvin Trial," interview by Ailsa Chang, NPR, March 29, 2021, https://www.npr.org/2021/03/29/982417659/the-trauma-of-george-floyds-killing-has-been-renewed-with-start-of-chauvin-trial?t=1641365893879.
8. Chaand Nagpaul and Sathish Jayagopal, "Doctors Call for Action on Racism in Wake of Covid-19 and Death of George Floyd," *British Medical Journal*, 2020, https://www.bmj.com/content/370/bmj.m3607.
9. Roy, "Pandemic Is a Portal."
10. On attribution of the quotation to Emerson, see "The Purpose of Life Is Not to Be Happy but to Matter," http://quoteinvestigator.com/2014/11/29/purpose/.
11. Thomas Moore, *Care of the Soul* (London: Piatkus, 1992), 304.
12. Bertrand Russell, *Political Ideals* (New York: Century, 1917), 23.
13. Toni Morrison, "No Place for Self-Pity, No Room for Fear," *The Nation*, March 23, 2015, https://thenation.com/article/archive/no-place-self-pity-no-room-fear/.

CHAPTER 2

Dislocating Gratitude

A Meditation from a Blasted Mountain

Patricia O'Connell Killen

> The ground moved a little bit and then, oh my God, the whole mountain took off.
>
> —Robert Rogers, recreational climber

> So far beyond human experience that what I perceived and what the pictures show were two completely different things.
>
> —Gary Rosenquist, rescue helicopter pilot

May 18, 2020, only a few months into the COVID-19 pandemic, marked the fortieth anniversary of the deadliest volcanic event in US history, the eruption of Mount St. Helens.[1] The most active volcano in the Cascade Range of North America, St. Helens is just one of several that grace the skylines of the Far West's major cities.[2] The pandemic overshadowed the anniversary of what might seem a regional event, insignificant in relation to the convulsive global disruption of COVID-19. Yet like the pandemic, St. Helens's eruption, in philosopher Kathleen Dean Moore's words, "undercut the conceit that humans are at the center of creation."[3] Volcanic eruptions and global pandemics destabilize, dislocate, undo, and, perhaps, redo. Both make clear that there is no escape from mortality.

At the time of this writing, in what is now the third year of the pandemic, the US death toll has topped a million and continues to climb. Worldwide, the number has surpassed 5 million.[4] We know in our bodies and souls that humanity is undergoing profound disruption on a global scale across all dimensions of material, psychic, social, and spiritual life. We are too close, too entirely saturated with what is transpiring to be able to enumerate all its effects, to grasp the contours of the suffering it has occasioned, or to take the full measure of its meaning. We are awash in accumulating data and tentative, preliminary narratives, and are unable to weave a fabric of coherent meaning from what humanity and the earth are undergoing.[5] Acknowledging the truth of now, this chapter turns to the 1980 eruption of Mount St. Helens and its aftermath as a metaphor through which to probe the possibility and dynamics of gratitude, injury, and repair in a pandemic age. Metaphors, as the poet Jane Hirshfield puts it, allow us to "feel and know something differently." They are "handles on the door of what we can know and what we can imagine."[6]

Metaphors are "neither true nor untrue in any ordinary sense," but they "can feel right or wrong."[7] To some, the Mount St. Helens eruption, a natural disaster, may feel wrong because systemic human agency was not a significant contributing factor as it has been in the COVID-19 pandemic. Still, the eruption's starkly different character may allow a different kind of seeing into our pandemic age. The vantage from a blasted mountain offers perspective on the possibility of the human experience of gratitude amid cataclysm, on the subtle interior movements that tend to lead to gratitude amid events that disturb and dislocate, crush and create. St. Helens's eruption invites attention to the reality that, sometimes, when gratitude arises amid cataclysm, destabilization and decentering are integral to the experience of gratitude itself.

BOUNDARY EXPERIENCES: COVID-19 AND A BLASTED MOUNTAIN

The COVID-19 pandemic and the eruption of Mount St. Helens are boundary experiences. They confront us with our contingency, our finitude, with the reality that we need not exist and that we live in the face of death. Boundary experiences shine a spotlight on the fragility of human existence. While the scale of the COVID-19 pandemic and the eruption of Mount St. Helens differ, both are cataclysmic, outsize in their effects. As boundary experiences, they dislocate and decenter human beings. Like other boundary experiences, they take us outside of ourselves and so can be thought of as ecstatic. The intensity and effects of boundary experiences differ, depending on the nature of the event, on its duration, on whether it is experienced by an individual or a group, and on the social imaginary of those who undergo it.

Theorists of religion and theologians have long focused on boundaries, and on how humans are located with reference to them, in explaining religion as a human phenomenon. Catherine Albanese and others posit that religion emerged from early humans' encounters across boundaries while engaging in trade. Building on Joachim Wach's writings, Albanese defines religion as a symbolic system of ideas (creed), ethical practices (code), ritual and devotional forms (cultus), and communal structures (community) that orients and situates humans in relation to ordinary and extraordinary boundaries, and helps humans cross them. Ordinary boundaries are those that are part of the structures of cultural and social life, and historically have been reinforced by religion; extraordinary boundaries are those that portend irrevocable change, with birth and death being the two most obvious. Religion is about what happens as humans approach any boundary, be it physical, social, intrapersonal or communal. Boundaries are places of danger and possibility. Implicitly, or explicitly, they confront human beings with their contingency and finitude: We need not exist, and we will die.[8]

The dislocation and decentering that individuals and communities undergo at boundaries provoke questions about transcendence and about the meaning of the human person in the face of transcendence. History provides examples of this impulse. In Europe the Black Death of 1347–51 killed an estimated 30–60 percent of the population, spurred new religious movements within Christianity, and weakened the Roman Catholic Church's control.[9] The great Lisbon earthquake of 1755 with its accompanying flooding tidal wave killed an estimated fifty thousand people, fueled the Enlightenment, and accelerated the spread of atheistic and materialistic views in the West.[10] As these two examples illustrate, human responses to cataclysm include innovations in and abandonment of religion. Varied interpretations of the current COVID-19 pandemic, religious and otherwise, continue to emerge: for example, witchcraft, divine punishment for personal moral transgression, and just desserts for humans' destruction of the environment and unjust treatment of each other.

For humans, then, cataclysm is a context of multiple, intensified boundaries, boundary awareness, and unvoluntary boundary crossing. Using the eruption of Mount St. Helens as metaphor, this chapter contemplates the human experience of gratitude amid experiences of cataclysm. It draws on the writings of artists and scientists, many of whom lived in the Pacific Northwest at the time of the eruption and, in 2005, at its twenty-fifth anniversary, camped together for four days in the volcano's blast zone. The artists and scientists observed, conversed, and contemplated the eruption's vast disruption and its aftermath. Then they attempted to express meaning in the face of a reality where, as Moore puts it, "hope rides the back of horror, the two of them galloping in such perfect synchrony that they might be one thing."[11]

MOUNTAIN AS FACT: MOUNT ST. HELENS, MARCH INTO JUNE 1980

Beginning in March 1980, small tremors on Mount St. Helens signaled imminent possible volcanic activity. In May and June, the mountain showed itself to be very much alive. The volcano's most spectacular performance occurred on May 18. The magma that had been pushing up under the north flank of the mountain triggered a massive landslide that traveled "twelve miles down the Toutle River valley, burying more than twenty square miles under rock, mud, and broken forest." The mountaintop's collapse unleashed a "super-heated groundwater system" that had been building within the volcano. It shot a "steam-driven blast" to the north, "ripping away the forests closest to the vent." A bit farther away, the "blast snapped off trees, toppling them in patterns that mapped the direction of the force. The heat seared forests as many as seventeen miles from the mountain. . . . Searing hot pyroclastic flows spewed from the crater mouth," creating a vast pumice plain. "Massive mudflows raced down rivers that drained the volcano, some traveling seventy-five miles to the Columbia River." Thirteen hundred feet of the mountain's top blew off in an instant. A cloud of gray volcanic ash "boiled into the atmosphere and rode the wind to the northeast." Then "ash darkened the day and rained from the sky over a vast area of eastern Washington and beyond."[12] By the end of the day on May 18, the nine-hour explosive eruption had killed fifty-seven people, obliterated unknown numbers of other creatures, devastated 230 square miles of forest, shot a gas cloud fifteen miles into the atmosphere, and spewed 540 million tons of ash into the air. The ash fell over twenty-two thousand square miles.[13] In some places it fell to earth as large shiny mica-like flakes; in others, as specks finer than talcum powder and so dense that each quart weighed ten pounds. The May 18 eruption, along with two smaller subsequent ones on May 25 and June 12 that spewed more ash, crippled transportation and commerce in Portland, Vancouver, Spokane, Yakima, and surrounding towns, and affected agriculture in parts of Washington and Oregon for various lengths of time and to different degrees. Fallen ash made roads impassable, clogged air filters on combines and other vehicles, rendered automated teller machines inoperable, and created health hazards, especially for vulnerable populations.

News reports in the hours immediately following the May 18 eruption predicted that the ash falling across the region was acidic and when rained upon would decimate forests, crops, and other vegetation.[14] This initial news evoked terror in those who call the region home, whose psyches are imprinted with its myriad shades of blue and green and gray, and whose livelihoods would not survive such an effect. The mountain was undoing a place. Families and communities grieved the fifty-seven people who died on May 18. Many people mourned the untold number of other creatures, plants, and forests that perished; the loss of beauty; the obliteration of the mountain's snow-capped symmetry. Those whose memories included annual occasions at family cabins, youth camps, or campgrounds on the mountain, especially around Spirit Lake, grieved too. As writer Christine Colasurdo puts it, "But not only had I lost an entire landscape, I myself was lost—a stranger in what should have been familiar land."[15] Widespread disorientation prevailed. The eruption undid worlds in myriad ways, many of which have taken years to register.

ON THE MOUNTAIN: DESTABILIZING GRATITUDE

In 2005, twenty-five years after that eruption, a group of artists, philosophers, and social and natural scientists made a foray to Mount St. Helens. They carried shared questions to be explored from and across diverse disciplinary perspectives: what the mountain might teach about the meaning of cataclysmic loss and the profound injury of all kinds that it entails, what it might teach about healing, and whether understanding the mountain's changes could teach something about human loss and recovery.[16] While the contributors' reflections, published in the volume *In the Blast Zone: Catastrophe and Renewal on Mount St. Helens,* have distinct foci—butterflies, linguistic precision, geological change, human mortality—all address disruption and possibility, dislocation, and what follows dislocation. Cumulatively, a thematic pattern runs through their ponderings.

A confrontation with mortality begins the pattern. The Mount St. Helens eruption, as the current pandemic is doing now, confronted people with their contingency—that is, they need not exist and will cease to exist. This is a primal religious experience, the definitive boundary experience. The group members of "the foray," as they denominated themselves, responded to both the explosive power of the mountain, so visible in its destructive effects, and to what had transpired on the mountain in the intervening quarter century with fear and awe, responses that led some to gratitude.

The writer Ursula K. Le Guin began by sharing a memory of her first post-eruption visit to St. Helens in 1981, sixteen months after it exploded. Then she had felt a "metaphysical fear" in the face of the scale of "the awful simplicity of death" that she encountered and found "beyond comprehension." Returning in 2005, she found the explosion of life on the mountain equally incomprehensible and disorienting: "It was just as hard to comprehend that all that silent dead landscape was changed—was green—had come alive. Had always been alive." Cognitive dissonance took hold. The stark contrast between the vast death and destruction she had witnessed in 1981 and the riot of new life, an enlarged "variety and energy of the biota of the mountain" she encountered in 2005, disoriented her.[17]

Le Guin's memory reawakened her earlier metaphysical fear and had led to feelings of foreboding in anticipation of the 2005 sojourn. "But," she writes, "when I was there, getting ready to lie down and sleep on the volcano, any such thoughts and fears were entirely gone. I have no explanation. I guess I felt: well, now I'm here, I'm hers. I'm part of her, like all her trees and birds and lakes and dirt. So what she does I do, and that's OK."[18] Le Guin's sentences convey a level of acceptance, even an embrace of her mortality, borne in the experience of feeling part of something much larger than the human.

The ecologist Robin Wall Kimmerer found the mountain "too terrible to look at, too beautiful to look away." Her language expresses awe and terror, sentiments associated with encountering the transcendent. Kimmerer writes, "The size and power of the blasted land rolled over me like the shockwave that had vaporized the land. I found that looking directly at the steaming mountain made me weak with a visceral desire to run fast and run far. I swallowed hard and could bear only a sideways glance at her looming presence, the crater like an all-seeing eye." Traversing the pumice plain of the blast zone was "a walk between wonder and abject terror." Yet in the end, she confesses, the landscape "would not let me take cover behind denial of what I feared most. I felt myself surrender to its truth."[19]

Le Guin and Kimmerer describe the visceral dimension of their encounters with finitude and contingency in the blast zone—fear-terror-wonder-surrender. Kathleen Dean Moore also pondered surrender. She muses, "Someday everything I love will be folded back into the Earth. . . . Every person I love, every song I sing, every beloved child, every poem will be folded back into the roar of Earth's fire and disappear forever." She asks whether, given the human trait of "cling[ing] to the significance of small lives," there is any comfort in what the mountain shows: "That no matter how fragile and finite small lives may be, no matter how we grieve foresight of our own deaths, Life itself is a powerful force that will not be turned away."[20] Environmental philosopher Tony Vogt answers Moore with a no. He took no consolation in the "wonder" and "delight at the mountain's marvels" of new life. Time on the mountain, he writes, "calls forth more troubling emotions" and the hard truth "that death for some means life for others." The mountain is "about mortality and suffering, about impermanence."[21] Le Guin, Kimmerer, and Moore recognize Vogt's "hard truth" and respond in a different tone.

Vogt's reluctance to assert a strong claim of hopeful meaning for humans from his experience on the mountain gestures toward another way St. Helens confronted the sojourners with their finitude and contingency—that is, the realization of their inability to comprehend the multifaceted character of the mountain or to take its measure. Geologist Frederick Swanson emphasizes this in two ways. He, along with other scientists in the foray, notes that Mount St. Helens undid scientific predictions about what would happen during and after a cataclysmic volcanic explosion: "Preconceptions about how volcanic landscapes behave in the aftermath of eruption were blown away." For Swanson and his peers, as for all in the COVID-19 pandemic, facing what they did not and do not know was itself a boundary experience. Further, Swanson chafes at the limits and inaccuracy of language used to talk about the eruption. The first news reports were replete with images: "'the devastated area', 'the zone of devastation', 'a moonscape'." Their emphasis on destruction obscured the reality. Missed was the fact that within days of the 1980 eruption, "surviving organisms and surprising pioneers appeared."[22]

Scientists attempt to comprehend the world, from subatomic particles to the cosmos. Generally, scientific knowledge comes through incremental steps toward answering well-defined questions. For the scientists of the foray, some of whom made academic careers of studying Mount St. Helens from the 1980 eruption forward, the encounter with the mountain nurtured a robust humility about understanding cataclysmic events. Plant expert Charles Goodrich observes, "An alpine grotto full of spring wildflowers is beyond composition." It leaves one "aware of his limits."[23] Or, as forest research scientist Jerry Franklin puts it, most of "[my] pretty good ideas about how the post-eruption landscape would evolve, and most of my preconceptions proved dead wrong."[24] The encounter with finitude and contingency, then, occurs at the limits of one's existence, at the limits of knowledge, and at the limits of possibilities that can be imagined.

ON THE MOUNTAIN: CHANGE, DESTRUCTION, DEATH, RESILIENCE, CREATION, NEW LIFE

The scientists preferred the word "change" to speak of what transpired on Mount St. Helens.[25] To their ears it carried a more neutral connotation, unencumbered by the value-laden and human emotion–saturated connotations of words such as "destruction," "death," "resilience," or "creation." Even the scientists knew, however, that all language falls short in summing the meaning of simultaneous utter destruction of life and emergence of life. The mountain confronted the sojourners with the truth that destruction and creation are inextricably intertwined.

Naturalist Susan Zwinger contemplates that "some scientists believe that life may have begun in a volcanic setting, that the heat and chemistry set off chain reactions [that yielded amino acids, proteins, and complex polymers,] which then organized themselves into structures capable of metabolism."[26] Or, as Moore writes, "disturbance kicks the world into motion." Still, neither Moore nor Zwinger will relinquish the words that ecologists deemed "human projections onto the landscape": "destruction, creation, catastrophe, renewal, sorrow, and joy."[27]

Moore vividly describes the members of the foray watching lightning dance over the crater during a thunderstorm with heavy rain and high wind. While keeping a tent pole anchored with the force of his weight, a geologist reminded them that "lightning creates the conditions for life." He explained that the lightning-filled gas cloud over the 1980 eruption "charged the nitrogen in the ammonia and ozone." So "when the ash fell, it was nitrogen rich and ready to fertilize new plants."[28] A destructive and feared force is necessary for life. Poet and naturalist Tim McNulty expresses the destruction-creation moment in verse: "The mountain is a window open on the moment of creation. / From its ragged skirts a fresh and hungry world unfurls."[29] On the mountain, change is what is most real, and change is necessary for the very existence of the beings, thoughts, and feelings that humans relinquish only with reluctance and often great grief.

The blasted mountain itself gestured toward the trustworthiness of humans' refusal to relinquish emotion-saturated language. Scientists discovered that what mattered most for the evolution of life on the mountain after the eruption were those things that had survived.[30] In all disruptions, writes forest scientist Franklin, what survives, or the "biological legacies," are more significant than the scope or character of disturbance.[31] What survives are the beginning of regrowth and the place to which animal life will anchor. Such biological legacies are "refugia," or habitats that facilitate the survival of plants or animals.[32]

Unable to "hold the gaze of the mountain," ecologist Kimmerer sought solace in focusing on what she knew best—plants. What she found was wonder. On the leeside of the "skeleton of a single tree," she spied a "knothole," a "damp depression." Growing in it was a type of moss whose normal "home" is "old-growth" forests, and "sprouting from the fist-sized moss garden was a tiny fern." A knothole on the leeside of a now-dead tree had protected the moss from the blast. Kimmerer reflects: "Life itself is so improbable, and on that May morning, so was survival." But only days after the eruption, "ferns, faithful to spring, pushed through the ash" toward sunlight and "made a place for spiders to land." Twenty-five years later, the abundance of life in the blast zone testified to the improbable survival of seeds and plants, having been protected from the blast by a knothole on the leeside of a now-dead tree or by late snowpack, layers of humus, or Earth itself. "Life persists and perishes this way, protected by layers and layers of chance." While "there is no such thing as safety," Kimmerer writes, there is resilience. "The mountain says that recovery does not come from outside, but from within. It is what is left behind that matters."[33]

The foray members' expressions of awe, wonder, and surrender, and their meditations on the intricately interwoven nature of destruction and creation on the mountain, speak to the complicated nature of the questions of injury and repair that are central to this volume's exploration of meaning and possibilities in this pandemic age. Forest scientist Franklin observes that the term "recovery" with reference to the mountain's landscape was misplaced, precisely because the word carries the connotation of "a return to some preexisting condition," an impossibility on Mount St. Helens. There could be no returning the mountain and the life it hosts to the state that existed before the eruption. Instead, the flora and fauna on Mount St. Helens twenty-five years after the eruption were more diverse and plentiful than before it.[34] The blast made possible the proliferation of the rare butterfly, Leona's little blue; the explosion of pearly everlasting, "a wildflower that thrives on disaster"; and the arrival of western meadowlarks to the mountain.[35]

The scientists and artists pondered a dance of death and life, of absence and teeming, of horror and beauty during their time on the mountain. The death and destruction of the eruption have not been erased by the animal and plant life that emerged and now thrives, no matter how riotous. The fact of injury remains, even as the wound of a blasted dead tree provided safety and sustenance for moss and fern. For the mountain, newness of life is a kind of repair, though it is not restoration. For the mountain, for the natural world, if anything counts as healing, it is the process of evolution through which life continues.

But what about for humans? What can count as repair after injury? What options exist beyond escape into denial? What offers a new purchase on the reality? Environmental philosopher Vogt is not sure. He urges resisting the temptation "to embrace the story of the eruption and its aftermath as one of cataclysm and recovery," and generalizing it "to a moral about the irrepressible persistence of life, and by extension find a parable for human hope and ultimate triumph in the face of cataclysm." Yielding to the temptation, he writes, would foreclose stories yet to be uncovered.[36] A premature, overarching narrative would deny fact and dishonor the dead. Moore also wrestles with the question: "Lord knows, I'd like to see the world the way ecologists do. If all of us thought of death as change rather than catastrophe, could we blunt Earth's edge of sorrow? And isn't this a source of hope, that the forces of nature turn death into life again and again, unceasing?" She wants to go there but cannot. Instead, she recalls familiar words of an old Christian hymn—"Above Earth's lamentation, / I hear the sweet though far-off hymn / That hails a new creation"—and tells us that she cannot hear the singing "for the crying of small birds in the back of my mind."[37] Le Guin and Kimmerer do not write of wrestling with these questions. They testify to their "surrender" to the mountain, describing the internal shifts that brought them to it, but choose not to speak beyond their personal experience.

Cataclysmic events are injurious in myriad ways, some of them irreparable. With Mount St. Helens, human injury involved fifty-seven deaths, job loss, heightened anxiety, fear, grief-saturated memories, destruction of long-standing family camping traditions, aggravated pulmonary and respiratory disease, and psychological and spiritual harm. None could be repaired where repair means restoration, with recovery understood as a return to the state that existed before the cataclysmic event. The same is true for the pandemic. As the writer Arundhati Roy points out, the COVID-19 pandemic, as with pandemics in the past, is a historic global rupture of systems and reality. This renders it "a gateway between one world and the next." Standing in that gateway, Roy says, humans face a choice: to make a feeble and ultimately destructive attempt to "stitch our future to our past [while] refusing to acknowledge the rupture" or "to rethink" the world "we have built for ourselves," to "imagine [our] world anew."[38] So what counts as repair? Is an alternative sense of "repair" applicable to post-cataclysmic eras, including to our post-COVID era?

Here is one take on repair, drawn from the writings of the artists and scientists of the foray. Repair begins in holding the facts of a situation unblinkingly—no denial, no escape—and engaging the human impulse to compose or discover meaning, which includes placing what individuals and communities undergo within a more textured, richer narrative frame that resists premature closure. For humans, as for the mountain, meaning and meanings unfold over time. In the case of Mount St. Helens, part of the unfolding of meaning was occasioned by what the data revealed. What was and is loss, and what was and is creative newness continue to be revised in the face of surprising findings and unanticipated developments. The narratives of the mountain's evolution, its medium of injury and repair, remain unfinished. Openness to discovery and to having their understandings revised, or entirely upended, is evident in the modest, even humble tone of the sojourners' essays. They resist premature closure.

The essays also point, I think, to dimensions of repair in a wider range of human experiences. An individual's or community's understanding of injury develops over time with new experiences, distance from the event, new questions, and accumulating insight. Repair is a process. The composition of narratives is an essential part of that process.[39] So, too, is resisting premature closure. Repair entails that those who underwent injury compose narratives that in some way redeem themselves and humanity from its uselessness and senselessness. The composition of those narratives tends to be provisional at first and often iterative through a lifetime. Trauma short-circuits this process, precisely because it stops the iterative development and refinement of narrative.[40] We live our questions and the keys to their answers long before we can put them into words; only when we find language both accurate and capacious enough to hold what we experience and feel do we move forward.[41]

RELOCATED GRATITUDE: BEING HUMAN WITHOUT BEING THE CENTER OF IT ALL

The mountain confronted those who made the foray with their finitude and contingency. It demanded that they confront unblinkingly the inextricably interwoven character of destruction and creation, of the moment of death and emergence of new life. The fear and awe that the sojourners experienced on the mountain, the pain and tenderness that suffused their contemplation of death and new life relocated them. They came down the mountain holding and practicing being human in a different way.

In his essay, geologist Scott Russell Sanders reflects on dislocation and relocation, on being in place and out of place. Sanders broke the rules on the foray. While crossing the pumice plain, a piece with moss growing in it caught his eye. "I persuaded myself that this lump of pumice, no larger than a hen's egg, could serve the cause of conservation by helping me tell the story of nature's recuperative powers. So I put the stone in my pocket and carried it home"—home to Indiana, where he attempted to nurture the moss in the pumice. But out of place, no "combination of moisture and sunlight" that he tried could "keep them alive." The dead pumice stone now sits next to a piece of Indiana siltstone on his desk. Eyeing the two stones, Sanders is struck by the fact that the pumice he took to demonstrate "life's resilience" became a "symbol of life's fragility" and the importance of "adaptation to the conditions of a particular place." Recognizing his intellectual hubris in taking the stone, he writes, "My stone was out of place; it belonged back on the talus pile next to Ghost Lake, downwind from the volcano."[42]

But Sanders does not end with confession. He situates the two stones within a larger, more complex narrative. They "remind me that Earth is restless, powerful, forever casting up new materials and forms." Sanders himself is "merely one of those ephemeral shapes," yet "his passage [is] all the more precious to him for being so brief." In the face of his own finitude Sanders feels "reverence for this wild, creative, mysterious flow of things. Our lives, our civilization, everything we can touch or imagine is part of that flow, a wave lifted for a moment above the current, and then drawn back to the source." Sanders has relocated himself and all of humanity within a longer, larger, older, mysterious story. Standing within the frame of this narrative, he declares that humans "cannot save the world for it is not ours to save; the best we can do is to honor its magnificent energy."[43]

"Reverence," not fear, is Sanders's response to the realization that humans are part of something the measure of which they do not comprehend. A grateful tone permeates his declaration of release from the obligation to save the world. Instead of shouldering an impossible burden, Sanders says that humans can ally themselves with the magnificent energy of life's flow by preserving "the living abundance that we all inherited at our birth."[44]

Three months after the foray, one of its participants, naturalist Ann Zwinger, suffered a serious stroke. Her daughter, Susan, also a naturalist, traveled into the blast zone herself to understand the "catastrophe" of her mother's event. She camped on Windy Ridge at Ryan Lake, "fifteen miles from the Mount St. Helens crater." Sitting "with three feet of Kalama ash" under her, Susan recalled that twenty-five years before, the explosion "charred three campers sleeping here." She turned her thoughts from those deaths to the power of water, writing: "Now ducks and shorebirds gurgle; passerines twitter. How quickly life comes back in water. Past violence breeds beauty.

Immanuel Kant spoke of beauty and terror, of horrendous power and multiplicity creating awe."[45]

Awe also moves Zwinger to a confession of faith of sorts:

> On this glorious fall morning, as brilliant colors lash the ash-dark background, I believe in life's resilience. I breathe deeply, imagining the dynasty of anaerobic microbes, which ate the oxygen and created stinking lake soups. This morning I believe in the refreshing rains, snows, groundwater, and tricklets falling into these lakes to dilute the organics, restoring them to normal oxygen levels. . . . I believe in the simple power of streams, which cut down through nine feet of ash to the organic soil, bringing up buried seeds still viable years later.[46]

Trust in water's process gives Susan hope for her mother's recovery, which, she writes, "will parallel the biological force" that was rapidly bringing green back to the mountain. "Such metaphors do not lessen our loss," she muses, "but Nature's shaking keeps me steady."[47] Zwinger, like Sanders, situates being human within a narrative of the powerful mysterious force of nature and finds in this relocation solace and strength.

Relocation for the writer Le Guin brought freedom from fear through her feeling that she belonged to the mountain.[48] Hers was a progression from dissonance and foreboding to settling into a new place. "I'm grateful to the mountain," she says, "because it gives me the opportunity to pray."[49] Ecologist Kimmerer also was relocated through "surrender to [the mountain's] truth," part of which was recognizing that "whether we deny it or not, there is no such thing as safety." She moved from anxiety and fear to peace in the knowledge that while she could die on the mountain, she also could live on the mountain. Humans live, writes Kimmerer, "on the ridge between creation and destruction."[50]

Humans exist on a plane where destabilizing, dislocating experiences and encounters are part of the fabric of being and necessary to new life. The clarity with which we recognize this reality, and how we respond to it, may have a different texture depending on whether one is camped on a blasted mountain, is confined to home space in the morass of global pandemic, or is risking all as a frontline worker in a hospital, grocery store, or meatpacking plant. In whatever way this reality confronts human beings, the result of the confrontation is relocation to a fear-infused anxious hardness that demands the restitching (restoration) of past conditions, whatever the cost, or, relocation to a freer, more modest way of holding being human. Self, life, and world are experienced differently from these two standpoints. In the frustration being played out at school board meetings across the country and in the raging fear of those who attacked the US Capitol on January 6, 2020, we see the fruits of relocation to anxious hardness. With Le Guin, Kimmerer, Sanders, and Zwinger, who write in grateful tones of being relocated to freedom, peace, solace, release, and savoring of beauty, we see being relocated to a more modest way of being human.

This relocation is both out of our control and a choice we make. Which space we occupy—and most humans vacillate between the two over time—depends in no small part on our material circumstances and on how we have learned to grieve, to bear loss, to discern glimpses of meaning and the preciousness of love in all the circumstances of our life narratives with all their aspirations, victories, losses, and deaths. This is the journey of life in the face of mortality.

Moore captures how this relocation happens, repeatedly, in each confrontation with the reality of death and its connection to life. Yes, says Moore, the mountain undoes "the belief that human lives are the measure of time," and it laughs at "the confidence that global events are under human control." She continues, "We fear loss so desperately" because we "have such a love for the Earth and its life, for our own lives. . . . Would we be so afraid of our own deaths, if we didn't love life so urgently?" Perhaps the "fear of losing it all can lead us to a place of rejoicing, a recognition of how deeply we value the living, changing world, how lovingly we cling to our place in it." Moore recommends to herself, and so to her readers, three practices: "when I'm afraid, to be open to wonder"; "when I'm grieving, to be amazed by beauty"; and "when I'm caught up in my human-scaled sense of time and significance, to remember that my life is part of the endless flow of fiery rock." She seeks "to be astonished and grateful" throughout her life.[51]

DISLOCATING GRATITUDE

Only two of the sojourners, writer Le Guin and philosopher Moore, use the word "gratitude." Yet the impulse toward gratitude comes through in the reflections of the other members of the foray. It arises in the intensity of the sojourners' visceral experiences of fear and awe, their contemplation of death and new life, their feelings of being dislocated and relocated, and their sensing of a different way to hold being human in the world. Gratitude bubbles up in a surprising freedom, solace, peace, honesty, and savoring that flows from facing mortality through the destruction and riotous life of the mountain. Gratitude, when viewed from the blasted peak, seems as wild, as unbidden, as the mountain itself. And it comes amid vulnerability, tenderness, loss, and delight.

This view of gratitude—with the potential that it can be, in its own way, a form of repair or healing possible even during injury, even during cataclysm—is subject to critique. It can rightly be questioned as a fantasy of the economically and culturally privileged, or as yet another form of oppression manufactured by the positive thinking industry, or both. There seem to be no limits to humans' capacity for self-deception or to corporate capitalism's capacity to manipulate human impulses. Other colleagues' contributions to this volume develop critiques of gratitude and its relation to dimensions of injury and repair in a pandemic age, notably when gratitude is coerced or conventionally demanded in a relationship of differential power and freedom. Structural injustice and oppression are real, and their effects crush body and soul. And still, from the blast zone of Mount St. Helens, the social and personal suffering and devastation that colleagues' critiques of our current situation disclose so powerfully are not the full story. The metaphor of the blasted mountain invites listening, even in the madness of our pandemic age, to the "still, small voice" within that, while perhaps only faintly audible, draws us to notice courage, tenderness, love, and grief in our midst as signposts, like the moss-nurtured fern in the knothole of a dead tree, of alternative possible futures, the beginnings of new stories.

NOTES

1. The two quotations opening this chapter are from interviews in "The Eruption of Mount St. Helens," *Minute by Minute*, A&E Network, aired 2001 (accessed on YouTube, March 2022, https://www.youtube.com/watch?v=fArB5Jz2wos). In addition to the members of the symposium group, I want to thank Paul Blankenship; Eugene V. Gallagher; Stephen Lantry, SJ; Heidi McCormick; and Carol Simon for feedback on earlier versions of this chapter.
2. The Cascade Range with its volcanoes and regular seismic activity is part of the "ring of fire" that circles the Pacific Ocean, marking where tectonic plates of the land masses meet those under the sea. See the U.S. Geological Survey, "What Is the 'Ring of Fire'?," https://www.usgs.gov/faqs/what-ring-fire. The Pacific Northwest awaits both the eruption of the next active volcano and an anticipated massive earthquake that, based on past patterns, could occur within the next fifty years. See "Ring of Fire," *Encyclopedia Britannica*, September 5, 2022, https://www.britannica.com/place/Ring-of-Fire.
3. Kathleen Dean Moore, "In Endless Song," in *In the Blast Zone: Catastrophe and Renewal on Mount St. Helens*, ed. Charles Goodrich, Kathleen Dean Moore, and Frederick J. Swanson (Corvallis: Oregon State University Press, 2008), 27. References to the edited volume are hereafter cited as *In the Blast Zone*.

4. The numbers cited in the chapter are from the spring of 2022; I retained them to preserve the nature of this writing as a product of its moment. The estimated number of deaths from COVID as of February 28, 2023, are 1.1 million in the United States and 6.8 million worldwide. See Jennifer Kates and Josh Michaud, "Ten Numbers to Mark Three Years of Covid," Henry J. Kaiser Family Foundation, March 6, 2023, https://www.kff.org/coronavirus-covid-19/fact-sheet/three-years-of-covid-19.
5. On attempts to take the measure of COVID's impact, see John Mooallem, "What Happened to Us," *New York Times Magazine*, February 26, 2023, 26–37, 51. Not only has COVID-19 been a direct cause of suffering, death and disruption, but the pandemic also has been a catalyst for wider recognition of the urgency of other "pandemics," including police violence, economic disparity, racism, and the climate crisis—topics that other contributors to this volume address.
6. Jane Hirshfield, "The Art of Metaphor," TED-Ed, September 24, 2012 (accessed on YouTube, March 2022), https://ed.ted.com/lessons/jane-hirshfield-the-art-of-the-metaphor.
7. Hirshfield.
8. Catherine Albanese, *America: Religion and Religions*, 5th ed. (Belmont CA: Wadsworth, 2012), 1–10, provides a succinct presentation. See also Joachim Wach, *Sociology of Religion*, 1st edition 1944, Routledge Library Editions: Sociology of Religion (New York: Routledge, 2019), for a fuller presentation.
9. See John Aberth, *The Black Death: A New History of the Great Mortality in Europe, 1347–1500* (London: Oxford University Press, 2020).
10. See Nicholas Shrady, *The Last Day: Wrath, Ruin, and Reason in the Great Lisbon Earthquake of 1755* (New York: Penguin, reprint edition, 2009); and Susan Neiman, *Evil in Modern Thought: An Alternative History of Modern Philosophy* (Princeton NJ: Princeton University Press, 2002).
11. Moore, "In Endless Song," in *In the Blast Zone*, 23.
12. Description taken from Charles Goodrich, Kathleen Dean Moore, and Frederick Swanson, "Introduction," in *In the Blast Zone*, x–xi; and the US Geologic Survey, "1980 Cataclysmic Eruption," accessed April 2021, https://www.usgs.gov/volcanoes/mount-st,-helens/1980-cataclysmic-eruption.
13. US Geological Survey, "How Far Did the Ash from Mount St. Helens Travel?," June 9, 2009, podcast, https://www.usgs.gov/media/audio/how-far-did-ash-mount-st-helens-travel.
14. See Joanne Omang and Thomas O'Toole, "Mount St. Helens Broke All Rules on Environment," *Washington Post*, May 22, 1980.
15. Christine Colasurdo, "Everlasting Wilderness," in *In the Blast Zone*, 78.
16. Goodrich, Moore, and Swanson, "Introduction," in *In the Blast Zone*, xiii.
17. Ursula K. Le Guin, "Coming Back to the Lady," in *In the Blast Zone*, 4–7.
18. Le Guin, 7, 8.
19. Robin Kimmerer, "On the Ridge," in *In the Blast Zone*, 41, 45.
20. Moore, "In Endless Song," in *In the Blast Zone*, 23.
21. Tony Vogt, "In the Zone: Notes from Camp," in *In the Blast Zone*, 50, 51.
22. Frederick J. Swanson, "Languages of Volcanic Landscapes," in *In the Blast Zone*, 105, 109.
23. Charles Goodrich, "A Gardener Goes to the Volcano," in *In the Blast Zone*, 56.

24. Jerry F. Franklin, "Evolutionary Impacts of a Blasted Landscape," in *In the Blast Zone,* 62.
25. Charlie Crisafulli, "Change, Survival, and Revival: Lessons from Mount St. Helens," in *In the Blast Zone,* 10.
26. Susan Zwinger and Ann Zwinger, "Nature's Shaking Keeps Me Steady," in *In the Blast Zone,* 101.
27. Moore, "In Endless Song," in *In the Blast Zone,* 25.
28. Moore, 25.
29. Tim McNulty, "The Way to Windy Ridge," in *In the Blast Zone,* 20.
30. Kimmerer, "On the Ridge," in *In the Blast Zone,* 46.
31. Franklin, "Evolutionary Impacts," in *In the Blast Zone,* 64.
32. Goodrich, "Gardener Goes," in *In the Blast Zone,* 57.
33. Kimmerer, "On the Ridge," in *In the Blast Zone,* 44, 43, 45, 46.
34. Franklin, "Evolutionary Impacts," in *In the Blast Zone,* 67, 66.
35. John Calderazzo, "Mount St. Helens," in *In the Blast Zone,* 35; and Colasurdo, "Everlasting Wilderness," in *In the Blast Zone,* 82.
36. Vogt, "In the Zone," in *In the Blast Zone,* 51.
37. Moore, "In Endless Song," in *In the Blast Zone,* 25, 26.
38. Arundhati Roy, "The Pandemic Is a Portal," *Financial Times,* April 3, 2020, https://www.ft.com/content/10d8f5e8-74eb-11ea-95fe-fcd274e920ca.
39. See Mark Yaconelli, *Between the Listening and the Telling: How Stories Can Save Us* (Minneapolis: Broadleaf Books, 2022) on the importance of storytelling after cataclysmic events.
40. See contributions by Susan Abraham, Edward Donalson, Kristi Lee, and Doug Peduti in this volume for discussions of trauma.
41. See Charles Davis, *The Body as Spirit: The Nature of Religious Feeling* (London: Hodder & Stoughton, 1976), 1–17.
42. Scott Russell Sanders, "Two Stones," in *In the Blast Zone,* 96, 98.
43. Sanders, 98.
44. Sanders, 98.
45. Zwinger and Zwinger, "Nature's Shaking," in *In the Blast Zone,* 100, 101.
46. Zwinger and Zwinger, 102.
47. Zwinger and Zwinger, 103.
48. Le Guin, "Coming Back," in *In the Blast Zone,* 8.
49. With this line from Le Guin, poet and natural history writer Tim McNulty opens his "Way to Windy Ridge," in *In the Blast Zone,* 17.
50. Kimmerer, "On the Ridge," in *In the Blast Zone,* 46.
51. Moore, "In Endless Song," in *In the Blast Zone,* 27.

CHAPTER 3

"Grateful to the Proselyte"

Jews among Gentiles in an Age of Injury

Nathanael Vette

Writing at the turn of the second century CE, the pseudonymous author of 4 Ezra was in the throes of an existential and theological crisis:

> I beseech you my lord, why have I been endowed with the power of understanding? For I did not wish to inquire about the ways above, but about those things which we daily experience: why Israel has been given over to the gentiles as a reproach; why the people whom you loved has been given to godless tribes, and the Law of our fathers has been made of no effect and the written covenants no longer exist; and why we pass from the world like locusts, and our life is like a mist, and we are not worthy to obtain mercy. But what will he do for his name, by which we are called? It is about these things that I have asked.[1]

The Roman army, led by Vespasian and then Titus, had left Judea in ruins, the temple destroyed along with its priesthood, Jerusalem trampled upon by gentiles, and its inhabitants dispossessed. Josephus, who was present at the temple's destruction in 70 CE, estimates the number of dead at over a million.[2] Survivors now found themselves as refugees or slaves, without a holy city, temple, or priesthood, and at the mercy of gentile victors who spared no effort in humiliating the vanquished with decrees, triumphs, and punitive taxes. To some Jews, God's favor for the Jewish nation was suddenly open to question, if not in doubt. Why had God allowed the temple to be destroyed by the gentiles, now for a second time? Had God reneged on his covenantal promises to the Jewish people?

To address these questions, our author followed apocalyptic convention by adopting the voice of the fifth-century BCE prophet, Ezra, drawing an analogy between the Babylonian exile and the experience of Jews in the late first century CE. But whereas other apocalyptic seers sought refuge in theodicy, assigning causes for the tragedy and taking comfort in secret heavenly plots working behind the scenes for the good of the Jewish nation, Pseudo-Ezra found such thinking simple and futile. Why God had given Babylon (Rome) dominion over Zion (Jerusalem), despite the faithlessness of the former and the faithfulness of the latter, could not be answered. When the angel Uriel attempts to explain that God's ways are inscrutable, Pseudo-Ezra falls on his face in exasperation: "It would be better for us not to be here than to come here and live in ungodliness, and to suffer and not understand why."[3] The sudden absence of Jerusalem and the temple marked such an incalculable loss that no rationalization could account for it. Pseudo-Ezra speaks as someone whose world had been unmoored from its foundations:

> For you see that our sanctuary has been laid waste, our altar thrown down, our temple destroyed; our harp has been laid low, our song has been silenced, and our rejoicing has been ended; the light of our lampstand has been put out, the ark of our covenant has been plundered, our holy things have been polluted, and the name by which we are called has been profaned; our free men have suffered abuse, our priests have been burned to death, our Levites have gone into captivity, our virgins have been defiled, and our wives have been ravished; our righteous men have been carried off, our little ones have been cast out, our young men have been enslaved and our strong men made powerless. And, what is more than all, the seal of Zion—for she has now lost the seal of her glory, and has been given over into the hands of those that hate us.[4]

While not every Jew across the empire would have shared in Pseudo-Ezra's anguish at the temple's destruction, the effects of its loss were nevertheless universally felt. Whereas adult males had once paid a tax to the Jerusalem Temple, the Romans now levied the punitive *fiscus Iudaicus* (Jewish tax), payable by all Jews between the ages of three and sixty-two years old, the funds of which went toward the upkeep of the pagan Temple of Jupiter Capitoline in Rome. The introduction of the fiscus marked the beginning of a slow but steady decline in the rights of Jews in the Roman Empire, culminating in the anti-Jewish legislation of Christian emperors in the sixth century that barred Jews from most civic and public life and circumscribed Jewish worship. After the losses of 70 CE and the subsequent failure of Simon Bar Kokhba's revolt, living as a Jew in the gentile world of late antiquity became increasingly perilous.

There is a tendency, however, to read Pseudo-Ezra's grief-stricken response as normative for late antique Judaism. On this "lachrymose" reading, all Jewish experience in the postrevolutionary period is filtered through the prism of moral injury. Wounded by the events of 70 CE and 135 CE, or by the success of their Christian rivals, Jewish communities are thought to have turned inward in response to injury, spurning the gentiles they had once welcomed and focusing instead on self-preservation through rigid identity markers.

This simplistic—and, ultimately, supersessionist—narrative of moral injury and decline fails, however, to do justice to the vignettes of Jewish life found in our sources. Far from signaling the withdrawal of Jews from Greco-Roman and later Babylonian society, the sources show a continued, albeit cautious, engagement between Jews and their gentile neighbors that was tempered by the painful lessons of the past while at the same time demonstrating a remarkable openness toward non-Jews or, as Pseudo-Ezra calls them, "those that hate us." One later midrash goes so far as to say that God is grateful for the gentile proselyte in ways that he is not for Israel.

To hear these stories of moral repair, and the lessons they may hold for our own injurious pandemic age, we must first survey what life was like for Jews living in a gentile world before and after 70–135 CE.

JEWS IN A GENTILE WORLD: 164 BCE TO 135 CE

There are two ways of telling the history of Jews in the gentile world of the ancient Mediterranean. One emphasizes the uneasy, if not adversarial, relationship between Jewish communities and their pagan gentile neighbors and ruling authorities, and is usually told through a series of successful and then unsuccessful independence movements. The other emphasizes the fluid ethnic and religious boundaries of the ancient world, in which Jews and gentiles often lived, worked, and worshipped cheek by jowl and participated in each other's cultures, so that a rigid distinction between the worlds of Judaism and paganism cannot be maintained. Histories have generally focused on the former at the expense of the latter, but both readings must account for two facts: First, the era began with an independent, or semi-dependent, Jewish nation and ended without one. Second, most Jews did not live in Palestine but in the Mediterranean and Babylonian Diaspora, where separation from gentile culture and religion was impossible, nor were Jews insulated from the dominant gentile culture in the land of Israel.

These narratives of conflict and confluence continue in parallel throughout the period. Having rebelled against Seleucid interference in the affairs of state and temple in the mid-second century BCE, the Hasmonean rulers of Judea carved out for themselves a kingdom greater than that of David and Solomon, expanding into neighboring regions and compelling gentile inhabitants, such as the Idumeans, to adopt Jewish customs. At the same time, the Jewish nation found an ally in the rising Mediterranean power of Rome, and when the Hasmonean dynasty descended into civil war, it was the Roman general Pompey who intervened to resolve the fracas. However, many saw Pompey's fateful decision in 63 BCE to enter the Holy of Holies, in which no gentile (or non-priestly Jew) was supposed to step foot, as a repeat of the sacrilege of the Seleucids a hundred years earlier. And yet by the time the Judean conflict was decided in the favor of the Idumean—namely, Herod—the Jewish nation had become a subject of Rome.[5] During his tumultuous reign, Herod sought a delicate balance between loyalty to Rome and Jewish nationalism, overseeing the restoration of the Jerusalem Temple, with extensions to rival the temples of the Hellenistic world, while also funding the construction of gentile cities and pagan festivals and temples. The power vacuum left after Herod's death, however, led to fresh calls for independence, replacing the pro-Roman Herodian government with theocracy. The opposite came to pass: While the Herodian dynasty continued to exercise nominal rule in the region, real power would be concentrated in a Roman prefect stationed in Judea. The Judean struggle for independence from gentile interference in the affairs of state and temple faced an uncertain future.

Nevertheless, by the beginning of the first century CE, Jews had grown in number and influence across the Mediterranean. Jewish customs had become a part of everyday life in the cosmopolitan Hellenistic city, with some gentiles adopting Jewish practices such as observing the Sabbath, attending synagogue, and even traveling to Jerusalem to visit the outer court of Herod's Temple. Although Jews did not appear to wage a large-scale effort to win over proselytes, some gentiles voluntarily underwent circumcision or baptism to become Jews, while still more non-Jews associated with and patronized Jewish communities or incorporated the Jewish God into their pantheon.[6] Confluence gave way to conflict, however, when Alexandrian Jews objected to the erection of statues of the emperor Caligula in their synagogues, prompting gentile mobs to massacre Jewish residents and confine them to a quarter of the city. Caligula's solution was to order a statue of himself placed in the temple in Jerusalem, an order that, had it not been for the emperor's timely assassination, would have led to open revolt in Judea and throughout the Diaspora.[7]

After years of corruption and misrule by Roman procurators in Judea, however, revolt broke out. The conflict began not in Judea but Caesarea, where the Roman procurators had issued laws denying Jewish residents the same privileges afforded to gentiles. This sparked a deadly conflict that quickly spread to Jerusalem, where a Judean mob massacred the Roman garrison and radical priests barred gentiles from offering sacrifices in the temple and halted the daily sacrifice for the emperor. While some advocated a return to peace with Rome, the movement for independence gained fresh momentum, and by 66 CE the revolutionary spirit had swept the countryside from Judea to Galilee. The revolt saw the violence between Jews and gentiles, first seen in Caesarea, spread throughout the region, and those in majority-gentile cities massacred Jews in their midst while those in majority-Jewish cities in turn massacred gentiles. Those in Judea advocating friendly relations with gentiles and peace with Rome either faced persecution or fled, while the revolutionary party took up residence in the courts of the temple, in which gentiles could no longer step foot.

The successes of the revolutionary forces were, however, short lived. When Rome's civil war was decided in the general Vespasian's favor, Jerusalem was at war with itself. A fragile alliance between the feuding parties was unable to withstand the army of Titus, the new emperor's son, when it finally arrived in Jerusalem on Passover of 70 CE By the end of summer, much of the city lay in ruins, and the temple was reduced to ashes and rubble, destroyed by Titus's troops, with the Romans having won a decisive victory over the revolutionary forces.

On the one hand, the temple's destruction plunged Judaism into its greatest theological crisis since the Seleucids defiled the temple. New literature emerged to make sense of the tragedy, offering theodicy by way of apocalypse. Works attributed to figures from Israel's (and Rome's) past—Ezra, Baruch, Abraham, and the Roman Sybil—gave readers a behind-the-scenes glimpse of the divine blueprint of history, explaining why Jerusalem, the temple, and the priesthood had to fall to the gentiles and why, despite all appearances, victory over the gentiles would soon be granted to the Jewish nation.

On the other hand, the post–70 CE period was something of a golden age for Jew-gentile relations. Even though Jews had been dispossessed of their ancestral homeland, deprived of their temple, and burdened with the punitive fiscus, gentiles appear to have flocked to Jewish communities around the Mediterranean in ever larger numbers. The practice of adopting Jewish customs was apparently so widespread it attracted the ire and suspicion of figures as dissimilar as Juvenal and Epictetus.[8] Judaism could even claim proselytes in the imperial household—for example, Flavius Clemens and Flavia Domitilla—though their conversions would become the pretext for their downfall.[9] What led to the growth in popularity of Judaism during this period is not clear.[10] There is, again, no evidence of a concerted Jewish effort to win converts. The destruction of the temple would have been a hindrance to conversion, not a boon, as some have argued.[11] And yet while Jerusalem and its temple lay in ruins, some pockets of Jewish life in the ancient Mediterranean appear to have been flourishing.

The attraction of gentiles to Judaism prompted a backlash, however, especially in the elite classes, and there appear to have been measures—in addition to the deterrent fiscus—enacted to discourage Roman citizens from abandoning their ancestral customs to become Jews. Some male Jews took the step of hiding their circumcisions while in the bathhouse, apparently fearing the social or political consequences.[12] Armed conflict broke out afresh in Trajan's reign and then again in Hadrian's reign, as Jews responded to the emperor's plans to demolish the ruins of the temple and build a new temple to Jupiter. Jewish revolutionaries recaptured part of Judea and briefly established a messianic kingdom under the leadership of Simon Bar Kokhba. The days of the messianic kingdom were cut short, however, when Hadrian's forces arrived in Judea boasting ten legions and proceeded to massacre the Jewish inhabitants of Palestine. By 135 CE, the bloodshed had eclipsed even that of the first revolt, and the painful episode ended with the execution of the leading sages—Rabbi Akiva and his ten colleagues—leaving Jews once again without a holy city, leadership, or temple.[13]

AN INWARD TURN AFTER INJURY?

The suffering of the Jewish community did not escape the notice of its critics. After the defeat of Bar Kokhba's rebellion, one gentile Christian could gloat, "You dashed down the Lord; you were dashed to the ground, and you lie dead."[14] Such triumphalist anti-Jewish rhetoric would remain a feature of the elite Christian response to Judaism from 135 CE onward. The rabbis, though still mourning the loss of the temple, produced a body of literature primarily concerned with the religious demands of everyday life. One well-known commentator goes so far as to call the Mishnah, the first major work of the period, "ahistorical."[15] So what effect, if any, did these successive injuries have on relations between Jews and gentiles?

The classic theory of retrenchment asserts that Judaism responded to these tragedies by retreating in on itself, withdrawing from the Greco-Roman world and the gentiles it had once welcomed.[16] Whereas non-Jews had once flocked to the temple and patronized synagogues, Jewish communities now focused on the preservation of their ethnic and religious identity, taking extraordinary measures to avoid contamination from the pagan world it inhabited (the *Avodah Zarah* tractates of the Mishnah, Tosefta, and Talmudim are usually cited disparagingly in this regard). The breakdown in relations following the destruction of the temple and the defeat of Bar Kokhba had effectively ended Jewish efforts to engage gentiles, clearing the field for the Christians, who would emerge victorious in the fourth century CE.

The story of Judaism retreating as Christianity advanced is rooted in supersessionism. European writers of the late nineteenth and early twentieth centuries, Protestant and Catholic alike, wrote from the conviction that with the advent of Christianity, Judaism no longer had a place in the world. All evidence was interpreted through this lens. The extensive *adversus Iudaeos* literature of the early church, with its proscriptions against adopting Jewish customs and attending the synagogue, was seen, not as a sign of the popularity and force of Jewish arguments, but as an elaborate fiction for the clarification of the church's own positions.[17] Jewish communities, wounded and withdrawn after the defeats of 70 CE and 135 CE, posed no real threat to Christianity's success in winning gentile converts.[18] With Judaism in decline, the stage was set for Christianity's inevitable triumph.[19]

The period following the Second World War saw the emergence of an alternative account to the classic retrenchment theory.[20] It postulated that Judaism, or at least one branch of it, was for the most part unaffected by the losses of the two revolts and continued to proselytize gentiles, competing alongside Christians for the prize. Scholars advocating the competition theory maintain a distinction between the conservative Judaism of Palestine that turned inward in the wake of the tragedies and the liberal Judaism of the Diaspora that continued to attract and seek out gentile converts, with diminishing returns, until the anti-Jewish laws of the Christian emperors came into effect, ending the mission once and for all.[21]

On this reading, Jewish retrenchment occurred, not because of the tragedies of 70 CE and 135 CE, but because of the victory of the Christians, who bested Jews in a competition for gentile recruits.[22] Whereas the classic account of retrenchment positively casts the inclusivist Christians as the heroes against the exclusivist Jews, the competition theory favors the supposedly liberal Diaspora Jews over the narrow Palestinian Jews. The loss of the temple and the Jewish homeland is thought to have freed Diaspora Judaism from the constraints of ethnic particularism, increasing its appeal to potential gentile converts.[23] For the competition theorist, the triumph of Christianity and the retrenchment of Judaism were not inevitable but the result of a hard-fought struggle in which Christianity eventually gained the upper hand.

While the competition theory attempts to correct the classic retrenchment theory, it repeats its fatal flaw, telling a story of Christian vitality and Jewish decline.[24] For both, the success of a religion is judged by its ability to draw converts. A caricature of rabbinic particularism becomes the foil for either the universalism of Christianity or an idealized version of Diaspora Judaism. Both theories assume, often without evidence, that Judaism was a missionary religion until either the tragedies of 70 CE and 135 CE or the laws of the sixth century CE put an end to missionary activity. The loss of the proselytizing spirit is thus seen as a deficiency of post-retrenchment Judaism. Both theories construct amorphous, monolithic categories of "Judaism" and "Christianity" or "synagogue" and "church" in pursuit of an unquestioned narrative of Christian triumph and Jewish atrophy taking place over centuries and across continents.

AN OUTWARD TURN AFTER INJURY?

Our sources do not present a unified Jewish experience; then, as now, such reconstruction is impossible. They do, however, provide a window into how some Jewish communities traversed the hazardous terrain of an increasingly hostile gentile world both inside and outside the Roman Empire and after its fall. The following discussion is limited to rabbinic literature, sources that are often taken by the retrenchment and competition theorists as evidence of Jewish withdrawal. And while there is no shortage of negative comments pertaining to non-Jews, the sources generally maintain a positive attitude toward gentiles wishing to join Jewish communities while at the same time noting the change in relations between Jews and gentiles after the destruction of the temple and the exile of Jews from Jerusalem.[25]

The most positive assessment of the Roman conquest of Judea and the exile of Jews from the land appears in a discussion of Hosea 2:23: "I will say to Lo-ammi (not my people), 'You are my people.'" The Gemara attributes the following saying to the second-century CE *tanna* (sage, ca. 1–200 CE), Rabbi Eleazar ben Azariah: "The Holy One, blessed be he, exiled the Israelites among the nations only so that converts should join them."[26] And yet the same passage describes the Romans as worrying, day and night, about how to destroy the Jewish people.

Nevertheless, the sources speak of the benefit to gentiles of Jewish exile. According to the third-century CE Amoraic sage Rabbi Simeon ben Lakish, Abraham, symbolizing Israel, is a blessing to the world: "[God said,] 'I will set up a cinnamon tree in the world. Just as in the case of a cinnamon tree, so long as you manure and hoe it, it will produce fruit, so in the case of Abraham.'"[27] And again, "even the other families on the earth enjoy blessings only on account of Israel . . . even the ships that sail from Gaul to Spain are blessed only on account of Israel."[28] But the blessing may also proceed in the other direction, from the gentiles to Jews. To this end, the Yerushalmi offers a parable where righteous gentiles among the Jewish people are likened to beautiful saplings planted by a king in his son's garden.[29] Here the attraction of gentiles to the Jewish community is a blessing from God and a reward for righteousness. Elsewhere prominent proselytes of Israel's past are cited as proof of the benefits gentile converts bring the Jewish people: "The Holy One, Blessed be He, said to Abraham: I have two good shoots to graft onto you: Ruth the Moabite, the ancestress of the house of David, and Naamah the Ammonite, whose marriage with Solomon led to the ensuing dynasty of the kings of Judea."[30] In the present age, however, it is primarily gentiles who have reaped the benefits from the exile of Jews among the nations.

Traditions about conversion are, however, careful to note the dangerous predicament of Jews living in the period after 70–135 CE. According to the sages of the Tannaim, "They are valid proselytes only if they are converted under the presently-prevailing conditions [of repression] . . . only he who lives with you in your misery will be settled among you, and no other."[31] Sources attest to the practice of first attempting to dissuade potential converts from joining the Jewish community, citing the example of Naomi, who attempts to dissuade Ruth from leaving the land of Moab for Judah.[32] The Gemara attributes the rule to sages in the generations following the temple's destruction.[33] It says, "Our rabbis have taught on Tannaite authority: A person who comes to convert at this time—they say to him, 'How come you have come to convert? Don't you know that at this time the Israelites are forsaken and harassed, despised, baited, and afflictions come upon them?' If he said, 'I know full well, and I am not worthy [of sharing their suffering],' they accept him forthwith."[34]

And again:

> If a man wishes to become a proselyte he is not accepted at once but they say to him, "Why do you want to become a proselyte? Do you not see that this people are debased, oppressed and degraded more than all other peoples, that diseases and chastisements come upon them and they bury their children and children's children, that they are slaughtered for [observing] circumcision, immersion and the other precepts [of the Torah] and cannot hold up their heads like other peoples?[35]

While the practice of dissuading potential proselytes can be seen as a way of testing their sincerity, and to deter "calculating converts" or even Roman spies from joining the community, it also alerts the would-be convert to the dangers of being a Jew in a hostile world.[36] This shows, not just a concern for the safety of the Jewish community, which could be threatened by the presence of proselytes,[37] but a concern for the well-being of potential proselytes themselves. Elsewhere the sages struggle to explain "how come gentiles at this time are harassed, and sufferings come upon them."[38] There is an awareness that the conversion of gentiles was unusual given the ongoing suffering of Jewish communities as well as the unique threats faced by proselytes. As the Gemara tersely states: "Conversion is uncommon, death is routine."[39]

But the surprising persistence of proselytes despite these hindrances afforded them a special place in Jewish communities. The *Sifra* on Leviticus 19:18 offers the following interpretation: "Just as it is written of Jews 'and you shall love your fellow as yourself,' so it is written of proselytes 'and you shall love him as yourself.'" Likewise, the *Mekhilta* maintains that "beloved are the strangers [i.e., proselytes]. For in ever so many passages Scripture applies to them the same designations as it does to the Israelites."[40] Tradition criticizes the first-century BCE sage Shammai for dismissing a would-be convert, whereas Hillel is praised for having compassion on the gentile and for bringing them "under the wings of the Divine Presence."[41]

The sources also speak of God's special love for proselytes. They are likened to lilies handpicked by God from the garden of the nations.[42] The midrash speaks of this love: "The proselyte is beloved because the Holy One had [the following] written about himself: 'Why are you like a proselyte in the land?' [Jer. 14:8] The Holy One said: Thus do I love the proselyte."[43] The *Mekhilta* goes so far as to say God loves the gentile proselyte in ways he does not love Israel: "Now, who is the greater, he who loves the king or he whom the king loves? You must say: It is he whom the king loves. And it is written: 'And loveth the stranger' [Deut. 10:18]."[44] The Targum explains why the proselyte is exceedingly precious to God, saying of Ruth:

> [You] left your gods and your people, your father and your mother and the land of your birth, and have gone to become a proselyte and to dwell in the midst of a people with whom you were unacquainted before. May the Lord reward you well in this world for your good work, and may you receive full recompense from the Lord, the God of Israel, in the world to come, because you have come to be a proselyte and to seek shelter under the shadow of His Glorious Presence.[45]

One later midrash offers a striking parable of God's love for the proselyte, speaking of God's gratitude for the gentile who has unexpectedly joined the flock of Israel.[46]

> The Holy One, blessed be He, greatly loves the proselytes. To what may this be compared? To a king who had a flock which used to go out to the field and come in at even. So it was each day. Once a stag came in with them. When the flock came in to the fold he came in with them; when they went out to graze he went out with them. The king was told: "A certain stag has joined the flock and is grazing with them every day. He goes out with them and comes in with them." The king felt an affection for him. When he went out into the field the king gave orders: 'Let him have good pasture, such as he likes; no man shall beat him; be careful with him!" When he came in with the flock also the king would tell them, "Give him to drink"; and he loved him very much. The servants said to him: "Sovereign! You possess so many he-goats, you possess so many lambs, you possess so many kids, and you never caution us about them; yet you give us instructions every day about this stag!" Said the king to them: "The flock have no choice; whether they want or not, it is their nature to graze in the field all day and to come in at even to sleep in the fold. The stags, however, sleep in the wilderness. It is not in their nature to come into places inhabited by man. Shall we then not account it as a merit to this one which has left behind the whole of the broad, vast wilderness, the abode of all the beasts, and has come to stay in the courtyard?" In like manner, ought we not to be grateful to the proselyte who has left behind him his family and his father's house, aye, has left behind his people and all the other peoples of the world, and has chosen to come to us? Accordingly He has provided him with special

> protection, for He exhorted Israel that they shall be very careful in relation to the proselytes so as not to do them harm; and so indeed it says, "Love ye therefore the proselyte" [Deut. 10:19].[47]

MORAL INJURY AND THE OUTWARD TURN

The differences in date, provenance, and style prevent these sources from offering a unified picture of Jew-Gentile relations in the era following 70–135 CE. They do, however, effectively dismantle the retrenchment theorist's caricature of rabbinic literature as withdrawn and particularistic in contrast to the gregarious universalism of Christianity or an idealized Diaspora Judaism. The tragedies of the temple's destruction and Bar Kokhba's defeat, and the marginalization of Jews thereafter, did not end Jewish engagement with the gentiles; nor was it unaffected by them. Rather, Jewish communities appear to have cautiously welcomed voluntary converts, nevertheless warning them of the difficulties faced by Jews after losing their land and temple. Proselytes should be under no illusion of the suffering experienced by Jews in a hostile world. But if gentiles were still willing to join the Jewish people, despite these disclaimers, they could become the recipients of love, even gratitude, not only from the community but also from God.

Why a community or an individual would continue to welcome those belonging to a group responsible for their suffering cannot be easily explained by historical criticism, let alone theology. While a psychological analysis based on such fragmentary literary evidence is impossible, the study of trauma theory is able to offer analogies that cast fresh light on the question. Moral injury, broadly construed, is a subject of trauma theory and concerns the effects of physical or emotional wounds that violate a person's core moral beliefs and expectations. For those studying religions, trauma theory has particular value in its ability to describe and account for the role of ritual in identity shaping and preserving acts in response to traumatic experience.[48] The figure of Pseudo-Ezra, introduced at the beginning of this chapter, clearly experienced the loss of the temple and the land as a moral injury. Pseudo-Ezra can speak of their joy as having been ended.[49] The memory of this moral injury is preserved in rabbinic literature: The Tosefta states that there were those who refused to eat meat or drink wine since the temple was destroyed.[50] Still, in an early medieval midrash we read: "As long as the kingdom of Edom [Rome] abides, there will be no rejoicing on the earth."[51]

But it is the corollary of moral injury, moral repair, that is most illuminating for our analysis of Jewish responses to gentiles in the postrevolutionary period. As an organic response to injury, moral repair attempts to bridge the experience of the injured person or group before and after trauma, preserving and strengthening identity markers while also reinterpreting ritual and tradition so that acts take on a purificatory and restorative significance. For example, the loss of the temple and the land required that the traditional means of restoration be reimagined.[52] A famous example is recorded in the *Avot d'Rabbi Natan*.

> Once as Rabban Joḥanan ben Zakkai was coming out from Jerusalem, Rabbi Joshua followed after him and saw the temple in ruins. "Woe to us!", Rabbi Joshua cried, "that this place where atonement was made for the sins of Israel, is laid waste!"; "My son," Rabbi Joḥanan said to him, "Do not be sad; for we have another atonement as effective as this. And what is it? It is acts of loving-kindness, as it is said, 'For I desire mercy and not sacrifice' [Hos. 6:6]."[53]

Whereas there is an extensive literature and vocabulary on moral repair within individual persons and communities, moral repair between persons has received less attention, so it often functions as a touchstone that is "not closely analyzed and [is] not situated in a broader perspective on moral relationship."[54] Nevertheless, one can observe the language of interpersonal repair in the acceptance of gentile proselytes into Jewish communities after 135 CE, wherein certain ritualized elements appear to have held a purificatory and restorative significance. On the one hand, there is a recognition of the change in circumstances for Jews living after the loss of the temple and the land, and its ongoing emotional and political effects on the community. The proselyte may not enter without acknowledging this experience. On the other hand, there is an awareness that the desire of the proselyte to join the community is both rare and precious, earning them the love and gratitude of the community and God.

MORAL REPAIR IN THE PANDEMIC AGE

In this chapter, I have attempted to recover a narrative of moral repair in a history often told as a series of successive injuries. In doing so, I had hoped that it might say something urgent to our own injurious and polarized pandemic age. There are some clear parallels: Now as then, we see communities that have experienced nothing but hostility from others respond to injury by offering the cautious hand of fellowship to "those that hate them." It reflects both the desire that injury be acknowledged and the recognition that repair can be elusive but remains imperative. And on those rare occasions when moral repair does take place between persons, and between communities, it can create the conditions for profound and surprising expressions of gratitude. But perhaps the lesson for our own day is the value of listening to narratives of moral repair, as fragmentary as they may be, especially when narratives of injury can seem to overshadow everything. The pandemic age has seen the proliferation of new injuries and held a fresh and much needed light to old ones. Nevertheless, there have been heartening stories of moral repair, though they can be harder to hear.[55]

At the beginning of this chapter, we met Pseudo-Ezra in the throes of an existential crisis, having witnessed their world destroyed by gentiles. And yet our author chose the pseudonym "Ezra," adopting the persona of the scribe who led exiles back from Babylon to Judea, having been charged by a gentile king to rebuild the house of God in Jerusalem. On the other side of injury, repair awaits. Whereas Pseudo-Ezra claimed to have written after the destruction of the First Temple, it is another book purporting to come from the destruction of the Second that expresses this hope most clearly. The priest Rabbi Ishmael is said to have been called up to heaven on the eve of the tragedy in 70 CE, whereupon he received this vision: "At once Israel shall be saved from among the gentiles and the Messiah shall appear to them and bring them up to Jerusalem with great joy. Moreover, the kingdom of Israel, gathered from the four quarters of the world, shall eat with the Messiah, *and the gentiles shall eat with them.*"[56]

NOTES

1. 4 Ezra 4:22–25.
2. Josephus, *War*, trans. H. St. J. Thackeray (LCL 203, 487, 210; Cambridge, MA: Harvard University Press, 1927–28), 6.420.
3. 4 Ezra 4:12.
4. 4 Ezra 10:21–23.
5. Narrated in books 14–15 of Josephus's *Antiquities*, trans. Ralph Marcus (LCL 489; Cambridge, MA: Harvard University Press, 1963).
6. Feldman, *Jew and Gentile*, 288–382.
7. There are two contemporary responses to the crisis from the Alexandrian Jewish philosopher Philo: *Against Flaccus*, trans. F. H. Colson (LCL 363; Cambridge, MA: Harvard University Press, 1954); and *On the Embassy to Gaius*, trans. F. H. Colson (LCL 379; Cambridge, MA: Harvard University Press, 1962).
8. Juvenal, *Sat.* 14:86–106, trans. Susanna Morton Braund (LCL 91; Cambridge, MA: Harvard University Press, 2004); and Epictetus, *Disc.* 2.9.20–21, trans. W. A. Oldfather; LCL 131; Cambridge, MA: Harvard University Press, 1925).

9. Dio Cassius, *Rom. Hist.* 67.14.1–2, trans. Earnest Cary and Herbert B. Foster (LCL 176; Cambridge, MA: Harvard University Press, 1925).
10. One possibility is the dispersion of Judean refugees around the Mediterranean after the war led to a renewed interest in Judaism.
11. Most notably Simon, *Verus Israel,* 3–11, 28–53, 301.
12. Martial, *Ep.* 7.82, trans. D. R. Shackleton Bailey (LCL 95; Cambridge, MA: Harvard University Press, 1993).
13. On the bloody aftermath of Bar Kokhba's revolt, see Cassius Dio, *Rom. Hist.* 69.12.1–14.3. The classic account of Rabbi Akiva's martyrdom is found in b. Ber. 61b.
14. Melito, *Peri Pascha* 99–100 (Stuart George Hall, *Melito of Sardis: On Pascha and Fragments,* Oxford Early Christian Texts [Oxford: Clarendon, 1979], 57).
15. Neusner, *Judaism.*
16. Renan, *Histoire des origines du christianisme,* 5:5, 11–16; and Harnack, *Mission and Expansion,* 18.
17. Harnack, "Die Altercatio Simonis Judaei," 77–78; Krüger, *Geschichte der altchristlichen Litteratur,* 69; and Jordan, *Geschichte der altchristlichen Litteratur,* 240.
18. Harnack, *Geschichte der altchristlichen Literattur,* 1:2.58.
19. Critiqued in Cohen, "Adolph Harnack's 'The Mission,'" in Pearson, *Future of Christianity,* 168–69.
20. Surveyed in Baumgarten, "Marcel Simon's 'Verus Israel,'" 472–73.
21. Goodenough, *Jewish Symbols,* 44; Simon, *Verus Israel,* 378–84; anticipated in Schürer, *Geschichte des jüdischen Volkes,* 3:162; and Freimann, "Die Wortführer des Judentums," 555–85.
22. Simon, *Verus Israel,* 371, 384.
23. Simon, 3–11, 28–53, 301.
24. Taylor, *Anti-Judaism,* 8–11.
25. See Porton, *Stranger within Your Gates.*
26. b. Pes. 87b.
27. Gen. Rab. 46:2.
28. b. Yeb. 63a. The same passage maintains that calamities befall gentiles only because of the Jewish people.
29. y. Ber. 8:2.
30. b. Yeb. 63a.
31. b. Yeb. 24b.
32. Tg. Ruth 1:10–18; y. Qid. 3:15; b. Yeb. 47b; and Ger. 4:3. For Ruth as the model proselyte, see Tg. Ruth. 2:10–14; and b. Yeb. 63a.
33. For dating, see Cohen, "Rabbinic Conversion Ceremony," 186–87.
34. b. Yeb. 47a.
35. Ger. 1:1.
36. b. Avod. Zar. 24b; Hoenig, "Conversion," in Eichorn, *Conversion to Judaism,* 52; and Cohen, "Rabbinic Conversion Ceremony," 188–90.
37. b. Nid. 13b; b. Qid. 70b; and Kal. Rab. 2:4.
38. b. Yeb. 48b.
39. b. Git. 85a.
40. Mekh. on Exod 22:20.
41. b. Shab. 31a; and par. ARN 15:3.
42. y. Ber. 8:2.

43. Midr. Tanḥ. B, Lech Lecha 6:3.
44. Mekh. on Exod. 22:20.
45. Tg. Ruth 2:11–12.
46. The Torah Shelemah attributes a version of this parable to the third-century CE Palestinian sage Rabbi Alexandri.
47. Num. Rab. 8:2.
48. Kelle, "Moral Injury," 121–44.
49. 4 Ezra 10:22.
50. t. Sot. 15:10–15.
51. Midr. Ps. 97:1.
52. Geringer and Wiener, "Insights into Moral Injury," 67.
53. ARN A, 4.
54. Walker, *Moral Repair*, 22.
55. To give one example from the United States and another from the Philippines, see Langhout et al., "Teaching and Learning," 249–65; and Espartinez, "Emerging Community Pantries," 926.
56. 3 En. 48:10. Italics added.

BIBLIOGRAPHY

Baumgarten, Albert I. "Marcel Simon's 'Verus Israel' as a Contribution to Jewish History." *Harvard Theological Review* 92 (1999): 465–78.

Cohen, Shaye J. D. "Adolph Harnack's 'The Mission and Expansion of Judaism': Christianity Succeeds Where Judaism Fails." In *The Future of Christianity*, edited by Birger A. Pearson, 163–69. Minneapolis: Fortress, 1991.

———. "The Rabbinic Conversion Ceremony." *Journal of Jewish Studies* 41 (1990): 177–203.

Espartinez, Alma. "Emerging Community Pantries in the Philippines during the Pandemic: Hunger, Healing, and Hope." *Religions* 12 (2021): 926.

Feldman, Louis H. *Jew and Gentile in the Ancient World: Attitudes and Interactions from Alexander to Justinian*. Princeton NJ: Princeton University Press, 1993.

Freimann, M. "Die Wortführer des Judentums in den ältesten Kontroversen zwischen Juden und Christen." *Montasschrift fur Geschichte und Wissenschaft des Judentums* 55 (1911): 555–85.

Geringer, Kim S., and Nancy H. Wiener. "Insights into Moral Injury and Soul Repair from Classical Jewish Texts." *Pastoral Psychology* 68 (2019): 59–75.

Goodenough, E. R. *Jewish Symbols in the Graeco-Roman Period*. Vol. 1, *The Archaeological Evidence from Palestine*. New York: Pantheon, 1953.

Harnack, Adolf von. "Die Altercatio Simonis Judaei et Theophili Christiani nebst Untersuchungen über die antijüdische Polemik in der alten Kirche." *TU*. Leipzig: J. C. Hinrichs, 1883, 1:77–78.

———. *Geschichte der altchristlichen Literattur bis Eusebius*. Vol. 1, *Die Uberlieferung und der Bestand*. Leipzig: J. C. Hinrichs, 1893.

———. *The Mission and Expansion of Christianity in the First Three Centuries*. Translated by James Moffat. London: Williams & Northgate, 1908.

Hoenig, Sidney B. "Conversion during the Talmudic Period." In *Conversion to Judaism: A History and Analysis*, edited by David Max Eichorn, 33–66. New York: Ktav, 1965.

Jordan, Hermann. *Geschichte der altchristlichen Literatur*. Leipzig; Quelle & Meyer, 1911.

Kelle, Brad E. "Moral Injury and Biblical Studies: An Early Sampling of Research and Emerging Trends." *Currents in Biblical Research* 19 (2021): 121–44.

Krüger, D. Gustav. *Geschichte der altchristlichen Litteratur in den ersten drei Jahrhunderten*. Freiburg, 1895.

Langhout, Regina Day, et al. "Teaching and Learning during a Pandemic: How One Graduate Community Psychology Class Quickly Incorporated Healing Justice into Our Practices." *Community Psychology* 28 (2021): 249–65.

Neusner, Jacob. *Judaism: The Evidence of the Mishnah*. Chicago: University of Chicago Press, 1981.

Porton, Gary G. *The Stranger within Your Gates: Converts and Conversion in Rabbinic Literature*. Chicago: University of Chicago Press, 1994.

Renan, Ernst. *Histoire des origines du christianisme*. Vol. 5, *Les Evangiles et la seconde generation chrétienne*. Paris: Michel Levy Freres, 1877.

Schürer, Emil. *Geschichte des jüdischen Volkes im Zeitalter Jesu Christi*. 3 vols. 3rd ed. Leipzig: Hinrichs, 1909.

Simon, Marcel. *Verus Israel: A Study of the Relations between Christians and Jews in the Roman Empire AD 135–425*. Translated by H. McKeating. Liverpool: Liverpool University Press, 1986.

Taylor, Miriam S. *Anti-Judaism and Early Christian Identity: A Critique of the Scholarly Consensus*. Studia Post-Biblica 46. Leiden: Brill, 1995.

Walker, Margaret Urban. *Moral Repair: Reconstructing Moral Relations after Wrongdoing*. Cambridge: Cambridge University Press, 2006.

CHAPTER 4

Conflicting Civil Religions

Bellah, Lincoln, and the Alt-Right—Today's American Dilemma

James Spickard

This volume grows out of a project titled "Gratitude, Injury, and Repair in a Pandemic Age: An Interreligious Dialogue." Some of these terms are easier to grasp than others. We are certainly living in a pandemic era. Since 2020, the United States has suffered at least four major waves of COVID-19, and hundreds of people continue to die each day. Though the public has moved on, experts now worry about the next pandemic and wonder whether the world is even less ready for that one than it was for COVID-19.[1] Industries have been upended, and economies have crashed, recovered, and crashed again. Few people have been untouched. Many continue to live with a sense of impending crisis.

There are other injuries. The United States continues to suffer political polarization arising from a norm-shattering Trump presidency that laid bare the country's racism and ended with an alt-right mob's attack on the US Capitol. Some people struggle mightily to fulfill America's promise of equality and justice. Others rally around an authoritarian White Christian nationalism that seeks to restore "God's order" and ensure America's world dominance. Still others line their pockets while chaos reigns. Pundits tell us that the American public is more politically and culturally divided now than it has been since the 1960s or even since the Civil War.[2] Our times easily pass Fintan O'Toole's "Yeats Test" for direness: "Things fall apart; the centre cannot hold / . . . The blood-dimmed tide is loosed, and everywhere the ceremony of innocence is drowned."[3] People worry, hope, and pray for health and tranquility to return.

Pandemic, injury, and a hope for repair. Where is gratitude in this picture? It is at least hiding: Recent polls show that a majority of Americans think that the country is headed in the wrong direction, as similar polls have shown for most of the last fifty years.[4] People are not grateful for the way things are.

Yet the country has deep and complicated cultural resources. There has long been an ethos of self-correction in American political life that allows hope for a better future. This is not the only ethos at work, however. We also find anger, fragility, conflict, and despair. Can we be grateful, even if the social and political picture is as dark as it appears?

To find out, we must revisit a time when the United States faced another great trial. The 1960s were, like now, an era of racial unrest, when America was challenged to give equality to its long-oppressed Black citizens. Many Whites resisted that challenge, as they do today. The 1960s also saw civil unrest against the country's longest (until then) imperial war in Vietnam. Together, these issues brought down Lyndon Johnson's otherwise successful presidency and fed the divisions that haunt us still. What sources of hope and gratitude emerged then that might succor us now?

In a 1967 response to that crisis, the sociologist Robert Bellah wrote a justly famed article, "Civil Religion in America." In it he outlined what the journal's editor called "the one religion in America that is broad enough for all citizens to accept." This civil religion was, Bellah claimed, both the imaginative glue that holds the country together and the moral guide that lays out its national mission. He saw it as a source of hope in a time of darkness.[5]

Bellah's article was, in fact, a critique of the Vietnam War. In the article he painted a convincing picture of a nondenominational civil religion that was embodied in national creeds and rituals, and contained an explicit theology of national purpose. He showed how that purpose developed through what he called America's first two "times of trial." The first trial was gaining independence and seeing whether the country could become self-governing and what kind of nation would emerge. That trial's early prophets and saints were George Washington, Benjamin Franklin, Thomas Jefferson, and the other "founding fathers" who created the democracy that the United States has mostly enjoyed.

The second trial was over the question of slavery and, more broadly, whether the country would extend democracy to all. Its prophet and saint was Abraham Lincoln, who used America's religious heritage to frame and reframe the nation's direction through the Civil War. In Bellah's telling,

Lincoln connected the nation's purpose with God's transcendent will without, however, descending into self-righteous nationalism. Lincoln's life, words, and martyrdom returned America, *in potentia,* to its transcendent mission as an "almost chosen people."[6]

Bellah argued that this mission bound America to a higher-than-national purpose. It differentiated the United States from the "old nations" of Europe, just as the Hebrews' willingness to follow God's pillars of smoke and fire to the Promised Land differentiated Israel from Egypt. He saw the Vietnam War as a misstep in the country's "third time of trial," which he described as "the problem of responsible action in a revolutionary world." Would the United States continue down an imperial path, as it was doing in Vietnam? Or would it heed the civil religion's warning that "our nation stands under higher judgment"? Bellah's hope—and implicit gratitude—rested on his analysis that "American civil religion is not the worship of the American nation but an understanding of the American experience in the light of ultimate and universal reality."[7]

Does this civil religion still exist? Can it or its successors be a source of gratitude and hope in our current calamity? That is our question to explore.

BELLAH'S CIVIL RELIGION

Bellah borrowed the term "civil religion" from Jean-Jacques Rousseau's insight that societies are held together by a shared sense of the sacred.[8] Bellah wrote, "I used the phrase [civil religion] to describe the religious dimension of American political life that has characterized our republic since its foundation, and whose *most central tenet is that the nation is not an ultimate end in itself but stands under transcendent judgement* and only has value insofar as it realizes, partially and fragmentarily at best, a 'higher law.'"[9] This central tenet distinguished America's civil religion from mere nationalism.

Bellah began his essay with a close reading of John F. Kennedy's 1961 inaugural address, in which the president invoked God three times as a witness and arbiter of his future presidential conduct. He swore "before God" to uphold the Constitution. He identified God, not the state, as the source of "the rights of man." And he ended the address with the recognition that "here on earth God's work must truly be our own." None of these statements was said parochially. "God" in this passage was not the Catholic, the Baptist, nor even the Christian God; nor was it יהוה, nor الله, विष्णु, ੧ਓ, nor any other specific supreme being.[10] Symbolically, the term stood for them all. It reminded listeners that American democracy is based on more than just the will of the people. For the American civil religion, wrote Bellah, the people's will "is not itself the criterion of right and wrong. There is a higher criterion in terms of which this will can be judged. . . . The president's obligation extends to the higher criterion."[11]

Kennedy did not invent this obligation. Bellah traced it to America's founding documents—the Declaration of Independence, the Constitution, and the writings of Franklin and Jefferson—and to the major speeches that all presidents have given on ritual occasions. Washington, for example, said in his first inaugural address, "The propitious smiles of Heaven can never be expected on a nation that disregards the eternal rules of order and right which Heaven itself has ordained." No subsequent president's inaugural failed to mention God or a transcendent being, and none mentioned Jesus or Christ.[12] Bellah wrote, "The God of the civil religion is not only rather 'unitarian,' he is also on the austere side, much more related to order, law, and right than to salvation and love. . . . He is [also] actively interested and involved in history, with a special concern for America."[13] Doing justice is more important to this God than are lesser national affairs.

The term "civil religion" here is apt. Gods do not make religions; people do. These religions express their people's sense of the sacred through origin myths and the lives of the saints whom they hope to emulate. The Boston Tea Party, Paul Revere's ride, the Battle of Bunker Hill, Valley Forge, and so on are all key parts of America's independence myth—Bellah's "first trial"—that defined the nation as opposing tyranny and being dedicated to freedom. No matter that the famous "tea party" was not a tax protest but a tea smugglers' attempt to eliminate low-cost competition.[14] Nor that Revere never finished his famous ride, and the Bunker Hill battle was mostly fought on the next hill over. Myths need not be accurate to inspire.

Civil religions also use sacred texts. Like Genesis's two myths of creation, America's core texts are internally inconsistent: The Declaration of Independence says that "all men are created equal," while the Constitution counts a Black male slave as only three-fifths of a man. This contradiction was well noted at the time.[15] It grew over the next seventy years until its tension erupted in a brutal civil war, whose Union victory changed the Constitution to match the declaration's promise. The North's failure to support Reconstruction, however, doomed for another eighty-seven years the legal equality that the civil religion demanded.

America had, however, other civil religious possibilities. From the beginning, Bellah's version had to compete with what Philip Gorski called "a conquest narrative," a different "promised land" motif that used Israel's martial exploits against the Canaanites to justify the displacement and slaughter of North America's natives. Historians have debunked Governor William Bradford's claim that Plymouth Colony had been set down into "a hideous and desolate wilderness, full of wild beasts and wild men," but the image lived on in iconic literature and fed the colonists' drive to "tame" the "new world."[16] Andrew Jackson's Indian removal policy drew on conquest themes, as did expanding cotton slavery, the Mexican-American War, and the growth of America' first overseas empire.

Slavery was important politically as well as economically because its growth maintained the South's power vis-à-vis the more populous North.[17] Antebellum Southern politicians such as John C. Calhoun emphasized the Constitution's plural reference to "states" and its official subordination of the Black labor force rather than the declaration's call for equality. This was a republican vision rather than a democratic one that called for a limited government dominated by a virtuous social elite dedicated to opposing both tyranny and majority rule.[18] Historian George Van Cleve contrasts Calhoun's myth of the United States as "a political union of states dedicated to preserving political and moral freedom" (for Whites) with the myth that Bellah described of "a progressively improving nation . . . based on a constitution founded on *and subordinate to* a religiously grounded (or ethically universalist) higher law."[19]

Abraham Lincoln came of age in the midst of this mythic competition. He favored the declaration's equality over the Constitution's compromise, and he abhorred slavery and consistently opposed its expansion. However, he also steadily argued that "the Congress of the United States has no power, under the constitution, to interfere with the institution of slavery in the different States."[20] America's adherence to law was a national virtue that he did not wish to discard.

Lincoln did not, however, take this as evidence that the declaration limited equality to Whites:

> They [the writers] did not mean to assert the obvious untruth, that all were then actually enjoying that equality [of rights], nor yet, that they were about to confer it immediately upon them. In fact they had no power to confer such a boon. They meant simply to declare the right, so that the enforcement of it might follow as fast as circumstances should permit. They meant to set up a standard maxim for free society, which should be familiar to all, and revered by all; constantly looked to, constantly labored for, and even though never

> perfectly attained, constantly approximated, and thereby constantly spreading and deepening its influence, and augmenting the happiness and value of life to all people of all colors everywhere.[21]

He thus opposed the Dred Scott decision as misreading the Constitution, history, and American ideals. He saw the Constitution's slavery clauses as compromises made to begin a "more perfect union" that required yet fuller perfection. Lincoln realized that this idea—that the declaration's principles required the Constitution's eventual change—meant that the United States was governed by higher standards than simply its founding laws. This was also the view Jefferson expressed in his December 1806 message to Congress, where he called for the abolition of the slave trade by "withdraw[ing] the citizens of the United States from all further participation in those violations of human rights which have been so long continued on the unoffending inhabitants of Africa, and which the morality, the reputation, and the best interests of our country have long been eager to proscribe."[22]

Congress abolished the trade in 1807, but that trade did not stop until 1862, when Lincoln enforced capital punishment against a slave trader.[23] The president was more tentative in freeing Southern slaves, basing the Emancipation Proclamation on his powers as commander in chief to undercut the Southern economy. Slavery was not fully abolished until the Thirteenth Amendment was ratified after his death.

Bellah did not discuss this part of Lincoln's history in his essay, though he recognized it. The passage he quoted at length came from Lincoln's second inaugural. It carries a more complex and overtly religious tone:

> If we shall suppose that American Slavery is one of those offences which, in the providence of God, must needs come, but which, having continued through His appointed time, He now wills to remove, and that He gives to both North and South, this terrible war, . . . shall we discern therein any departure from those divine attributes which the believers in a Living God always ascribe to Him? Fondly do we hope—fervently do we pray—that this mighty scourge of war may speedily pass away. Yet, if God wills that it continue until all the wealth piled by the bond-man's two hundred and fifty years of unrequited toil shall be sunk, and until every drop of blood drawn with the lash shall be paid by another drawn with the sword, as was said three thousand years ago, so still it must be said "the judgments of the Lord, are true and righteous altogether."[24]

This is clearly a religious passage. Alongside the Gettysburg Address, it is the source of Lincoln's stature as a civil theologian.[25] He argued that the United States has a higher calling than mere nationalism, just as Bellah did a century later.

Bellah also saw Lincoln as a character in this religious drama. He noted that Lincoln's words and his sacrificial death added a symbolic Christian element to what had previously been a rather Hebraic civil creed. Indeed, the timing of Lincoln's shooting—on Good Friday—led preachers of the time to liken him cautiously to Christ.[26] Lincoln had himself, in his Gettysburg Address, underscored the Union soldiers' deaths as a sacrifice of "those who here gave their lives, that the nation might live." Bellah quoted Robert Lowell's analysis of that address as joining "Jefferson's ideals of freedom and equality . . . to the Christian sacrificial act of death and rebirth. . . . [T]his is a meaning that . . . is now part of our lives as a challenge, obstacle and hope."[27] In Bellah's view, America's civil religion reads Lincoln as dying not just for his country but also for his country's transcendent ideals. This puts those ideals above national interests. This is a good model both for gratitude and for the fortitude to right wrongs.

Bellah devoted the last third of his essay to criticizing the Vietnam War as a violation of America's calling to be a force for justice in the world. He decried his country's support of "a repressive and unstable military dictatorship" that American leaders illegitimately presented as "the free people of South Viet-Nam." He wrote, "We have in a moment of uncertainty been tempted to rely on our overwhelming physical power rather than on our intelligence, and we have, in part, succumbed to this temptation. Bewildered and unnerved when our terrible power fails to bring immediate success, we are at the edge of a chasm the depth of which no man knows."[28]

Six years later, he compared Richard Nixon's second inaugural address with both Kennedy's and Lincoln's, finding Nixon's to be "a form of national self-worship without any element of [God's] higher judgement": "Better indeed it would be for us if our present chief magistrate was not congratulating himself on peace with honor but was instead telling his people that this was America's most criminal war for which we have already paid a terrible price and for which we will continue to pay the wages of sin for decades and generations to come."[29]

For Bellah, this sense of standing under higher judgment was what gave the United States its world-historical importance. Following "the better angels of our nature" meant casting aside our tempting devils to follow a higher, more ethical path. That was, for him, a source of gratitude that should carry the United States through its "third time of trial."

A personal aside: I was a first-year college student when Bellah wrote his article, though I only learned of it a decade later. I knew, however, about America's civil religion. I came out of high school headed for a career in foreign service as a way to support my country's positive role in the world. For me, as for Bellah, the Vietnam War made it impossible to defend my government. I experienced both the hope and the betrayal of the civil religion's promise of justice to all.

COMPETING RELIGIONS

Bellah's version of American civil religion spoke most strongly to those elite policymakers for whom America's historical ideals matter. He quoted the country's founders, presidents, and high officials whose roles and educations trained them to view public service as a transcendent good. Despite being a sociologist, he did not consult ordinary people's views. He articulated and deployed an elite vision to get the elite to change its ways.

What alternative civil religious elements do we find among ordinary people that might support—or oppose—Bellah's elite view? I have already mentioned the conquest narrative that justified America's westward expansion and the oppression of both Native peoples and African slaves. A related stream involves the glorification of violence in American life, a problem with which we still contend.

In a series of masterful histories, Richard Slotkin traced the growth of a popular frontier "myth of regeneration through violence," which he saw as "the structuring metaphor of the American experience."[30] He wrote, "The first colonists saw in America an opportunity to regenerate their fortunes, their spirits, and the power of their church and nation; but the means to that regeneration ultimately became the means of violence . . . when men like Davy Crockett became national heroes by defining national aspirations in terms of so many bears destroyed, so much land preempted, so many trees hacked down, so many Indians and Mexicans dead in the dust."[31]

Slotkin argued that America's true founding fathers were not "those eighteenth-century gentlemen who composed a nation at Philadelphia."

> Rather they were the rogues, adventurers, and land boomers; the Indian fighters, traders, missionaries, explorers, and hunters who killed and were killed until they had mastered the wilderness; the settlers who came after, suffering hardship and Indian warfare for the sake of a sacred mission or a simple desire for land; and the Indians

> themselves, both as they were and as they appeared to the settlers. . . . [These figures'] concerns, their hopes, their terrors, their violence, and their justifications of themselves, as expressed in literature, are the foundation stones of the mythology that informs our history.[32]

Slotkin's *Regeneration through Violence* traced the growth of this mythology from 1600 through the start of the Civil War. His later book, *Gunfighter Nation,* showed how it became a dominant theme in twentieth-century popular culture and politics, where it shaped several generations of White Americans' views of their country and of themselves. Solidified by Teddy Roosevelt's "Rough Rider" imperialism and particularly dominant in the decades when the United States banned non-White immigration (1924–65), it gave "manifest destiny" a conceptual six-shooter to enforce US hegemony around the world. It became even more virulent as the civil rights movement and the 1965 Immigration and Nationality Act began to transform US law and demographics in line with Bellah's cosmopolitan values.

Just look at Southern Whites' official and officially condoned violence against "uppity" African Americans. Trace the shifts in the National Rifle Association's policies on gun control from its 1920s advocacy of "responsible" gun ownership, training, and licensure to its support of unfettered access to heavy weapons "for protection" today.[33] Look at the string of police killings of unarmed Black people, even after the public murder of George Floyd forced these killings into the public eye. Look at recurring White vigilantism, as individuals such as Timothy McVeigh and Kyle Rittenhouse take violent retribution into their own hands.[34] Look at the culminating scenes of the popular films *High Noon, The Godfather* trilogy, the original *Star Wars* trilogy, *Independence Day,* and *Fight Club*. A major stream of American culture sees violence as a solution to problems, not as their origin.

To this we must add the South's post-Reconstruction "religion" of the "Lost Cause."[35] This was a direct descendant of Calhoun's republic of freedom (for Whites) and of his justification for White rule. It was more than just a matter of elite male politicians erecting monuments and memorials to the dead Confederacy as a way to keep Black people down. It also involved what Karen Cox called "Lost Cause Motherhood," with Southern women creating a White supremacist civic culture through education and literature. Novelists and writers portrayed antebellum life as good for slaves and decried both Reconstruction and Northern "tyranny." White women's clubs spread such views, including images of a benevolent antebellum patriarchy and a heroic postwar Klan defending Southern honor. Neither they nor their male counterparts openly advocated slavery's return; however, they did emphasize White people's (imagined) benevolent generosity and the supposed rightness of their continued rule.[36]

This civil-religious strand was explicitly Christian, as were several other movements that took political form. For example, historian Kevin Kruse charted the rise of a 1940s and '50s alliance between anti–New Deal business leaders and nonfundamentalist evangelicals to promote a Christian libertarianism that advocated small government and "traditional" moral codes. He showed how that alliance convinced an increasing share of the public that the "American way of life" was under threat not just from "godless Communism" but also from the welfare state and from (supposedly) antireligious liberal elites. Thus was the present tie between White Evangelical Christianity and pro-capitalist "conservative" politics begun.[37]

To this we must now add class resentment, especially from Southern and midwestern working-class Whites. Joe Bageant explored this theme in *Deer Hunting with Jesus,* where he showed how rural Virginia elites convince people to vote against their own interests while simultaneously stoking their resentment against the urban elites they see as oppressors. Arlie Hochschild found the same pattern in her study of Calcasieu Parish, Louisiana, where she focused on her informants' sense that they were playing by the rules of the game while "line jumpers" from less worthy demographic groups—Blacks, immigrants—supposedly benefitted from the federal government's largesse.[38]

Some people have indeed benefitted economically over the last forty years, though few Blacks and immigrants are among them. Instead, income and wealth have flowed to the richest 20 percent of America's population, which owes its success to its elite education, the key factor in the new knowledge economy.[39] These members of the top 20 percent are not just economically different; they are culturally different as well. In William Galston's description, "Racial and ethnic diversity does not faze these [elite] people, nor do changing social norms. Relatively few are social conservatives. They do not understand why anyone would object to equal treatment for LGBTQ individuals. If they identify with any religious dominations, it is with those whose doctrines and practices align with upper-middle-class sensibilities."[40]

These attitudes are common among coastal and urban elites and less common among Whites living in "flyover country." The latter are less educated and less wealthy; they are also more Christian, more rural, and more working class. Here, Galston found "the growth of a potent new locus of right-wing resentment at the intersection of race, culture, class, and geography. . . . Social conservatives and white Christians feel maligned and beleaguered. The working class has lost ground, and many members of the middle class fear that they are next. Many small towns and rural areas wonder whether they have a future."[41]

These people see themselves losing ground to others whose values they deplore. Thomas Edsall described these increasingly reactionary Whites as "driven by a sense of status loss and entitlement as well as resentment of minority groups that are viewed as a threat."[42]

America's alternate civil religion—populist rather than elite—pulls these strands into a semi-coherent whole. It imagines a White-dominated America built by "good Christians" who only want to give their families a stable middle-class life. It blends the Southern Lost Cause and right-wing Christian libertarianism with America's cultural emphasis on regeneration through violence to create a hatred of the elites whom they believe have robbed them of the American dream. It emphasizes freedom and a don't-tread-on-me ethic as a key part of White America's heritage. In the words of political scientists Alexandra Homolar and Georg Löfflmann, its adherents see themselves as "an idealized community of shared origin and destiny, the 'pure people,' who have been betrayed and humiliated because what is represented as their way of life and righteous place in the world has been lost."[43] The hotheads among them are ready to fight to restore "their" country. On January 6, 2021, some of them assaulted Congress to "stop the steal" that they thought threatened to take their country away from them.

JESUS TRUMP SUPERSTAR

Welcome to the new American dilemma. The old one, articulated in 1944 by Gunnar Myrdal as "the Negro problem and modern democracy," has not disappeared.[44] We see it still in discrimination, police violence, and the various forms of structural racism that permeate American society. And we recognize it in the title of Ta-Nehisi Coates's famous essay about Donald Trump, "The First White President": He was the first man to become president because he is White rather than because his race helped him accomplish things in other fields.[45]

Yet the mob that invaded the US Capitol, spurred on by then-president Trump's lies about a "stolen" election, tells us that something more is afoot. After attending a pro-Trump rally at the White House on the day that Congress had gathered to certify Joe Biden's election win, a largely White crowd marched to the Capitol building. A significant number of them attacked the building, overwhelmed the police, and entered, carrying handcuffs, weapons, and various US, Confederate, Trump, and Jesus flags. They terrorized lawmakers and came close to capturing Vice President Mike Pence, for whom they had erected a gallows in a courtyard outside.[46]

Reporters quickly noted the riot's large number of religious images, from the banners proclaiming "Jesus 2020" and "Jesus Is My Savior, Trump Is My President" to anti-Semitic T-shirts and to the numerous crosses, one of which declared in large letters "Trump Won." Just before the attack, members of the Proud Boys, a militant right-wing gang, "stopped to kneel in the street and pray in the name of Jesus . . . for God to bring 'reformation and revival.' . . . [They] asked God for the restoration of their 'value systems' and for the 'courage and strength to both represent you and represent our culture well.'" They rose, their leader told the reporters to "get the hell out of my way," and they moved on the Capitol.[47]

The key phrase here is "the restoration of their 'value systems.'" Over and over, rioters and their supporters talked about "taking back America" from the godless elites who, they claimed, have used it for their own purposes for too long. Reporters interviewed an evangelical Christian from Texas who said, "We are fighting good versus evil, dark versus light," and declared (in the reporters' words) that she was "rising up like Queen Esther, the biblical heroine who saved her people from death."[48]

New York Times columnist Thomas Edsall wrote in late January that "the Capitol insurrection was as Christian nationalist as it gets."[49] He cited sociologists Andrew Whitehead and Samuel Perry, who wrote:

> Christian nationalism is a cultural framework—a collection of myths, traditions, symbols, narratives, and value systems—that idealizes and advances a fusion of Christianity with American civic life. But the "Christianity" of Christian nationalism is of a particular sort. . . . It includes assumptions of nativism, white supremacy, patriarchy, and heteronormativity, along with divine sanction for authoritarian control and militarism. . . . [It] contends that America has been and should always be distinctively "Christian" from top to bottom—in its self-identity, interpretations of its own history, sacred symbols, cherished values, and public policies—and it aims to keep it this way.[50]

Where Bellah's civil religion saw God standing in judgment over America's misdeeds, Christian nationalists draw a parallel with God's blessings on ancient Israel's domination of Canaan. "America should fear God's wrath for unfaithfulness while assuming God's blessing—or even mandate—for subduing the continent by force if necessary."[51]

Yet Christian nationalism was just one of the January riot's themes. Confederate flags were as common as Christian symbols, and there were Gadsden flags, Second Amendment banners, and "Keep America Great" signs. Many participants, along with 14 percent of the US population, embraced the QAnon theory that "the levers of power are controlled by a cabal of Satan-worshiping pedophiles" against whom "American patriots may have to resort to violence" to "restore [the country's] the rightful leaders." White supremacy, racism, resentment against elites, the ideology of individual freedom, and the embrace of purifying violence—all played at least as large a role as Christian nationalism in the January insurrection.[52]

So did then-president Trump.

Sociologists have long had a professional bias toward bottom-up explanations of political phenomena. They look to class shifts, social strains, status resentments, and ordinary people's beliefs to explain what happens in the political sphere. These are important, but so are the actions of elites. The Tea Party Movement of the late 2000s to the mid-2010s, for example, was bankrolled by right-wing billionaires in an astroturfing parallel to the original Boston Tea Party's funding sources.[53] How did the complex mix of people and motives I have described in these pages coalesce behind an amoral, narcissistic, authoritarian plutocrat's claim that his "landslide" reelection was stolen and needed to be restored by those "great patriots" he called "very special" just before his Twitter account was suspended?[54]

Trump was (and is) a master of mobilizing White resentment by drawing on the alternate civil religious themes I have been tracing. His 2016 and 2020 presidential campaigns reverberated with the myths of an individualistic frontier liberty, a lost social dominance, and the need for regeneration that I outlined above. His economic appeals set elite "thieves" against "honest American workers." On the racial front, his appeals promised "to go back to a time when Whites were unquestionably at the top of the social hierarchy."[55]

The Christian front is most interesting, given the apparent contradiction between Trump's overwhelming support from White Evangelical Christian voters and his personal moral failings; yet there is biblical precedent for a pagan ruler helping God's people. Christian nationalists have referred to Trump as a new "King Cyrus" who will "restore the crumbling walls that separate us from cultural collapse." Cyrus, you may remember, was the emperor of Persia who conquered Babylon and freed the Jews. Though he ended up being killed by Scythians, who carried his head around in a skin full of blood, he remains, writes Katherine Stewart, "the model for a nonbeliever appointed by God as a vessel for the purposes of the faithful." She wrote that this identification "isn't a fringe thing." Polls show that a large number of White Protestants agreed that Trump was "anointed by God" to rule.[56]

Trump was (and is) a master at playing to such sentiments. Detailed analyses of his speeches show that he used religious language more than any president in the last hundred years, starting abruptly in his 2016 campaign. He especially used it in states with larger religious populations, where the odds of reaching his evangelical base were higher.[57] He also called on religious symbolism. Fintan O'Toole noted that Trump's late-campaign bout with COVID-19 had definite Christian overtones, even beyond his from-the-hospital claim that the treatments he received "look like miracles coming down from God": "In a grotesque parody of the Christian narrative, Trump presented his contraction of Covid-19 not as a consequence of his own narcissistic recklessness but as a Jesus-like self-sacrifice—he caught the virus on behalf of the people. Trump 'died,' was in the 'tomb' of Walter Reed hospital for three days and then rose again and appeared to many. This fable seems to have worked for his supporters, electrifying them with its evidence of their leader's indefatigability."[58]

In short, Trump articulated and shaped key elements of his followers' worldview. He did not create that worldview, but he cleverly spoke to those followers' preexisting way of seeing. For their part, those followers chose a candidate and then a president whom they believed spoke to their myths.

Indeed, those followers saw themselves as kingmakers. The January insurrection made it clear that, in O'Toole's words, the crowd of rioters was "both making a choice and defining the nature of political choice itself. It is to be decision not by election but by assertion, made not by the mere numerical majority but by 'we,' the patriots, the real Americans. Trump was at once the symbol of this power to choose and the vehicle for its enforcement."[59] To this crowd, elections do not matter if the wrong person wins.

The January insurrection was an act of popular political imagination, one that despises elites, distrusts their institutions, and demands the political power to restore the United States to its "traditional" path. Its participants claimed that only "real Americans" have the right to rule—and this means Whites, conservative Christians, and "the people who built this country" and "respect its freedoms." Trump's supporters were acting out the alternate version of America's civil religion.[60] To that religion, only the "right people" can belong.

Unlike Bellah's and Lincoln's civil religious vision, this alternate version does not worry that it might misread God's intent. Its adherents believe they are acting out God's will. Self-doubt is not part of their civil theology.

GRATITUDE AND HOPE

So we have intersecting pandemics: the COVID (and subsequent) viruses, the climate crisis, the increasing social inequality, the mass extinctions, the assaults on democracy in the United States and other parts of the world, and the frantic, not-quite-end of a Twitter-maniac presidency. Our anxiety grows as we doomscroll through these and other contagions, leaving us sleepless with worry and dread. Or we find ourselves "slouching toward quietus," to use Joan Didion's description of the turn-on/tune-in/drop-out side of the similarly apocalyptic 1960s.[61] It is no wonder that 20 percent fewer Americans agreed in 2021 that "God has granted America a special role in human history" than did so in 2013.[62] Constant crisis tries the faith of even the most optimistic among us.

Where is gratitude in this situation? Both sides of our political divide are grateful for the country's traditions, but they disagree about which ones. Bellah articulated a civil religion that warned the nation that it could be wrong and that its actions would be judged by a transcendent God whose aim was justice. This is not unique in human history, but it is rare; it is a gift to be part of a polity that seeks to atone for its misdeeds. The alternate civil religion lacks this self-corrective impulse, though it does emphasize individual freedom. Its followers are grateful for that freedom, but they see it as something to be defended for itself instead of for the justice it might bring. And for too many, that freedom belongs only to members of the American "tribe"—namely, native born, White, English-speaking Christians who believe that capitalism is the world's best economic system.[63]

As a sociologist, I find the alternate civil religion's faith in capitalism and individual freedom naively touching. Even Milton Friedman could only reconcile the two (in theory) by periodically disbanding corporations, but that does not happen. Thomas Piketty has charted the role that "patrimonial capitalism" plays in our growing economic and political inequality. Michael Lind describes the emergence of a "new class war" between transnational neoliberal elites and White working-class outsiders, the latter of whom agitate for a return to a utopia they imagine they once controlled. In his analysis, the odds of an alt-right rebellion benefiting any but the elites are extremely low.[64] The abstract ideal of "freedom" does not provide the traction that a positive social movement needs.

Thus, Bellah's turn to a justice-centered civil religion to oppose the Vietnam War was savvy, as was his choice to frame it in religious terms. The first focused attention on the nation's core values. The second made upholding those values a matter of transcendent duty, even for people who do not postulate an actual "Being" watching over America's deeds. Bellah's effort failed, and his next intellectual project examined the cultural sources of that failure, which he located in the growth of individualistic and utilitarian ways of thinking on the part of America's middle-class population.[65] As he put it in a retrospective interview, "There is a sense . . . that the article on civil religion was Minerva's Owl, taking off at dusk, and that [the civil religion] was described just as it was over."[66]

Yet we can be grateful for his effort and for the account that he laid out of the transcendent judgment that the civil religion's God sets over the nation. That tradition, despite the country's many failures, past and present, gives me hope that Americans can work toward justice in the future. Proverbs 29:18 speaks of the importance of prophetic vision in upholding a people's will to persevere. That vision tells us what we must do, and it goads us to work together to accomplish it. The vision of the nation being "not an ultimate end in itself but . . . only [having] value insofar as it realizes . . . a higher law" gives us an ideal toward which we can work.[67] It rescues us from the twin demons of anxiety and resignation. Those of us who share this civil religion find ourselves with ideals to which we can turn in times of trial.

How might we act on those ideals in the present moment? What injustices must we overcome to achieve the full extension of freedom and democracy for all and to act responsibly in an increasingly interconnected world? These questions reflect Bellah's second and third trials, which are with us still. Yet we need to go beyond Bellah on this and particularly beyond his Clintonesque call for liberal transnationalism.[68] In his emphasis on culture, he ignored the structures on which our current inequalities depend.

Personally, I think that repair needs to start with reparations, an inadequate but necessary way of giving justice to those from whom so much has been taken. This includes reparations for racial and class injustice, such as the thefts of land, capital, and wages that have prevented less powerful people from sharing our world's general progress.[69] It should also include reparations for climate injustice, perhaps by having wealthy countries develop and transfer climate-saving technology to those regions that lack access to nonpolluting energy sources.

Yet these reparations cannot come from the less educated, the working class, the rural Whites, or the others whom our neo-liberal economy has left behind. They must come from the elites who have benefitted the most from our current inequalities. As the self-described conservative columnist David Brooks remarked about the United States, "For the past several decades the economy has funneled money to highly educated people who live in large metro areas. That has created a ruinous class rift that divides the country and fuels polarization. [We need to] funnel money to the roughly two-thirds of Americans without a bachelor's degree—who work on road crews, in manufacturing plants, who care for the elderly and are disproportionately unemployed."[70] This would differentially benefit not only Blacks and other minorities but also the working-class supporters of the alt-right whom the current economy has abandoned. They have been harmed as well.

The transcendent version of our civil religion says that we should do this because it is right. It may bring political peace, or it may not. But doing right is the only way to expiate our collective corruption.

Like all religions, civil religion involves myths and structuring metaphors, symbols and symbolic universes, and "conceptions of a general order of existence" that shape people's imaginations and actions.[71] Though Bellah's account of America's civil religion was overdrawn, and he remained blind to much injustice, that religion's myths, metaphors, and symbols have not vanished. They live on in all of us who expect more of our country than it has delivered. We may no longer believe, with Lincoln, that God will call us to account for our misdeeds. Yet we can issue that call on our own. So long as we do so, and maintain its ideals, the best of that civil religion lives.

NOTES

1. IFRC, *Trust, Equity, and Local Action.*
2. For example, Thomas B. Edsall, "America Has Split, and It's Now in 'Very Dangerous Territory,'" *New York Times*, January 26, 2022, https://nyti.ms/3Z2SJB6; and Blake Hounshell, "Measuring America's Divide: 'It's Gotten Worse,'" *New York Times*, July 27, 2022, https://nyti.ms/3lA2vgk.
3. Yeats, "Second Coming," in *Michael Robartes*, 19–20. Fintan O'Toole wrote, "The more quotable Yeats seems to commentators and politicians, the worse things are." See O'Toole's "'Yeats Test' Criteria Reveal We Are Doomed," *Irish Times*, July 28, 2018, https://bit.ly/2ZgxJu3.
4. Gallup, "Satisfaction with the United States"; and "Poll Finds 71% of Americans Believe Country Is on Wrong Track," NBC News, January 30, 2023, https://nbcnews.to/3LK5q0D.
5. Bellah, "Civil Religion in America," 1–21; and Graubard, "Preface to the Issue," iii. Bellah's article generated an intellectual cottage industry that debated, expanded, and applied his argument to the United States and to countries around the world. See, for example, Richey and Jones, *American Civil Religion*; and Bellah and Hammond, *Varieties of Civil Religion*. Bellah contributed to that industry, but that was not why he wrote his original piece.
6. Lincoln, *Collected Works*, 4:236.
7. Bellah, "Civil Religion in America," 16, 17, 18.
8. Rousseau, *Du Contrat Social*, bk. 4, ch. 8. See Watson, "Damned Neighbors Problem."

9. Bellah, "American Civil Religion," 8. Emphasis added.
10. Okay, so I'm a typeface nerd: YHWH, Allāh, Vishnu, Ik Onkār.
11. Bellah, "Civil Religion in America," 4.
12. Washington, quoted in Bellah, 7. Bellah checked the speeches from Washington (1789) through Johnson (1965). I have checked subsequent speeches through Biden's address (2021); all follow the pattern.
13. Bellah, 7.
14. Carp, "Did Dutch Smugglers?"
15. Thus, Samuel Johnson's famous line, "How is it that we hear the loudest yelps for liberty among the drivers of negroes?" See Johnson, *Taxation No Tyranny*, 89.
16. On the "conquest narrative," see Gorski, *American Covenant*, loc. 487. On the "wilderness," see Johnston, "Puritan in the Wilderness," in MacDougall, *James Fenimore Cooper*, 60–63. See also Cronon, *Changes in the Land*. In Thoreau's words, "Generally speaking, a howling wilderness does not howl: it is the imagination of the traveler that does the howling." See Thoreau, "Allegash and East Branch," in Channing, *Main Woods*, 242.
17. See Wills, *Negro President*.
18. Gorski, in *American Covenant* (loc 1909–88), notes that Calhoun was a complex thinker whose "writings are replete with republican themes of virtue and corruption, and balance and faction, as well as with classical references to the historical experiences of ancient republics such as Sparta and Rome" (loc 1929).
19. Van Cleve, *Slaveholders' Union*, cited by Jamelle Bouie, "1820 Has a Lot to Tell Us about 2020," *New York Times*, September 25, 2020, https://nyti.ms/3zACGOo. Emphasis added.
20. Lincoln, *Collected Works*, 1:74–75 (1837), cf. 1:348 (1845), 2:247–83 (1854), and 3:39–76 (1858).
21. Lincoln, *Collected Works*, 2:406 (1857). This speech responded to a prior speech by Stephen A. Douglas; it was not part of the famous Lincoln-Douglas debates.
22. Jefferson, *Sixth Annual Message*. Article 1, section 9, clause 1 of the Constitution set January 1, 1808, as the first date at which Congress could ban the "importation of such Persons as any of the States now existing shall think proper to admit." ("Such persons" was recognized as meaning slaves, a word that the framers deliberately avoided.) By the time Jefferson sent his message, only South Carolina still imported slaves; it had previously abolished the trade between 1787 and 1803.
23. By the 1850s, the illegal slave trade was run out of New York by Portuguese and Brazilian businessmen. James Oakes reports that "despite an 1820 statute prescribing the death penalty for such crimes, no slave trader had ever been sentenced to die." Lincoln refused mercy to "Nathaniel Gordon, a ship captain who had been illegally trading in slaves for more than a decade. . . . The effect was immediate. His execution in 1862 sent [slavers] scurrying to close down their business and flee the country. US participation in the slave trade was effectively shut down." See Oakes, "Why Did the Slave Trade Survive," 39.
24. Lincoln, *Collected Works*, 8:333 (1865).
25. Elton Trueblood, for example, called Lincoln "the theologian of American anguish," while Sidney Mead called him "the most profound and representative theologian of the religion of the Republic" and "the spiritual center of American history." Reinhold Niebuhr wrote that Lincoln's achievement was his "affirmation of a meaningful [American] history along with religious reservation about the partiality and bias which human actors and agents

betray in their definition of that meaning." Trueblood, *Abraham Lincoln*; Mead, quoted by Endy, "Abraham Lincoln," 229; and Niebuhr, "Religion of Abraham Lincoln," 173.

26. Bellah, "Civil Religion in America," 10; and Noll, "Image of the United States," in Hatch and Noll, *Bible in America*, 44. Noll reported that those preachers also cited most of the figures who had previously been used to memorialize George Washington: Abel, Jacob, Moses, Joshua, Othniel, Samuel, Abner, Elijah, David, Josiah, Jehoiada, Mordecai, Cyrus, and Daniel.
27. Bellah, 10; and Lowell, "On the Gettysburg Address," in Nevins, *Lincoln and the Gettysburg Address*, 88–89.
28. Bellah, 16, 15, 17.
29. Bellah, "American Civil Religion," 11, 12.
30. Slotkin, *Regeneration through Violence*, 6–7; see also Slotkin, *Fatal Environment*; and Slotkin, *Gunfighter Nation*.
31. Slotkin, *Regeneration*, 5.
32. Slotkin, 4.
33. Coleman, "NRA Supported Gun Control." See the NRA advertisement and its dog whistle embrace of White supremacy at Moyers and Winship, "NRA Issues Call."
34. See Charles M. Blow, "Rittenhouse and the Right's White Vigilante Heroes," *New York Times*, November 19, 2021, https://nyti.ms/3oFkUFS.
35. Osterweis, *Myth of the Lost Cause*; and Wilson, *Baptized in Blood*.
36. Cox, "Women, the Lost Cause, and the New South"; Gardner, *Blood and Irony*; and Johnson, "'Drill into Us,' 525–62.
37. Kruse, *One Nation under God*. At this writing, Amazon sells a "Less Tax, More Jesus" T-shirt from Libertarian Christian Tee Shirts for $19.99 "plus free returns" (https://amzn.to/3qj3jWO).
38. Bageant, *Deer Hunting with Jesus*; and Hochschild, *Strangers in Their Own Land*. Neither Bageant nor Hochschild wrote about race, though it was clearly part of the background in both places.
39. Reeves, *Dream Hoarders*; and Thomas B. Edsall, "Why Trump Still Has Millions of Americans in His Grip," *New York Times*, May 5, 2021, https://nyti.ms/33wT4Sh.
40. Galston, "Bitter Heartland."
41. Galston.
42. Thomas B. Edsall, "Why Trump Is Still Their Guy," *New York Times*, April 21, 2021, https://nyti.ms/2RZ0oDP.
43. Homolar and Löfflmann, "Populism."
44. Myrdal, *American Dilemma*.
45. Coates, "First White President."
46. For a seasoned political reporter's eyewitness description, see Danner, "'Be Ready to Fight.'" See photos at Brandom and Krales, "In Photos"; and Azi Paybarah and Brent Lewis, "Stunning Images as a Mob Storms the U.S. Capitol," *New York Times*, January 6, 2021, https://nyti.ms/3oJPAWp.
47. Elizabeth Dias and Ruth Graham, "How White Evangelical Christians Fused with Trump Extremism," *New York Times*, January 11, 2021, http://nyti.ms/35z5ryC.
48. Dias and Graham.
49. Thomas B. Edsall, "The Capitol Insurrection Was as Christian Nationalist as It Gets," *New York Times*, January 28, 2021, https://nyti.ms/3abURPA. For a more recent (and full) report, see Tyler and Seidel, *Christian Nationalism*.

50. Whitehead and Perry, *Taking America Back*, 10.
51. Whitehead and Perry, 11.
52. On QAnon among participants, see Giovanni Russonello, "QAnon Now as Popular in U.S. as Some Major Religions, Poll Suggests," *New York Times*, May 27, 2021, https://nyti.ms/34rHoAD. The three quotes come from the three core questions on a recent poll that showed 14 percent of Americans are QAnon believers; see PRRI, *Understanding QAnon's Connection*. On the list of themes, see Farhad Manjoo, "Finally, a President Acknowledges White Supremacists," *New York Times*, January 22, 2021, https://nyti.ms/3i5pU5h; Colin P. Clarke, "A New Era of Far-Right Violence," *New York Times*, January 24, 2021, SR9, https://nyti.ms/3uL5jWF; and Charles M. Blow, "Is America's Democracy Slipping Away?," *New York Times*, May 31, 2021, A18, https://nyti.ms/3p7D42Q.
53. Nesbit, *Poison Tea*; Alexander Hertel-Fernandez, Caroline Tervo, and Theda Skocpol, "How the Koch Brothers Built the Most Powerful Rightwing Group You've Never Heard Of," *The Guardian*, September 26, 2018, https://bit.ly/3uwT5kh; and Carp, "Dutch Smugglers."
54. The original tweets were removed when Twitter (now X) banned him from its platform. These phrases were preserved by Eliza Relman, Oma Seddiq, and Jake Lahut, "Trump Tells His Violent Supporters Who Stormed the Capitol 'You're Very Special,' but Asks Them 'to Go Home,'" *Business Insider*, January 6, 2021, https://bit.ly/3fy9Jvw.
55. Peter Baker, "More Than Ever, Trump Casts Himself as the Defender of White America," *New York Times*, September 10, 2020, https://nyti.ms/3vJjIE4. The quote is from political scientist Kevin Arceneaux (Edsall, "Still Their Guy").
56. Cyrus appears in Isaiah 45; Herodotus reported his fate, continuing that the Scythians kept him in blood "so that the thirst for power that had inspired him could now be quenched" (Frankopan, *Silk Roads*, 3). This paragraph's quotes come from Katherine Stewart, "Why Trump Reigns as King Cyrus," *New York Times*, January 1, 2019, A19, https://nyti.ms/3cFoiu5. Polling data comes from Djupe and Burge, "Trump the Annointed?"
57. Hughes, "Appealing to Evangelicals."
58. O'Toole, "Democracy's Afterlife." The "miracles" quote comes from Hughes, "Appealing." If you think this is a stretch, read anthropologists' accounts of their fieldwork in right-wing Christian communities. See, for example, Aho, *Politics of Righteousness*; and Harding, *Book of Jerry Falwell*.
59. O'Toole, "Trump Inheritance."
60. For a parallel analysis, see Bradley Onishi, "Trump's New Civil Religion," *New York Times*, January 19, 2021, https://nyti.ms/3sHuJo0.
61. Cited by Watercutter, "Doomscrolling."
62. Sixty-four percent agreed in 2013; 44 percent agreed in 2021. The drop was smaller for self-identified Republicans and larger for Democrats and independents. See Jones et al., *Competing Visions of America*, 8.
63. Jones et al., 11–14, 9, 17. The graph on page 12 unpacks the racial attitudes better than does the one on page 11.
64. Friedman, *Capitalism and Freedom*; Piketty, *Capital*; Piketty, Saez, and Zucman, "Distributional National Accounts"; and Lind, "New Class War."
65. Bellah, *Broken Covenant*; and Bellah et al., *Habits of the Heart*.
66. Bellah. "In God We Trust."

67. Bellah, "American Civil Religion," 8.
68. See Bellah, "Civil Religion in America," 18.
69. For an example, see Coates, "Case for Reparations." There are analogues for other dispossessed groups.
70. David Brooks, "The Heart and Soul of the Biden Project," *New York Times*, April 9, 2021, A22, https://nyti.ms/3uDpndC.
71. These elements come from Clifford Geertz's famous essay "Religion as a Cultural System," in Banton, *Anthropological Approaches*.

BIBLIOGRAPHY

Aho, James A. *The Politics of Righteousness: Idaho Christian Patriotism*. Seattle: University of Washington Press, 1990.

Bageant, Joe. *Deer Hunting with Jesus: Dispatches from America's Class War*. New York: Three Rivers Press, 2007.

Bellah, Robert N. "American Civil Religion in the 1970's." *Anglican Theological Review*. Supplement Series, no. 1 (1973): 8–20.

———. *The Broken Covenant*. New York: Seabury Press, 1975.

———. "Civil Religion in America." *Daedalus* 96, no. 1 (1967): 1–21.

———. "In God We Trust: Civil and Uncivil Religion in America." Interview by Rachael Kohn. *Encounter*, Australian Broadcast Corporation, October 17, 1999. https://ab.co/3atSLfb.

Bellah, Robert N., and Phillip Hammond, eds. *Varieties of Civil Religion*. San Francisco: Harper & Row, 1980.

Bellah, Robert N., Richard Madsen, William M. Sullivan, Ann Swidler, and Steven M. Tipton. *Habits of the Heart: Individualism and Commitment in American Life*. Berkeley: University of California Press, 1985.

Brandom, Russell, and Amelia Holowaty Krales. "In Photos: The Pro-Trump Mob's Invasion of Congress." *The Verge*, January 6, 2021. https://bit.ly/2Sp221q.

Carp, Benjamin L. "Did Dutch Smugglers Provoke the Boston Tea Party?" *Early American Studies* 10, no. 2 (2012): 335–59.

Coates, Ta-Nehisi. "The Case for Reparations." *The Atlantic*, June 2014. https://bit.ly/30g6PmL.

———. "The First White President." *The Atlantic*, October 2017. https://bit.ly/3nnQ3wN.

Coleman, Arica L. "When the NRA Supported Gun Control." *Time*, July 29, 2016. https://bit.ly/3wmcB49.

Cox, Karen L. "Women, the Lost Cause, and the New South: The United Daughters of the Confederacy and the Transmission of Confederate Culture, 1894–1919." PhD diss., University of Southern Mississippi, 1997.

Cronon, William. *Changes in the Land: Indians, Colonists, and the Ecology of New England*. New York: Hill and Wang, 1983.

Danner, Mark. "'Be Ready to Fight.'" *New York Review of Books* 68, no. 2 (February 12, 2021): 4–8.

Djupe, Paul A., and Ryan P. Burge. "Trump the Annointed?" *Religion in Public*, May 11, 2020. https://bit.ly/3fymRAJ.

Endy, Melvin B. "Abraham Lincoln and American Civil Religion: A Reinterpretation." *Church History* 44, no. 2 (1975): 229–41.

Frankopan, Peter. *The Silk Roads: A New History of the World.* New York: Vintage, 2017.

Friedman, Milton. *Capitalism and Freedom.* Chicago: University of Chicago Press, 1962.

Gallup. "Satisfaction with the United States." *Gallup Historical Trends,* 2021. https://bit.ly/3wj4ZAF.

Galston, William A. "The Bitter Heartland." *American Purpose,* March 31, 2021. https://bit.ly/3xRtMfs.

Gardner, Sarah E. *Blood and Irony: Southern White Women's Narratives of the Civil War, 1861–1937.* Chapel Hill: University of North Carolina Press, 2004.

Geertz, Clifford. "Religion as a Cultural System." In *Anthropological Approaches to the Study of Religion,* edited by Michael Banton, 1–46. London: Tavistock, 1966.

Gorski, Philip S. *American Covenant: A History of Civil Religion from the Puritans to the Present.* Kindle ed. Princeton NJ: Princeton University Press 2017.

Graubard, Stephen R. "Preface to the Issue 'Religion in America.'" *Daedalus* 96, no. 1 (1967): iii–vii.

Harding, Susan Friend. *The Book of Jerry Falwell: Fundamentalist Language and Politics.* Princeton NJ: Princeton University Press, 2000.

Hochschild, Arlie Russell. *Strangers in Their Own Land: Anger and Mourning on the American Right.* New York: The New Press, 2016.

Homolar, Alexandra, and Georg Löfflmann. "Populism and the Affective Politics of Humiliation Narratives." *Global Studies Quarterly* 1, no. 1 (2021): 1–11. https://bit.ly/3vqK5OR.

Hughes, Ceri. "Appealing to Evangelicals, Trump Uses Religious Words and References to God at a Higher Rate Than Previous Presidents." *The Conversation,* October 13, 2020. https://bit.ly/3fUJr5K.

IFRC. *Trust, Equity, and Local Action: Lessons from the Covid-19 Pandemic to Avert the Next Global Crisis.* Geneva: International Federation of Red Cross and Red Crescent Societies, 2023. https://bit.ly/3nad5er.

Jefferson, Thomas. *Sixth Annual Message to Congress, December 2, 1806.* The Avalon Project, Lillian Goldman Law Library, Yale Law School, New Haven CT. https://bit.ly/3qmZ20U.

Johnson, Joan Marie. "'Drill into Us . . . the Rebel Tradition': The Contest over Southern Identity in Black and White Women's Clubs, South Carolina, 1898–1930." *Journal of Southern History* 66, no. 3 (2000): 525–62.

Johnson, Samuel. *Taxation No Tyranny.* London: T. Cadell, 1775.

Johnston, Paul K. "A Puritan in the Wilderness: Natty Bumppo's Language and America's Nature Today." In *James Fenimore Cooper: His Country and His Art,* edited by Hugh C. MacDougall, 60–63. Oneata: State University of New York at Oneata, 1999.

Jones, Robert P., Natalie Jackson, Diana Orcés, Ian Huff, and Thea Holcomb. *Competing Visions of America: An Evolving Identity or a Culture under Attack?* Washington DC: PRRI, November 1, 2021. https://bit.ly/3kufmwY.

Kruse, Kevin M. *One Nation under God: How Corporate America Invented Christian America.* New York: Basic Books, 2015.

Lincoln, Abraham. *Collected Works of Abraham Lincoln.* Edited by Roy P. Basler, Marion Dolores Pratt, and Lloyd A. Dunlap. New Brunswick NJ: Rutgers University Press, 1953.

Lind, Michael. "The New Class War." *American Affairs* 1, no. 2 (2017). https://bit.ly/3dOXuHb.

Lowell, Robert. "On the Gettysburg Address." In *Lincoln and the Gettysburg Address: Commemorative Papers*, edited by Allan Nevins, 88–92. Urbana: University of Illinois Press, 1964.

Moyers, Bill, and Michael Winship. "NRA Issues Call for White Supremacy and Armed Insurrection." BillMoyers.com, June 29, 2017. https://bit.ly/34Ch6vq.

Myrdal, Gunnar. *An American Dilemma: The Negro Problem and Modern Democracy*. New York: Harper, 1944.

Nesbit, Jeff. *Poison Tea: How Big Oil and Big Tobacco Invented the Tea Party and Captured the GOP.* New York: St. Martin's Press, 2016.

Niebuhr, Reinhold. "The Religion of Abraham Lincoln." *Christian Century* 82, no. 6 (1965): 172–75.

Noll, Mark A. "The Image of the United States as a Biblical Nation, 1776–1865." In *The Bible in America: Essays in Cultural History*, edited by Nathan O. Hatch and Mark A. Noll, 39–58. New York: Oxford University Press, 1982.

Oakes, James. "Why Did the Slave Trade Survive So Long?" *New York Review of Books* 68, no. 6 (April 8, 2021): 38–39.

Osterweis, Rollin G. *The Myth of the Lost Cause, 1865–1900.* Hamdon CT: Archon Books, 1973.

O'Toole, Fintan. "Democracy's Afterlife: Trump, the GOP, and the Rise of Zombie Politics." *New York Review of Books* 67, no. 19 (December 3, 2020).

———. "The Trump Inheritance." *New York Review of Books* 68, no. 3 (February 25, 2021), 4–8.

Piketty, Thomas. *Capital in the Twenty-First Century.* Translated by Arthur Goldhammer. Cambridge MA: Harvard University Press, 2014.

Piketty, Thomas, Emmanuel Saez, and Gabriel Zucman. "Distributional National Accounts: Methods and Estimates for the United States." Working Paper 22945. Washington DC: National Bureau of Economic Research, December 2016. https://bit.ly/3DpCXGc.

PRRI (Public Religion Research Institute). *Understanding QAnon's Connection to American Politics, Religion, and Media Consumption.* Washington DC: PRRI, May 27, 2021. https://bit.ly/2SwZ2Ah.

Reeves, Richard. *Dream Hoarders: How the American Upper Middle Class Is Leaving Everyone Else in the Dust.* Washington DC: Brookings Insitution Press, 2017.

Richey, Russell E., and Donald G. Jones, eds. *American Civil Religion.* New York: Harper & Row, 1974.

Rousseau, Jean-Jacques. *Du Contrat Social; ou, Principes du Droit Politique.* Amsterdam: Marc Michel Rey., 1762.

Slotkin, Richard. *The Fatal Environment: The Myth of the Frontier in the Age of Industrialization, 1800–1890.* Norman: University of Oklahoma Press, 1985.

———. *Gunfighter Nation: The Myth of the Frontier in Twentieth-Century America.* Norman: University of Oklahoma Press, 1992.

———. *Regeneration through Violence: The Mythology of the American Frontier, 1600–1860.* Norman: University of Oklahoma Press, 1973.

Thoreau, Henry David. "The Allegash and East Branch." In *The Main Woods*, edited by William Ellery Channing, 174–327. Cambridge: The Riverside Press, 1906.

Trueblood, Elton. *Abraham Lincoln: Theologian of American Anguish.* New York: Harper & Row, 1972.

Tyler, Amanda, and Andrew L. Seidel, eds. *Christian Nationalism and the January 6 Insurrection.* Washington DC: Baptist Joint Committee for Religious Liberty and the Freedom from Religion Foundation, February 9, 2022. https://bit.ly/3zy7O4m.

Van Cleve, George William. *A Slaveholders' Union: Slavery, Politics, and the Constitution in the Early American Republic.* Chicago: University of Chicago Press, 2011.

Watercutter, Angela. "Doomscrolling Is Slowly Eroding Your Mental Health." *Wired,* June 25, 2020. https://bit.ly/3qAoOTk.

Watson, Micah. "The Damned Neighbors Problem: Rousseau's Civil Religion Revisited." *Religions* 10, no. 349 (2019).

Whitehead, Andrew L., and Samuel L. Perry. *Taking America Back for God: Christian Nationalism in the United States.* New York: Oxford University Press, 2020.

Wills, Gary. *Negro President: Jefferson and the Slave Power.* New York: Houghton Mifflin Harcourt, 2003.

Wilson, Charles Reagan. *Baptized in Blood: The Religion of the Lost Cause, 1865–1920.* Athens GA: University of Georgia Press, 1980.

Yeats, William Butler. "The Second Coming." In *Michael Robartes and the Dancer,* 19–20. Churchtown, Dundrum: The Cuala Press, 1920.

CHAPTER 5

On Not Letting a Pandemic Go to Waste

Theory for the Sick and Dying

Susan Abraham

> After all, the reader might think that to read without facility, to speculate without devotion, to investigate without wonder, to consider without exultation, to work hard without piety, to have knowledge without love, to have intelligence without humility, to study without divine grace and to observe without divinely inspired wisdom might be enough.
>
> —Saint Bonaventure

PANDEMIC THOUGHTS

The global pandemic has shocked us with a sense of collective pain and trauma. However, it is very important to remember that this is not the first time that human beings have experienced a global pandemic. Many cultural theorists are appalled at how the lessons from the AIDS/HIV crisis have been forgotten. Yet the impact of COVID-19 has been staggering. In many ways, the speed with which disinformation, fear, and anger are stoked deviously is what is different, though the intentions of those employing these tactics are recognizable as an opportunistic grab for continued cultural power into the future. Others, writing directly in response to COVID-19, challenge the idea that human beings have a right to expect a pain-free life. As an educator, drawing on theological traditions that teach courage, resilience, and gratitude as habits to be cultivated and developed, I wondered if something was to be learned from critical theory as it responds to pandemics. I chose to study two theorists: the queer feminist Eve Kosofsky Sedgwick and Korean-born, Germany-based, cultural studies philosopher Byung-Chul Han. Both offer distinctive points of conversation as they think through the cultural politics of disease, illness, and death. Primarily, they present the convictions that global pandemics are an occasion to reexamine our commitments to writing and reading, an occasion to repristinate our theoretical apparatuses for the sake of ethical living, and, finally, an occasion to provide a constructive view of how we must live in the face of death and dying. Neither thinker speaks directly about gratitude, even as they speak about and with hope in the futures they envision. For both thinkers, the goal is to cultivate a habitus of thought and practice, to relativize the significance and importance of the ego and self, precisely in the context of pandemic. Their intent is to create the conditions to hear and see the truly othered in our communities, because pandemics affect these others in ways that are unimaginable to the rest of us.

My intent is to explore critical theory's relevance in contemporary classrooms where we teach reading, writing, and thinking in an age marked by multiple global pandemics. For some time now, I have become increasingly disenchanted with the predominance of attitudes of negativity and the dismissal of religious and theological texts under the guise of critical thinking. Critical thinking, meant to advance equity and inclusion of marginalized groups, has become distorted as the simple stance of "I don't agree, because I don't see my experience reflected in the text." Often such a stance is adopted by privileged groups that are subtly using the mechanism of critical thinking to further consolidate forms of neoliberal and secular power. Reading that truly challenges, especially reading that is theological, is dismissed as irrelevant to contemporary experience. Take the epigraph at the beginning of this chapter, for example. In various classrooms that I have inhabited, students resist any complex speech about the Christian tradition as "too Christian, too punitive, not acknowledging of the psychological reasons for vices; not *critical* enough." How may we read texts, especially texts that may surprise and even dismay us? How may we read critical theory that may challenge our contemporary self-confidence? And why read during a pandemic unless it directly relates to my survival? Is there room for theology? For ideas on living from other religious traditions? For spirituality? For the cultivation of dispositions such as gratitude? These questions animate this chapter.

As the epigraph from Bonaventure's *Itinerarium* makes clear, reading in the Christian tradition is a sacred activity. Reading leads to self-transcendence and invites us to think about the nature of transcendence, including divine transcendence. However, critical thinking, a feature of contemporary academic institutions, in emphasizing the inequities of social structures, is a form of contemporary self-transcendence. Such a form of critical thinking is evident in the work of the two thinkers I explore. Moreover, their delineations for critical thinking are not without a grasp of the spiritual. Hence, critical thinking is more than thinking about the material conditions of human living. Critical thinking need not be resolutely secular.

A very early thinker in this regard was Eve Kosofsky Sedgwick (1950–2009), whose essay "Paranoid Reading and Reparative Reading, or, You're So Paranoid, You Probably Think This Essay Is about You" set off a firestorm of scholarly responses for and against the idea that "the intellectual baggage that many of us carry around under a label such as the 'hermeneutics of suspicion' needs unpacking and revisioning."[1] Her specific critique is that many so-called critical thinkers bring "an unmystified, angry view of large and genuinely systemic oppressions" that nevertheless does not "enjoin that person to any specific train of epistemological or narrative consequences."[2] In other words, critical reading alone, in her estimation, does not provide for transformation. Her challenge to what is an inflexible norm in academic contexts is not that academics stop critical thinking but that other methods of reading also be brought into play to effect transformation and change. She is a "queer" thinker but one whose queerness surprises and challenges epistemic and disciplinary pieties.

Others such as Byung-Chul Han, a contrarian and ferocious critic of neoliberal capitalism, argue that the problem is that human beings in our time have come to think of ourselves as the center of the universe. Thus, the reaction to COVID-19 globally is based on the avoidance of pain that human beings have cultivated as a result of the economic frameworks that condition and form us. He is invested in being a "heretic" in the culture wars and advises that nothing is more important than developing a "heretical consciousness." His heretical stance pushes against many liberal convictions. And that is his point: Liberalism is so entangled in a global capitalist network of extractive and exploitative mechanisms that it capitulates to being formed by such capitalism in unthought ways. Of course, his thought then pushes relentlessly beyond forms of recognizable liberalism into territory one may think belongs to forms of leftist libertarianism but with very important questions that could be considered by liberal thinkers, especially in the academy.

PANDEMIC QUEERING

Eve Kosofsky Sedgwick is particularly important in a pandemic time. Her work as a queer theorist arose in the simultaneous context of the AIDS/HIV pandemic and her own diagnosis of breast cancer. Stephen M. Barber and David L. Clark in the introduction to an anthology of collected essays on Sedgwick's work write that her commitment to a political space for those who were ill with a disease that was so identity changing was to reveal the complex engagement with body, race, gender, and sexuality.[3] Her continued relevance is her insistence that as an author, her job was to give voice to those whose stories are conveniently forgotten, especially those whose identities were enacted in complex intersections of body, gender, and sexuality. Hence, she claimed "queer" as an identity, even though she was married to a man and remained married to him until her death in 2009:

> [I am] a queer but long-married young woman whose erotic and intellectual life were fiercely transitive, shaped by a thirst for knowledge and identifications that might cross the barriers of what seemed my identity. It was also of someone who had it at heart to make decisive interventions on two scenes of identity that were supposed not to have to do with each other: the scene of feminism, where I "identified" and which I knew well; and the scene of gay men's bonding, community, thought, and politics, a potent and numinous scene, which at the experiential level was at the time almost totally unknown to me.[4]

Queer performativity infuses all of Sedgwick's writing. But it was also deeply intertwined with her illness. In her book *Tendencies*, she writes of how the experience of being diagnosed with breast cancer, then having surgery and chemotherapy, has "also proven just sheerly interesting with respect to exactly the issues of gender, sexuality, and identity formation that were already on my docket."[5] Her experience of the cancer diagnosis deepens her commitment to queer thinking, which "was [also] very much shaped by AIDS and the critical politics surrounding it, including the politics of homophobia and queer assertiveness."[6] Thus, her emphasis on queerness came out of her awareness of her own mortality and of identifying her theoretical and intellectual work with the lives of those who were dying of AIDS: "The AIDS activist movement . . . owed much to the women's health movement of the 70s; and in another turn an activist politics of breast cancer, spearheaded by lesbians . . . emerged on the model of AIDS activism."[7] Illness, then, became the catalyst for her work on critical writing and reading. As she declares, "The need I brought to books and poems was hardly to be circumscribed, and I felt I knew I would have to struggle to wrest from them sustaining news of the world, ideas, myself. . . . Becoming a perverse reader was never a matter of my condescension to texts, rather of the surplus charge of my trust in them to remain powerful, refractory, and exemplary."[8] She calls such reading "overreading," "ardent reading," and "queer reading."

In a different essay published in *Tendencies*, Sedgwick speaks of gratitude in a poem that she struggled to write. She writes of this poem: "A particular unfinished long narrative poem, a sulky problem child of my own, itself going on nine, 'child' in *many* senses 'of my right hand,' and joy, whose swollen proportions are only—in a society that hates fat kids—less a shaming badge of my maternal deficits of nurture and discipline than has been its virtual failure in the last two years to grow any *more*."[9] Sedgwick's unblinking gaze on herself as a writer and poet, a self-described "fat writer and poet" as she constantly reminds the reader, is the contingency she brings in her body to the work of reading and writing.

As she writes in *The Warm Decembers*,

Waking as an adult, now, who has an art.

An adult, I mean, who's not depressed.
For whom a vacant, distended, paper-light globe
called "gratitude," fills up the inner space
(gratitude as it were for water and for sleep:
for being able not to loathe "the sweet approach
of even or morn, or sight of vernal bloom,"
"or flocks, or herds")
—gratitude without an object, too, since these
good things—love of our life—
are our own true birthright if we've *any* right.
Gratitude, *positive happiness,* not the less for that.
Positive, meaning not good necessarily
either, but—now surplus, outside. What
isn't, although it must have been once, me
but is now rented or is lent to me,
is paid as wages for the "work" I therefore "love." I do,
I "love" the work that lets me like the world,
"love" the indenture that I call my "gift,"
almost as much as simply fear
the blinding loss of it.
. . .

To have,
as excess, the thing you might as easily not have
propels you forward with the impulse from behind,
the place you cannot see, but others can.[10]

The poem initially was written as a response to Sedgwick's growing understanding of how society disciplines and shapes bodies and queer sexualities, but it also blooms into the realization of her vocation as a thinker, writer, and reader. Gratitude is the expression that follows her sense that the gifts of writing and reading were given to her to repair and heal the world, even as she begins to sicken from breast cancer.

Reading and writing thus were in service of bringing to light queer experiences and queer life through embodied differences. It is important here to note the move Sedgwick is making. Rather than "representation" in a simple sense, she understands the acts of writing and reading as acts that ought to speak about queer survival in the face of AIDS and gay bashing. She is a queer thinker because her ethical commitments demand that she do so: "I think [we are] trying in our work to keep faith with vividly remembered promises made to ourselves in childhood: promises to make invisible possibilities and desires visible; to make the tacit things explicit; to smuggle queer representation in where it must be smuggled and, with the relative freedom of adulthood, to challenge queer eradicating impulses frontally where they are to be so challenged."[11] Texts therefore have a responsibility to give voice and space to those who were being erased. Reading, concomitantly, arises from the same ethical basis: One reads because one must necessarily believe that texts have "to remain powerful, refractory, and exemplary."[12] Only "ardent reading" would bring both the contingent reader's commitment and the text's exemplariness to light. Ardent reading therefore is queer reading.

Even as Sedgwick brings queer performativity into her reading practices, she complicates the way critical theory has taken over the reading enterprise. Critical theory has its source in Paul Ricoeur's "hermeneutics of suspicion," which "asserted that consciousness for Marx, Nietzsche and Freud is hidden-shown . . . or, simulated-manifested."[13] That is, all hidden consciousness must be brought to the surface. In any given text, the idea of suspicion has been used to demonstrate that opaque drives for mastery inhibit any direct access to meaning. Suspicion, an affect, is the way in which we expose the "falsification of the man of guile," and the consequence of such an attitude is another affect—paranoia. But, as Sedgwick avers, paranoid readings are stating the blindingly obvious: "In a world where no one need be delusional to find evidence of systemic oppression, to theorize out of anything *but* a paranoid critical stance has come to seem naïve, pious, or complaisant."[14] She emphasizes here that the word "paranoid" is not to be contained in its pathological sense alone; paranoia when reading should not stand in for all critical theoretical inquiry. Paranoid readings are one kind of position one occupies when reading. Other positions must also be mobilized to help.

It is important to understand why Sedgwick chooses to use the psychoanalytic term "paranoia," given that it would be negatively perceived. Her point is that homophobic writing requires paranoia to be recognized as such. Paranoid reading unearths how homophobic language is naturalized. In *Tendencies*, she tracks the meaning of an innocuous word—"family." She writes, "Religion, state, capital, ideology, domesticity, the discourses of power and legitimacy" all line up to create "family" as

> a surname
> a sexual dyad
> a legal unit based on state-regulated marriage
> a circuit of blood relationships
> a system of companionship and succor
> a building
> a proscenium between "private" and "public"
> an economic unit of earning and taxation
> the prime site of economic consumption
> the prime site of cultural consumption
> a mechanism to produce, care for, and acculturate children
> a mechanism for accumulating material goods over several generations
> a daily routine
> a unit in a community of worship
> a site of patriotic formation.[15]

Such a construction of the category "family" is shot through with homophobia. It would necessitate a paranoid reading of such naturalized meanings to uncover the idea that family buries queer identity as it normalizes heteronormativity.

Nevertheless, for Sedgwick, paranoia is only one kind of "epistemological practice" among many. In this key idea for Sedgwick, "epistemologies of enmity" reveal that knowledge constructs and forms: "I suppose this ought to seem quite an unremarkable epiphany: that knowledge *does* rather than simply *is*."[16] Thus, the defenses of queer thinkers against Christian homophobic attacks are paranoid, anticipating rejection and exclusion. Yet this need not be the lone response to an oppressive system. In the first place, she agrees that a paranoid position in relation to oppressive systems is useful because it can "offer unique access to true knowledge."[17] In the second place, however, "disarticulated, disavowed, and misrecognized" ways of knowing are also simultaneously practiced by those who engage in paranoid positionality.[18] The paranoid position, though, does not call enough attention to the multiple ways in which texts may be read and often seem to have a "monopolistic" hold on the act of reading. Further, and most damningly, academic theory follows the paranoid disposition, creating frameworks that dismiss any possibility of other and constructive ways of reading. In other words, Sedgwick is pointing to the limits of critical thinking.

These other ways of reading, which Sedgwick terms "reparative," are about pleasure and amelioration. Reparative positions teach us "the many ways selves and communities succeed in extracting sustenance from the objects of a culture—even of a culture whose avowed desire has often been not to sustain them."[19] The reparative position cultivates hope, which can be "a fracturing, even a traumatic thing to experience."[20] The interplay of paranoid and reparative reading is "queer reading," less sexual-drive oriented (without minimizing the significance of sexuality) and more affect-cultivation oriented (without maximizing the effect of affect and emotions). Reading cultivates affect, especially the affects of mood and mental health. Paranoia is an example of affect. Her point is that only emphasizing paranoid readings cultivates deep negative affective behaviors in the reader when texts can do so much more. It is important to notice that Sedgwick is not dismissing the importance of the paranoid positionality. The paranoid position leads to a form of strong theory that is also affect—one that explains the affect of humiliation or humiliation and fear.[21] These affects are negative affects, and in balancing a theory that creates negative affects with positive ones, reparative reading provides such a theoretical frame.

Reparative reading is complex reading in view of repairing and building community. In *Tendencies*, Sedgwick tracks how her own sense of mortality quickened by the personally devastating diagnosis of breast cancer paralleled the sense of mortality members of the gay community felt with a diagnosis of AIDS. One is the overwhelming sense of being almost reduced only to body, one that could imminently disappear. With the diagnosis of breast cancer, she now feels female and feminized in a way she never did before. The regimen of taking medications creates a complex of affect and emotion:

> That pretty, speckled, robin's-egg blue pill with the slightly sinister name "Cytoxan"—it was developed during WWII as a chemical warfare agent; when, as per doctor's instructions, I drop four of this "agent" into my bloodstream every morning, the mildest way to describe what is happening is via the postmodernist cliché that I am "putting in question the concept of agency"! I have never felt less stability in my gender, age, and racial identities, nor, anxious and full of the shreds of dread, shame, and mourning as this process is, have I ever felt more of a mind *to explore and exploit every possibility [of the affects].*[22]

In other words, a paranoid stance would deepen the sense of alienation and grief she was feeling. Another kind of reading was necessary to help her balance her deep feelings of pain with other feelings of resilience and strength.

Simultaneously, the fact of being ill creates a renewed attention in ways that memorials commemorate the loves and relationships of people who have died. The "panels on panels on panels" of the NAMES Project AIDS Memorial Quilt capture some of this sentiment: "Love you! Kelly"; "Frederic Abrams. Such drama"; "Michel Foucault. Where there is power, there is resistance . . . a plurality of resistances . . . spread over time and space. . . . It is doubtless the strategic codification of these resistances makes a revolution possible."[23] Sedgwick writes then of her rage at the quilt, at the disease, at the dying of bodies and wonders if her own death (in 2009, almost twenty years away) will create in others the same anger, powerlessness, *and* sense of opportunity that she feels—the paranoid and reparative moments in twinned action. The textual evidence of celebrations of life and mourning for senseless death becomes the reason for her own writing.

It may seem as if Sedgwick's work is dated because now there are slightly more civil protections for queer people and much more research done on breast cancer. It is also better known that breast cancer does not only affect women. Hence, some of her critical views on reading with illness may seem out of date today. Yet Sedgwick's queer thinking gave rise to the very field of queer thought and repristinated many forms of critical theory since the 1990s. Further, her thinking fostered multiple contemporary reflections on the limits of critique. Hence, her point that illness and imminent death are occasions to reexamine critical theory's commitments remains a very pertinent one. Her own illness and imminent death also brought her to a study of Zen Buddhism. While I do not have the space here to explore this strand of her thought more fully, it is enough to note that Buddhist ideas of "not" and "no-self" became significantly important to her process of slow death rather than the "unremitting regimen of positive thinking" that exhorted cancer patients like herself to keep fighting and "win" the battle with cancer. Consequently, she began to fully inhabit the Bardo (a Tibetan word for "existence between death and rebirth") as the "pedagogy of Buddhism" marked by "silence, inexpressibility, and unteachability."[24] This position therefore ultimately "queers" secular feminist theory's avoidance of religion and spirituality.

Significantly, Sedgwick declared that the category "queer" would vanish in the future. In one way, she herself was writing as one beyond representative queerness. In another way, she was advocating for all critical theory to become more fully queer and examine the intrinsic sexual politics of all knowledge precisely as a response to the AIDS pandemic. Further, she complicated the sense of "I," which many thinkers and activists take for granted, in her strong identification with gay male creativity. Finally, as one of her dearest friends sickened and died of AIDS, she writes of how important it is to identify with people who are ill:

> It's as though there were transformative political work to be done just by being available to be identified with in the very grain of one's illness. . . . All of these may nonetheless be brought consciously, even if haltingly, into the world of people living with this disease—just as, whatever one's privilege, a person living with fatal disease in this particular culture is inducted ever more consciously, even more needily, yet with ever more profound and transformative revulsion into the manglingly differential world of health care under American capitalism.[25]

It would be a queer thing indeed for anyone to attempt to inhabit the world of someone sick and dying arising from a political commitment to think of health and illness beyond an individualist frame. It would be a queer thing indeed for anyone to be in actual, real, and engaged solidarity with the suffering and dying!

Representations of "queer," however, remain resolutely attached to an individualist frame, deepening the neoliberal emphasis of self-identity. First, "queer" signifies for many a very particular self-identification as an objective and empirical category governed by rules of evidence; that is, one *has* to be gay to be queer. But if that is the case, then the AIDS pandemic *only* happened to gay people, and that is evidently fallacious. This point is what Sedgwick is driving home with such clarity and force: Certain forms of identity politics and their critical stances actually limit the potential for larger and more robustly complex resistances and solidarities if we relegate (among other things) sexual illness to any one group of people. Identity politics also hides the way in which illness under specific economic and political regimes combines with state violence. Theory cannot remain a bystander! It must push and think beyond its many confinements and seek intersectional nexuses and possibilities for alliance. Second, the term "queer" has become domesticated and performative in a way that Sedgwick could not have imagined. In the past ten years, there has been a general widening of sexual identities, with many performances of acceptance and inclusion in politics, religion, and the academy, with visibility in popular culture. Of course, in many parts of the world, horrific violence continues to be displayed toward queer people, but the domestication of the term also means that queer has lost the theoretical sharpness that Sedgwick was pleading for in 1991. "Queer" in Sedgwick's work is a critical stance that seeks reparative amelioration of conditions of embodied sexual life, illness, pandemic, and ill health as entanglements of capitalism, liberal individualism, and judgmental condemnation of the sick and dying. However, traversing beyond the category of sexual identity, and unmooring "queer" from its allegiance to sexual identity alone, is a strategy that would make *all* politics queer. Sedgwick's hope for the term to become such an all-encompassing strategy has not come into fruition because the imploding fragmentation of the Left is itself a mechanism aimed at destroying the possibility of solidarity across the many constructed divisions of contemporary capitalism. Such fragmentation is actively managed through processes of violence and death, many of which Sedgwick had identified in the eighties and nineties. Consequently, other voices in the recent past have joined her voice in calling for political strategies and alliances beyond self-expressive identity categories, as we see below.

PANDEMIC HERESIES

"The virus is the mirror image of our society," declares cultural studies philosopher Byung-Chul Han. A Korean German philosopher, Han is the author of several books on topics such as hyper consumerism, hyper information culture, hyper transparency, and hyper positivity. He studied metallurgy at Korea University as an undergraduate. In graduate school, he studied philosophy, German literature, and Catholic theology in Freiburg and Munich. He currently teaches at the Berlin University of the Arts. Han's writing tends to the libertarian, espousing privacy, silence, and noncommunication to challenge the current mood of liberal societies that demand psychic and psychological knowledge from each other constantly.

Han came to global attention because of his first book, *The Burnout Society*.[26] Perhaps as a challenge to the formalism of academic writing, his writing is aphoristic, pithy, and tweetable. Stuart Jeffries, in an essay on contemporary philosophy in *The Guardian*, remarks that "Han cuts an intriguing figure. He rarely makes public appearances or gives interviews . . . and his Facebook page seems to have been set up by Spanish admirers, and only recently did he set up an email address which he scarcely uses. He is often heralded . . . as a wunderkind of a newly resurgent and unprecedently readable German philosophy."[27] In *The Burnout Society*, Han makes the (heretical) claim that today's society is no longer Foucault's disciplinary world of hospitals, madhouses, prisons, barracks, and factories.[28] Instead, we have become an "achievement society" in which we all have become "entrepreneurs of ourselves." As Jeffries observes, in relation to Han's slim volume, "In the West's deindustrialized, neoliberal era, [Foucauldian] biopolitics is obsolete. Instead, by deploying big data, neoliberalism has tapped into the psychic realm and exploited it, with the result that, as Han colorfully puts it, 'individuals degrade into the genital organs of capital.' . . . Instead of watching over human behavior, big data's digital panopticon subjects it to psychopolitical steering."[29]

Hyperactivity is one consequence of living in a society where our psychic worlds are so controlled from without. This is also because another feature of the burnout society is a manic drive to constantly be distracted, entertained, and fulfilled. He calls this the "excess of positivity," with an exceedingly distorted idea of freedom.[30] In an essay titled "The Crisis of Freedom," Han asserts that freedom is exploited by neoliberal interests: "Although the achievement-subject deems itself free, in reality, it is a slave. In so far as it willingly exploits itself without a master, it is an absolute slave. There is no master forcing the achievement-subject to work. Yet all the same, it is absolutizing bare life and labor . . . as the entrepreneur of its own self, the neoliberal subject has no capacity for relationships with others that might be free of purpose."[31] He goes on to remind us that for Marx, "individual freedom represents a ruse, a trick of capital," because it is simply capital relating to capital, not human being to another human being.[32] The resulting competitiveness, a source of deep anxiety and worry for the burnout society, is the visible sign of our current servitude to capital. The Hegelian master/slave dialectic is now vanquished because in contemporary Western society, "everyone is an auto-exploiting laborer in his or her own enterprise. People are now master and slave in one. Even class struggle has transformed into an inner struggle against oneself."[33] We are so busy curating aspects of ourselves to be put on display in this system that ethics and politics become self-referential and self-aggrandizing activities.

Han's is a deeply pessimistic and gloomy picture of human existence under neoliberal conditions. However, what is clear to him is that theory's role is to be agonistic to preserve the otherness of the other. Han has inveighed against global neoliberal economic frameworks in his writing, arguing throughout that we have become puppets who cannot read and write because we are held in thrall of a "psychopolitics" that contrasts with activities such as reading and writing.[34] Reading and writing have become the "mass media of the past" and have been replaced by the internet and social media, which emphasize display and exhibition. In his analysis of philosopher Bernard Stiegler's proposal, Han declares that "Steigler's overemphasis on television is problematic. . . . Strangely, Steigler hardly examines truly digital technology as the internet and social media, which prove fundamentally different than the mass media of the past. What is more, he barely pays attention to the panoptic structure of digital networks. As the result, he completely misses the workings of liberal psychopolitics, which employs digital technology on a large scale."[35] "Psychopolitics" is the neoliberal lure of endless self-optimization, self-regard, and self-display, or the culture of what may be termed "selfie-ness."

Given the context of psychopolitics, a global pandemic such as COVID-19 has created a "survival society," according to Han. His book *The Palliative Society* is a trenchant critique of our global culture's fear of pain—algophobia—which led first to the creation of the palliative society.[36] In our frenzied flight from pain, we are compelled to be happy, but happiness is construed in a highly interiorized and psychologized form: "It ensures that all are preoccupied with their own psyches rather than interested in critically questioning their social conditions."[37] This has then led to a "palliative democracy" rather than one in which people engage in robust debate with ideas that challenge and interrogate.[38] With COVID-19, the palliative society has morphed into a survival society where algophobia has transformed into thanatophobia, the fear of death.[39] Han's argument here is in service of a politics that can keep alive the vision of true democracies that accommodate debate and conversation about different and opposing points of view. The virus has escalated our slide into a mania for self-survival in which any other human being becomes a threat as a possible carrier of the virus. But, as he is careful to remind us, the problem is algophobia, with pain having been banished as an outrageous negative: "Pain is negativity par excellence. This paradigm shift is also present in psychology, where there has been a movement away from a negative psychology of suffering and towards a positive psychology concerned with well-being, happiness, and optimism."[40]

As a contrarian, Han wants to point out the inconsistencies that the pandemic has forced us into, specifically the crippling fear of contracting the virus even as we must continue to live in families and communities. A lack of faith and trust is overwhelmingly evident. He excoriates (Catholic) priests who social distance and wear masks, asserting that "virology deprives theology of its power."[41] The point is less that he is an anti-masker, given that his work was written and published very early in the pandemic; instead, he is interrogating what faith, trust, commitment, and service mean anymore. His challenge is that pain and death are the occasions to think about the good life—for all. He relativizes our sense of right to life as a primary right for any of us, reminding us that human beings as a species are basically living on top of a billion trillion bacteria and viruses, and barely separated from them by a thin skin:

> The pandemic demonstrates that the wall sheltering us from the elementary forces can break at any time. As the paleontologist Andrew H. Knoll puts it, "Human beings and other animals are 'evolution's icing,' and the 'bacteria are the cake.' Microbes threaten to break through the fragile surface, even to conquer it, at any time. . . . We take ourselves to be safe, but it is only ever a matter of time before we are pulled into the elements. In the Anthropocene, humans are more vulnerable than ever. Our violence toward nature returns and exerts itself upon us with even more force."[42]

It is a fact that human beings coexist with viruses and bacteria. All human beings, therefore, share responsibility for engaging in activities that puncture the thin veil between species. An overfocus on our individual survivability is a selfish and highly individualist way to live that forecloses the possibility of social, global, and concerted cooperation.

Han's writing deeply challenges. But he also invites us to constructive positions. Like Sedgwick, who asks us to occupy queer positions, Han invites us to occupy heretical positions. One of his heresies is to cultivate practices of "profound boredom."[43] He points to Walter Benjamin as a source for this idea—specifically, his notion that deep boredom is a "dream bird that hatches the egg of experience."[44] Boredom is "mental relaxation" and necessary for a time in which human beings live hectic and over-exhausted lives, drowning in multiple tasks, information, and expectations to achieve. Han's concern is that our burned-out condition erases the possibility of true listening and of listening communities: "The gift of listening is based on the ability to grant deep contemplative attention, which remains inaccessible to the hyperactive ego."[45] While he does not use the word, it is felicitous that a term such as "selfie-ness" captures our contemporary drive to be distracted by the gluttonous demands of the ego instead of engaging in deep mental and spiritual contemplation as a counterweight to the overstimulated lives we lead.

Deep contemplation is heretical activity in a culture that rewards frenetic activity. Scattered throughout Han's essays are various acknowledgements of the benefits of contemplation. For example, he asserts that contemplation, or paying attention, deepens our sensitivity to sight. In the essay "The Pedagogy of Seeing," Han invokes Friedrich Nietzsche's *Twilight of the Idols* and the three tasks of any teacher: to teach to see, to think, and to speak and write.[46] Seeing is a complex task, that requires great attention and perseverance. Han writes, quoting Nietzsche liberally:

> Learning to see means "getting your eyes used to calm, to patience, to letting things come to you." . . . Such learning to see represents the "first preliminary schooling for spirituality." One must learn "*not* to react immediately to a stimulus, but instead to take control of the inhibiting, excluding instincts." By the same token, "every characteristic absence of spirituality, every piece of common vulgarity, is due to an inability to resist a stimulus, the inability to set a *no* in opposition. Reacting immediately, yielding to every impulse, already amounts to illness and represents a symptom of exhaustion."[47]

The contemplative or reflective life cannot be lived in the "poverty of our times."[48] Han agrees with Hannah Arendt that "thinking has always been the privilege of the few," but that "few" is now "fewer" because of the "hyperactive restlessness, the franticness and unrest of today, does not do any good to thinking, and that thinking just reproduces always the same because of increasing time pressures."[49] The active life, or *vita activa*, has become an absolute value, driving everything that is not an act or activity out of life. It insists on accelerating the pace of life, driving human beings to a compulsion of labor. Han has interests in Zen Buddhist practices, and his focus on contemplation follows that strand of thought. Yet in most of his work, he depends on Western philosophical traditions to make his case, including among them, Christian theologians and mystics such as Thomas Aquinas and Meister Eckhart. Yet it is not a one-sided celebration of *vita contemplativa*; "rather, as in Meister Eckhart, a mediation between *vita activa* and *vita contemplativa* is the goal in mind."[50]

Then there is Han's injunction to accept pain in our lives. Of all his ideas, this one, developed in response to the COVID-19 pandemic, is the most challenging and potentially divisive. In the palliative society, "pain is interpreted as a sign of weakness."[51] Societies that privilege the vita activa find no meaning in the passivity of suffering because they are so focused on ability and performance. Thus, "today, pain cannot be expressed. It is condemned to be mute. The palliative society does not permit pain to be enlivened into a passion, to be given a language."[52] As he avers, in a "neoliberal dispositive," "be happy" is an injunction in which happiness is employed as positive emotional capital to ensure that individuals perform all the time. People hand over their freedom precisely because the principles of self-motivation and self-optimization create the conditions for "effortless domination."[53] Thus, freedom is not curtailed but exploited. The appeal to "be free" produces a compulsion that is far more devastating than the injunction to "be obedient."

The happiness mandate also gives rise to the "like" culture, another aspect of the culture of positivity that provokes Han's ire. Art, philosophy, thought—all are "vehemently forced into the straitjacket of the like," and artists (and philosophers) are pushed to become brands, to onform to the market, and to be "likeable."[54] What happens then is that the truly other is banished, as no one wants to deal with the pain of the unlikeable. However, "pain is the tear through which the wholly other can enter," and it is the negativity of pain that allows art and philosophy to provide a counternarrative.[55] Here is one of Han's more lyrical paragraphs:

> "Goosebumps," Adorno says, are the "first aesthetic image." They express the dawn of the other. A consciousness that is unable to shudder is a reified consciousness. It is incapable of experience, for experience "is in essence the suffering in which the essential otherness of being reveals itself in opposition to the tried and usual." A life that rejects all pain is also reified. Only the "act of being touched by the other" keeps life alive. Or else it remains in the hell of the same.[56]

Writing philosophy, and one could say also reading it, arises in pain. In another chapter in *The Palliative Society*, Han speaks of the "poetics of pain." He recounts the grief of various thinkers: Franz Kafka, Marcel Proust, Franz Schubert, Nietzsche. Since our cultures hasten to alleviate pain and tragedy, we are unable to produce great literature, art, or philosophy. A sense of tragedy that propelled earlier thinkers has vanished, leading us to forget how pain can be narrated or sung. Pain's poetics, its aesthetic dimensions, have been overtaken by a medical view of pain. The arts of reading and writing consequently suffer. Lest one thinks that Han is invested in forms of sadism or masochism, it is important to remember that he is drawing deeply from strands of Western philosophy and theology. Patience, the ability to wait, and the ability to renounce—these qualities have diminished or disappeared from our cultures of positivity. Writing and reading must be patient and cultivate habits of patience.

> The mental attitude that shows patience and is prepared to wait is eroding. It provides access to a reality which we are losing amid the compulsion of total availability. A waiting which remains patient within the enduring and slow exhibits a specific kind of intentionality. It is an attitude that resigns itself to the non-available. It is not a case of *waiting for* but of *waiting in*. . . . Renunciation is the fundamental trait of *intentionless waiting*. Renunciation *gives*. It makes us receptive to the non-available. It is opposed to consumption. . . . Pain is not a subjective sensation pointing to the lack of something but a reception, even the reception of being. *Pain is a gift*.[57]

Such receptivity opens us up to pain for the other. Thus, pain is not the pain of mine alone; pain also is the pain of another that I experience as mine. We experience a nakedness of the soul because "our digital bubbles shield us from the other."[58] Finally, to counter psychopolitics and its invidious consequences, Han invites us to "idiotism," which has nothing to do with stupidity or unintelligence. "Idiotism," he argues, "discloses a field of immanence of events and singularities for thought; this field eludes subjectivization and psychologization all together."[59] Philosophy, he writes, is a "history of idiotisms," where original thinking can expose one to derision and alienation. We live in a world of "compulsive and coercive communication and conformism," requiring the amelioration of idiotism. The idiot is the new heretic and, instead of nonstop conformist communication, fosters spaces of quiet and solitude where they can think in peace of what needs to be said. The idiot of today listens and lets others speak in the hope of repairing broken relationships. In a culture of hyper consumption and hyper production, what we have paradoxically given up is the ability to hear the other.

THEORY FOR THE SICK AND DYING

For Sedgwick and for Han, global pandemics are the occasion to remind critical theory of its primary responsibility—that of cultivating a sense of deep and complex commitment to the suffering of others by casting a critical and clear light on the systems that perpetuate their suffering. Sedgwick would have roundly castigated the global hand-wringing that was evident in the first months and year of the COVID pandemic, especially in Western contexts where the displays of outrage and the curtailing of "freedom" were evident. Han, writing more contemporarily, is very transparent about his contempt with such forms of self-indulgence. What both thinkers invite us to do is to create and think theoretically about the limits of capitalist-generated "freedom." Western capitalism with its fear of illness, dying, and disease hides the fragility of life while greedily consuming finite resources; however, it carefully constructs another kind of psychological fragility in which the very mention of pain, limit, and grief is considered an insult to the contemporary ego. The elusive ideal of "happiness" is touted as the cure for all pain, and when the ego suffers as such desire remains unfulfilled, it offers the pale consolations of a medicalized anthropology with its dreadful collections of pills and potions to help alleviate it. Sedgwick and Han roundly challenge these mechanisms, identifying them as disciplinary mechanisms of an inhumane and unsustainable economic and political order.

Our preoccupation with avoiding pain results in an overweening emphasis on personal survivability and personal success, achievement, productivity, and happiness. Our digital habits of consuming and circulating a stultifying sameness reflect the ruse of neoliberal capitalism, which has turned the mirror of truth into an artifact of self-regard. What interrupts such a "selfie culture" is illness and pandemic, where we are jolted out of our endless reverie of self-absorption. Sedgwick challenges us to think of illnesses such as breast cancer as illnesses that happen to us all, and Han challenges us to think of pandemics as evidence that we live and exist in a world deeply entangled with capitalism, consumption, extraction, and exploitation of each other and other species. Opening ourselves up to the reality of a global entanglement paradoxically creates the disposition of gratitude for the persistence of life despite its utter fragility and begins to repair a necessary sense of the whole. Other dispositions—uncannily sounding like spiritual dispositions of renunciation, of accepting pain and limit, of inhabiting heretical positions (to counter contemporary capitalist ones)—are practices that readers, writers, and thinkers can develop to deepen theoretical commitments for politics and ethics.

Theory for the sick and dying, therefore, as this chapter has tracked, is not simplistically secular. Or self-serving. Or productive. As the epilogue to this essay reminds us, intellectual work achieves balance only when interweaving spirituality alongside. Reading and writing are political acts of resistance inside and outside the classroom; they are acts that are queer and heretical. While they can be solitary activities, they parallel and counter forms of selfie-ness when they are done in service of imagining and healing the whole. The activities are solitary only because being countercultural and theoretically sophisticated may relegate one to an alone space, or—as Han colorfully puts it—the space of the idiot. Because they hint at forms of renunciative spirituality, such reading and writing will further alienate in a culture that breeds narrow conformism precisely through mechanisms of self-curation and displays of egoism. Reading and writing challenge regnant ideas of individualistic freedom because these practices help us understand how we are made to comply with a mirage of freedom, requiring instead an empathic and comprehensive grasp of complex ecosystems and interdependencies. Inhabiting the queer and the heretical, then, are acts that dissent in complex ways. Theory for the sick and dying, in such a view, is both a form of academic activism and a form of spirituality that brings bodily intelligence and dispositions of the spirit to the work of ethics and politics.

NOTES

Saint Bonaventure of Bagnoregio, "Journey of the Mind into God (*Incipit Prologus Itinerarium Mentis in Deum*)," *Opera Omnia S. Bonaventura*, trans. Simon Wickham-Smith, vol. 5 (Quaracchi edition, 1891), https://faculty.uml.edu/rinnis/45.304%20God%20and%20Philosophy/ITINERARIUM.pdf.

1. Sedgwick, *Touching Feeling*, 123–51.
2. Sedgwick, 124.
3. Stephen M. Barber and David L. Clark, *Regarding Sedgwick: Essays on Queer Culture and Critical Theory* (New York: Routledge, 2002).
4. Barber and Clark, 13.
5. Sedgwick, *Tendencies*, 12.
6. Sedgwick, 15.
7. Sedgwick, 15.
8. Sedgwick, 4.
9. Sedgwick, 178. Emphases in the original.
10. Sedgwick, 200. Emphases in the original.
11. Sedgwick, 3.
12. Sedgwick, 4.
13. Sedgwick, 4.
14. Sedgwick, *Touching Feeling*, 126. Emphasis in the original.
15. Sedgwick, *Tendencies*, 6.
16. Sedgwick, *Touching Feeling*, 127, 124. Emphases in the original.

17. Sedgwick, 130.
18. Sedgwick, 144.
19. Sedgwick, 151.
20. Sedgwick, 146.
21. Sedgwick, 133.
22. Sedgwick, *Tendencies*, 264. Emphasis added.
23. Sedgwick, 264.
24. Sedgwick, *Touching Feeling*, 174.
25. Sedgewick, *Tendencies*, 261.
26. Han, *Burnout Society*.
27. S. Jeffries, review of *Psychopolitics: Neoliberalism and Technologies of Power*, by Byung-Chul Han, and translated by Erik Butler, *The Guardian*, December 30, 2017, https://www.theguardian.com/books/2017/dec/30/psychopolitics-neolberalism-new-technologies-byung-chul-han-review.
28. Han, *Burnout Society*, 8.
29. Jeffries, review.
30. Han, *Burnout Society*, 1.
31. Han, *Psychopolitics*, 2.
32. Han, 3.
33. Han, 5.
34. Han, 23.
35. Steigler, *Taking Care*; and Han, *Psychopolitics*, 26.
36. Han, *Palliative Society*.
37. Han, 11.
38. Han, 2.
39. Han, 14.
40. Han, 2.
41. Han, 15.
42. Han, 26.
43. Han, *Burnout Society*, 12–15.
44. Han, 13.
45. Han, 13.
46. Han, 21–29.
47. Han, 21. Emphasis in the original.
48. Han, *Scent of Time*, 108.
49. Han, 108.
50. Han, 111.
51. Han, *Palliative Society*, 3.
52. Han, 3.
53. Han, 10.
54. Han, 4.
55. Han, 6.
56. Han, 6.
57. Han, 49. Emphases in original.
58. Han, 54.
59. Han, *Psychopolitics*, 81.

BIBLIOGRAPHY

Han, Byung Hul. *The Burnout Society*. Translated by Erik Butler. Stanford: Stanford Briefs, 2015.

———. *The Palliative Society*. Translated by Daniel Steuer. Cambridge: Polity Press, 2021.

———. *Psychopolitics: Neoliberalism and Technologies of Power*. Translated by Erik Butler. London: Verso Books, 2017.

———. *The Scent of Time: A Philosophical Essay on the Art of Lingering*. Translated by Daniel Steuer. Cambridge: Polity Press, 2009.

Sedgwick, Eve Kosofsky. *Tendencies*. Durham NC: Duke University Press, 1993.

———. (2003) *Touching Feeling: Affect, Pedagogy, Performativity*. Durham NC: Duke University Press, 2003.

Steigler, Bernard. *Taking Care of Youth and the Generations*. Stanford: Stanford University Press, 2010.

CHAPTER 6

Interdependence, Gratitude, and Justice

Hindu Perspectives

Anantanand Rambachan

INTRODUCTION: GRATITUDE AND DIGNITY

It would be unjust and untrue to speak about the meaning of gratitude in the Hindu tradition without acknowledging, at the outset, that there are millions of human beings for whom the Hindu tradition does not evoke a response of gratitude. For them, Hinduism is associated with teachings and practices that degrade and diminish their dignity and self-worth, and deny them the opportunities to realize the fullness of their human potential. Omprakash Valmiki, in his autobiography, *Joothan: An Untouchable's Life,* speaks for Dalits and other marginalized communities in a series of powerfully painful questions.

> If I really were a Hindu, would the Hindus hate me so much? Or discriminate against me? Or try to fill me up with caste inferiority over the smallest things? I also wondered why one had to be a Hindu in order to be a good human being—I have seen and suffered the cruelty of Hindus since childhood. Why does caste superiority and caste pride attack only the weak? Why are Hindus so cruel, so heartless against Dalits?[1]

He continues:

> Times have changed. But something somewhere continues to irk. I have asked many scholars to tell me why *savarnas* hate Dalits and Sudras, the lower castes, so much. The Hindus who worship trees and plants, beasts, and birds, why are they so intolerant of Dalits. . . . As long as people don't know that you are a Dalit, things are fine. The moment they find out your caste, everything changes. The whispers slash your veins like knives. Poverty, illiteracy, broken lives, the pain of standing outside the door, how would the civilized *savarna* Hindus know it?[2]

Valmiki's pain is not solitary; it is the cry of his community. We must acknowledge it as a consequence of the inhumanity, injustice, and oppression of the caste system that devalues some of our fellow human beings on the basis of birth and socially constructed norms of purity and impurity. We must admit how deeply the assumptions of caste have entered into teachings and practices of the Hindu tradition and the ways in which interpretations of religious teachings are invoked to legitimize caste. We must understand why gratitude would not be a word used by the so-called untouchables to describe their relationship with Hindus or the Hindu tradition. How could one be grateful for teachings and practices that diminish and undermine one's dignity and for persons who negate one's humanity?

That caste is a crushing and oppressive hierarchical ordering of human beings cannot be denied. We also cannot deny the invocation of the authority of religion to sanction this social order. We must understand also why some Dalits see the dismantling of Hinduism as a requisite of their freedom. They may be not aware of liberative teachings or influential movements that aim for reform and the overcoming of the caste system. In their eyes, such teachings exist only as abstract ideals, and reform movements have not had much success in removing caste. How may we then speak of gratitude in Hinduism? Are there teachings that subvert caste and offer an understanding of gratitude that does not imply the acceptance of the caste order?

GRATITUDE AND THE GIFT OF HUMAN EXISTENCE

The Hindu tradition, on the whole, regards human life as a blessing and a special gift that has its source in the divine. In the *Vivekacūḍāmaṇi*, a philosophical poem attributed to the theologian Śaṅkara (ca. eighth century CE), the teacher identifies three special gifts of God: one's birth as a human being, a longing for freedom from *avidyā* (ignorance), and a discipleship with a teacher.[3] If one receives the unique gift of human life, says Śaṅkara, and does not utilize it as an opportunity for overcoming ignorance about the nature of ultimate reality, then one, in reality, chooses self-destruction. In a similar vein, the poet Tulasīdāsa, in his retelling of the life story of Rama, who is regarded by a large number of Hindus as a divine descent, or incarnation (*avatāra*), speaks of human life as cause for joy, as a sacred opportunity for religious practice (*sadhana dhāma*), and as a doorway to liberation.[4] *Aitareya Upaniṣad* (2:3) twice uses the term *sukṛtám* (well made) to describe the human being.[5] It should be stated clearly, however, that the uniqueness of human life does not imply the power to instrumentalize all other sentient beings for human ends. We are unique because of our ability to gain knowledge of ultimate reality and to live with fulfillment, self-control, generosity, and love. With all of its challenges, and in spite of our capacity for inflicting pain and suffering, life is fundamentally good and a divine gift.

In the Upaniṣads, the universe and living beings are described as emerging from a wish on the part of infinite divine to become many, a wish for self-multiplication. In the words of the *Taittirīya Upaniṣad* (2.6.1), the One wished, "'Let me be many, let me be born.' He undertook a deliberation. Having deliberated, he created all this that exists. That (Brahman) having created (that), entered into that very thing." Since the Upaniṣads refute both the doctrine of dualism—that is, the existence of anything but the One prior to the emergence of the many—and creation from nonexistence (*asat*), all that exists emerge from the One alone. As the text above also states, the one Brahman entered into all that is created (*tadevānupraviśhat*).[6]

The Upaniṣads delight in detailing the rich and inexhaustible diversity that proceeds from the One. One text, for example, lists breath, mind, space, air, fire, Earth, divine beings, human beings, animals, birds, rice, barley, oceans, mountains, rivers, and corn! Another text speaks of the dark blue butterfly, the green parrot with red eyes, the thundercloud pregnant with lightning, and the revolving seasons. Diversity is a celebrative outpouring of the joyous fullness of the divine. God's capacity for bringing forth difference as self-expression is inexhaustible.

The implication of such a theology of creation, across Hindu traditions, is that the divine is present equally and identically in every being. In the words of *Bhagavadgītā* (13:29), "One who sees the Supreme God existing equally in all beings, the imperishable in the perishable, truly sees."[7] That the unfathomable, inexhaustible, timeless, and all-pervasive ground of existence chooses to be present in us is the most fundamental source of human dignity and worth. It is also the deepest reason for gratitude. My origin is from the infinite one, I am sustained moment by moment by that one, and my highest destiny is to return to that one. *Taittirīya Upaniṣad* (3.2.1) describes Brahman as "that from which all beings originate, that by which, after birth, they exist, and that to which they all return." Each human being is a unique gift of divine self-giving. Gratitude includes reverence for the self and for others that proceeds from an awareness of the sacred in all. The *Bhagavadgītā* (6:5) cautions against self-degradation (*nātmānam avasādayet*) and urges self-affirmation and self-worth (*uddhared ātmanātmanaṁ*). Human existence uniquely offers the opportunity for knowledge of the divine and for consciously joyful living that is the outcome of such knowledge. The divine is joy (*raso vai sah*) (*Taittirīya Upaniṣad* 2.7.1), and one attains joy by knowing the source of joy.

Although the Hindu traditions teach that the divine is present in all, there is the reality, as noted earlier, of ignorance and its dire consequences. We are unaware of the deeper truths of ourselves, the world, and the divine that exists within and unites us all. In the case of the non-dual (*advaita*) tradition, under the condition of ignorance we regard ourselves as separate and different from all else that exists. Without wisdom, we are not aware of our unity and ontological identity with others, with nature and the divine. In the *Chāndogya Upaniṣad* (6.14.2), the human condition under ignorance is likened to someone forcibly taken away from his beloved home, blindfolded, and left in the wilderness. A kind person answers his plea for help, removes his blindfold, and shows him the way home. In a similar manner, a compassionate teacher liberates the avidyā-bound individual by pointing out her unity with the limitless divine and with all beings.

Describing the human problem as one of ignorance does not minimize our predicament. The consequences of ignorance are both personal and social. (The Upaniṣads speak of the three-fold knots of the heart: ignorance, greed, and greedful action [avidyā, *kāma*, karma]). Ignorance generates greed because it engenders a false sense of separation, anxiety, incompleteness, and self-lacking. Desires for wealth, sense pleasures, fame, and so on are then generated to achieve completeness and self-value. The fulfillment of such desires, however, results in momentary experiences of completeness. Soon, new desires are generated, and the search for fullness becomes a race without a finishing line. The Hindu tradition does not condemn wealth and pleasure, but it is concerned with the personal and social consequences of greed. Greed generates actions and a legacy of structures that are destructive of the self and others. Although the consequences of ignorance are grave, ignorance does not point to a fundamental flaw in human nature. Ignorance can be overcome and, with that effort, greed as well. We are then liberated to live in joyous union, generosity, and love with all beings. The *Bhagavadgītā* (6:32) speaks of the liberated as owning the joys and sorrows of others as her own and as delighting in the flourishing of all (5:25). This means both owning the suffering of those who are marginalized and devalued in the Hindu tradition and working for their flourishing.

The ground, the most fundamental source, of gratitude is thankfulness for being, not nonbeing; for existence itself; for the privilege of living in and with sacred mystery; for recognizing and delighting in it in all beings; for knowing this mystery as the ground of all sense, mental and physical activity; and for experiencing it in the taste of water, the light of the moon and sun, the fragrance of the earth, and the brilliance of fire. It is gratitude for participating in the wonderous mystery of existence. In the words of the *Bhagavadgītā* 2:29, one contemplates sacred mystery with wonder, one speaks of it with wonder, and one hears about it with wonder. Even after hearing, no one fully understands.

DIVINE-HUMAN UNITY: THE DISMANTLING OF CASTE

The critical questions, however, that still need to be addressed directly are as follows: Are there teachings in the Hindu tradition that challenge and refute the assumptions of inequality and impurity that are at the heart of caste and that have the potential to transform human relationships? Do these teachings provide grounds for gratitude and rejoicing in existence? I believe that there are such teachings, and they were identified by the great Dalit leader Dr. B. R. Ambedkar.[8] Dr. Ambedkar, however, believed that Hindus lacked the will to reform Hindu society. The most fundamental of these teachings, the theological roots of which I described earlier, is the affirmation that the divine exists identically in every being. This truth of divinity abiding equally in all is the most important source and ground of the intrinsic dignity and equal worth of every human being. It is our theological antibody to the instrumentalization of human beings, the denial of their personhood, and their classification in unequal hierarchies. Positively, this teaching requires that we value others as we value ourselves, that we care for them as we care for ourselves, and that we labor together to overcome the causes of suffering. When we value and center our lives in the divine, who dwells within and enfolds every being, our relationships are transformed by love, service, and gratitude. As a contemporary Hindu monk, Swami Tyagananda puts it, "If God dwells in me and in everyone and everything in the world, then no matter who I am dealing with and who I am working for, I am really dealing only with God and working only for God."[9]

The famous Hindu teacher Sri Ramakrishna (1836–86), teacher of Swami Vivekananda, on one occasion spoke to his disciples about gratitude and service. In a discussion about compassion, Ramakrishna explained they should see serving others as serving God: "No, no; it is not compassion to *jivas* (living beings) but service to them as Shiva (God)."[10] Ramakrishna obviously wanted his students to understand service as a privilege and honor that must be exercised in humility and gratitude as a worshipful act. Of course, one could commend love, gratitude, and service within a hierarchical social order that is fundamentally oppressive. Our challenge is the transformation of both the personal and the social. We must not be content with virtues, such as gratitude, that are commended within deeply entrenched structures of injustice or virtues that are spiritualized and have no concern with transforming relationships in our world. The focus on ignorance (avidyā) as the cause of suffering has resulted in emphasizing the need for individual cognitive and ethical transformation without attending to the suffering that oppressive social and economic systems inflict and to the need to identify and transform these systems. The Hindu tradition must concern itself with such systemic sources of suffering.

Hindu teachings that are unambiguous about the divine being present equally in everyone, and the implications of such teachings for transforming personal relationships and oppressive social structures, sustain me as a Hindu practitioner and scholar. For such teachings I am grateful. But my gratitude is tempered with a deep regret that the liberating social implications of these teachings remain to be fully realized and that my tradition is not more aggressive about the work of dismantling caste structures. Our stance, unfortunately, is less self-critical, more defensive, and, for too many, indifferent.

GRATITUDE AND INTERDEPENDENCE

As noted earlier, the universe in the Upaniṣads is described as flowing from divine self-multiplication. The divine cause is present in every created effect, and every effect is moment to moment dependent on this cause for its existence and being.

Every effect, however, is present in and dependent on every other effect for its existence and sustenance. One of the important narratives on this truth occurs in the *Taittirīya Upaniṣad* 2.2.1, which offers a sequence of the emergence of the great elements and life from sacred mystery. The first to emerge is space. From space comes air, from air comes heat or fire, from fire comes water, from water comes the earth, from the earth comes vegetation, from vegetation comes food, and from food comes living beings. The divine, as the source of everything, is present in all, but we are also present in each other and exist because of each other. In the case of the great elements, for example, space is present in air; space and air in fire; space, air, and fire in water; and space, air, fire, and water in the earth. The original divine mode of self-multiplication is replicated, and everything is in everything. We are formed of the universe, represent it in our bodies, and always are organically connected with it. The earth is in everything solid in our bodies, water in all that is liquid, fire in the body's warmth and energy, and air in our breath. Dualistic ontologies and language that speak of human beings and the natural world as separate realities are both untrue and dangerous. It is false because we are an organic and integral part of the natural world and do not exist apart from it. The act of breathing unites us with the universe and every other being. Dualism is dangerous because it objectifies the natural world and contributes to the belief that we can destroy the natural world without destroying ourselves. The truth is that what we do to the natural world, we do to ourselves.

The interdependent character of existence that is the foundation of our existence includes our relationships with the community of human beings. The Hindu tradition describes every human being as owing his or her existence to others. We are never self-made beings; we do not develop our human potential outside of a human community. The interrelated community of beings to whom we owe our existence and our sustenance includes the divine as the ground of all reality: ancestors and parents, teachers, human caregivers, and the natural world. We exist and have possibilities for realizing our potential because we are a part of a generous and supportive interdependent whole. The proper response to this understanding of our unity, indebtedness, and interdependence is gratitude and commitment to the common good.

Gratitude in the Hindu tradition is a way of being in the world that is the outcome of understanding our interrelatedness and mutual dependence. There are several important Sanskrit terms that articulate the meaning of this way of being, including dharma, *lokasaṁgraham,* and *yajña.* At heart, gratitude is the response of generous self-giving in spontaneous response for one's unceasing receiving; it expresses the mutuality of receiving and giving. The *Bhagavadgītā* (3:11–12) describes this mutuality as ordained by the creator for human prosperity. It is represented by the *kāmadhuk,* or the wish-fulfilling cow of plenty that provides for all human needs. We attain the highest good by mutually caring, in gratitude, for each other.

Gratitude, Dharma, and *Yajña*

The language of gratitude in the Hindu tradition is the language of mutual obligations, or dharma.[11] We speak often of existence as interdependent without addressing sufficiently the ethical obligations that emanate from such a worldview. Hindu traditions, however, understand them as being inseparable. To exist is to do so interdependently, and the conscious understanding of this truth is embracing gratitude as a way of life.

Yajña is the Sanskrit term used in the *Bhagavadgītā* for this way of life, and the text commends sacred actions that are performed in the spirit of devotion, or the opposite of actions motivated by greed. *Yajña* describes a particular mode of Hindu worship in which a special altar is constructed, and upon this altar, a fire is lit. The fire symbolizes the divine reality; the worshippers, sitting at the fire, make offerings while reciting Veda verses (mantras). At the end of the ritual, food—some of which was offered into the fire—is distributed among the participants. Thus, food is received but only after it is worshipfully offered; it is to be enjoyed but only after it is shared. Later patterns of Hindu worship, or *pūja* in the home and temple, reflect a similar practice of giving and receiving. The basic structure of Hindu worship is receiving after giving.

In the *Bhagavadgītā* (3:9), Krishna observes, "Aside from action for the purpose of *yajña*, this world is bound by action. Perform action for the purpose of *yajña*, Arjuna, free from attachment." In the same text (3:19), he commends those who eat what is left after the practice of *yajñ*a and condemns those who eat only for themselves: "The virtuous who eat what is left after *yajña* are free from impurities; but the unrighteous, who cook only for their own sake, eat their own impurity" (3:13).

Ritual worship is held up here as a model for all actions. As we make offerings into the sacred fire or take offerings to the temple, we worship for the well-being of others, receiving, in turn, what we need for our own sustenance. The thief, says Krishna (3:12), is the person who enjoys the gifts of the world and does not give anything in return. It likens those who are not committed to the well-being of others to persons who selfishly cook only for themselves; virtuous persons cook both for themselves and for others. The food of the selfish is impure; the food of the virtuous is pure because it is shared.

Having said all of this, however, I recognize that I am commending an idealized version of the Hindu tradition articulated by those who came from more privileged places in the tradition. Acknowledging this truth does not discredit the insight of our human interdependent existence and its significance for gratitude. What it does not confess to is that the caste system limited the freedom of millions of human beings and made them involuntarily dependent on others. Entrenched social structures meant that they did not enjoy the same rights and opportunities as others to flourish and to realize their human potential. They were consigned to serving those who were on the higher rungs of the caste ladder. For such marginalized communities, talk of interdependence and gratitude is meaningless since their reality is one of an imposed dependence and not one of the freedom implied in interdependence. It is all too easy to speak of interdependence and to ignore the structural reality of multiple forms of dependence. In such contexts, discourse about interdependence and gratitude is hollow. If we must speak of interdependence and gratitude, let us see also the challenges that they present in oppressive and unjust environments. Interdependence is not meaningful without independence and the resources and opportunities to attain one's freely chosen goals.

Gratitude and the Common Good

Twice in the *Bhagavadgītā* (3:20; 3:25), Krishna uses the important expression *lokasaṁgraham* and urges that we consider it in every choice we make.[12] *Loka* is an inclusive word referring to the universe in its entirety, and *saṁgraham* means well-being. *Lokasaṁgraham* embraces not only all human beings but also the world of nature. It does not allow us to privilege unjustly the interests of a particular institution, nation, religion, race, or gender, and it excludes the pursuit of personal and institutional interests in ways that violently impede the flourishing of all, such as by trying to lift oneself or one's nation by crushing others. *Lokasaṁgraham* ensures that virtues are not privatized but applied publicly for peace, justice, and the flourishing of all. The common good is not served by economic systems that deplete our natural resources, eradicate our biodiversity, and adversely affect our climate. The public good becomes the measure of the meaning of all that we do. This moral concern for the common good ought not to be limited to actions of individual human beings. It must also become normative for the policies and practices of corporations, institutions, and states. When gratitude is translated into public policy, the outcome is what the tradition speaks of as *lokasaṁgraham.* To live from a place of gratitude is to constantly consider the implications of one's actions for the common good.

The theological ground of this commitment to the common good is the aforementioned interdependent nature of our existence. We are inseparable from the whole, which nourishes and sustains life, and we have moral obligations to contribute to the sustenance of the whole. Devotion to the common good is rooted also in the core teaching that the divine exists equally in all beings, uniting and holding all things together. The outcome of awakening to this teaching is a dedication to the flourishing of all beings, rejoicing when they prosper holistically and experiencing concern when they do not. Such dedication to the common good requires that we identify and work to overcome the causes that impede human flourishing, whether they are personal or embedded in social structures. It requires that we challenge any ideology and any political or social structure that denies the personhood and dignity of human beings and that condones injustice and irreverence. The case for justice includes but goes beyond the political and economic. It is also grounded in the divine presence in the heart of every human. Commitment to the common good thus is an act of worship. Today, the discernment of this divine presence calls us with urgency to reverence and care for our common home, the earth; to united efforts to halt its degradation; and to promote ecological responsibility in our nations, communities, and corporations.

Gratitude as a Divine Virtue

The Hindu tradition, as we have seen above, speaks of gratitude as a virtue appropriate in an interrelated community of beings that includes the divine, our ancestors, our teachers, other human beings, and the natural world. In relation to the divine, gratitude is usually described in ways that are nonreciprocal or asymmetrical. The divine is the object of human gratitude, but it is rare to find examples of an expression of gratitude by the divine to human beings.

There is, however, a beautiful example in the Hindu tradition of gratitude as a virtue of the divine. The example comes from the *Rāmacaritamānasa* by Tulasīdāsa. The text tells the life story of Rama, venerated by Hindus as a divine incarnation (*avatāra*). Rama is regarded as the exemplar of virtuous conduct, and Hindus look to his actions as sources of guidance. His humility in expressing gratitude is therefore significant as a model for human conduct.

Rama is the son of King Dasaratha of Ayodhya. As a consequence of palace intrigue and rivalries, he is banished to live an ascetic life in the forests for fourteen years.[13] He is accompanied by his wife, Sita, and his brother, Lakshmana. During their journey into the wilderness, Sita is abducted by Ravana, the king of Lanka, and kept prisoner in his island kingdom. A long search to find Sita ensues, led by Hanuman, the servant of Rama and the exemplar of love and service for God. With Hanuman's indefatigable service, Sita is located, rescued, and returned to Ayodha with Rama.

One of the poignant moments in the text occurs when Rama expresses his gratitude to his servant, Hanuman: "'Listen, Hanuman, no one has served me like you. What service can I do for you in return? When I think of it, I am unable to look you in the face. Upon reflection, my son, I have concluded that I can never repay you.' Again, and again, Rama looked at Hanuman, his eyes filled with tears and his whole body trembled with emotion."[14]

This moment in the text when the divine confesses gratitude to one of his creatures is powerful, but it is not the only occasion when Rama expresses his gratitude. He is always generous in his acknowledgement of even the smallest act of service. At the end of the text, before his friends return to their respective homes, Rama calls them together to express his thankfulness: "Most lovingly, he seated them by his side and addressed them in gentle words that were the delight of his worshippers. 'Very great is the service you have done me; but how can I praise you to your faces? You renounced your homes and comforts solely on my account; therefore, you have endeared yourselves to me.'"

Both passages are intense expressions of divine gratitude. Rama confesses his gratitude to be so overwhelming that he is unable to look into the eyes of his servant. He is emotional and on the brink of tears. He acknowledges that it is not possible to repay an act of gratitude. In his own response, Hanuman, when given the opportunity to receive a divine reward, asks only for the gift of love. "Love for you, is my greatest joy; bless me with never-ending love." The opportunity to serve was the deepest source of his gratitude.

Why is this story of Rama significant for our discussion? I have already noted the status of Rama as a divine incarnation and the relevance of his conduct for human beings. Hindus look to him in ways analogous to Christians drawing lessons from Jesus' conduct. Rama's conduct exemplified interdependence and the understanding that divine purposes are not accomplished without human cooperation. In his life story as narrated by Tulasīdāsa, he turns for help to the entire creation. His helpers are marginalized outcastes such as the tribal leader, Guha, and the members of the animal kingdom. Rama visits a woman, Shabari, who is described as the lowest of the low, as a woman and an outcaste. He soothes her fears and anxieties, and comforts her with the teaching that God's relationship is based only on love.

Such narratives from the story of Rama break boundaries of caste and patriarchy, even though such hierarchical structures are still evident in the text. The understanding that creation flourishes by the interdependent cooperation of every creature, and when there is gratitude for the work of every being, subverts hierarchies that value and privilege some groups over others and that support unequal access to resources. Divine gratitude is not transactional; it is delight in the intrinsic beauty and uniqueness of every being. Interdependence and gratitude affirm the equal dignity of all beings and challenge structural inequalities; thus, they are important for undermining caste inequalities.

Dhanyavād: Speech That Blesses

Although Sanskrit has many terms for gratitude or thanks, one of the most popular and commonly used is *dhanyavād*. *Dhanya* has a wide range of meanings that include "prosperity," "blessing," and "happiness." *Vād* (from verbal root *vac*, or "speak") indicates the spoken word. *Dhanyavād*, therefore, literally means "to speak of one's happiness, prosperity, blessing, or good fortune that has been caused by another." It is an acknowledgement of gifts received from another.

The word "dhanyavād" also conveys the important truth that while gratitude may be a thought or feeling, it becomes meaningful when it is conveyed through words or some other appropriate medium. Gratitude is a relational virtue and requires expression. It is an expression of value for the other.

While dhanyavād is a verbal acknowledgement of another's role in one's well-being, it may be translated also as blessed speech or speech that blesses. It is so described because it blesses both the speaker and the listener. The speaker is blessed because the truthful acknowledgement of the generosity of another helps to counter our spiritually debilitating egocentrism. In expressing our gratitude to another, we grow by learning to be generous. It also blesses the hearer by awakening her self-value. We have all experienced the deep satisfaction that comes when gratitude is genuinely expressed for something we did or said. It enriches our sense of life's meaning and purpose.

GRATITUDE AND THE LESSONS OF A PANDEMIC

The truth of our interconnectedness that is at the heart of the Hindu understanding of gratitude continues to be highlighted as we struggle with the challenges of a ravaging pandemic. We are all familiar with the butterfly effect that an American meteorologist developed to explain the possibility that small causes could have momentous effects. The underlying idea is that in complex and interrelated systems, phenomena occurring in one distant part may have implications for the entire system. The metaphor of a butterfly flapping its wings in the Amazon and causing a storm in Europe may not be literally true, but it helpfully describes the reality of our interconnectedness. The universe is likened in one Hindu sacred text to a spider's web. If we never understood this truth before, we cannot fail to understand it now under the conditions of a global pandemic.

One of the important lessons of the pandemic, however, is that while our interconnectedness offers us the opportunity for so much enrichment, it can also hurt. No human walls prevent a virus originating in one part of our world from rapidly spreading everywhere. The important corollary is that we cannot save ourselves without saving each other. Our lives are joined in both suffering and joy. Our motive for saving our neighbors ought not be limited to the desire to save ourselves, even though the pandemic reveals this truth of our interconnectedness. This chapter describes more fundamental reasons for care, rooted in teachings about divine immanence, joy, and life's unity. Such teachings are not incompatible with more pragmatic motives.

The pandemic has revealed, even more clearly, the fundamental inequities of our world and that the suffering is most acute where systemic structures of poverty make access to health care one of life's greatest challenges. Worldwide access to vaccines is necessary, but sustainable solutions to pandemics require global cooperation to address disparities in access to health care. Today, the common good cannot be limited to the national good; our commitment must be to the universal common good.

The pandemic has also intensified our human fallibilities and especially our tendency to blame our suffering on those in our community who are different. The pandemic has led to intensifying racism and xenophobia, and we have seen the rise of hate and violence in parts of our world. In India, for example, we saw instances of anti-Muslim violence after Muslims were blamed for spreading the COVID-19 virus. Combating scapegoating and xenophobia during this time is an obligation and a challenge for religious leadership. It is an opportunity for leaders of specific communities to speak on behalf of the human community and to commend caring and empathy.

There are times when the challenge of leadership is not so much the defense of one's own community but the willingness to risk speaking on behalf of those who are the victims of blame and violence by one's own community. Helping our communities in these times is about ensuring not only that they are safe from physical infection but also that their hearts grow in love and compassion for all human beings and especially for those who are marginalized and without access to the necessities for a decent human life. We must also inoculate against the virus of hate. We should all aspire to come safely through this pandemic as better human beings.

While our particular communities of faith will always have special meaning and significance for us, we are now required to enlarge our understanding of *we* to include our neighbors everywhere. Historically, our religions have been quite adept at championing and defending the interests of those who belong to the fold or those of specific groups within that fold. The area of concern rarely extended beyond the theological divide to include people of other faiths or with commitments different from our own. The boundaries of community and the application of ethical values were fixed by allegiance to text, doctrine, or ritual. Our religions spoke out when their own rights were affected but were usually inattentive to the oppression of the other. Now that the pandemic has painfully reminded us that our lives are irrevocably joined, one of the significant challenges to each tradition is the tension of preserving its unique historical identity while also affirming an inclusive *we* that transcends theological boundaries. The theological resources and symbols within each tradition that underline the unity and inclusive character of our existence need to be highlighted and examined in relation to those that are narrow and divisive or that emphasize the value of one community over another. In our context of a changing world and the growth of diversity in nations that were minimally heterogenous, what are our obligations, especially as religious communities? Most important, who do we represent? Who do we speak for? Politicians, with increasingly narrow visions, prioritize the interests of their nations and parties. Leaders who see the world as divided into competing races speak for their own race group. Managers of global corporations speak for the interests of their shareholders.

On whose behalf do religious leaders speak? We certainly have obligations to speak on behalf of the interests and concerns of our distinctive communities, but we cannot, as too often happens, stop at these boundaries. In a world dominated by narrow interests, religious voices are among the few that can speak for the human community and especially those human communities that are marginalized, that are the object of hate speech and actions, and that suffer the most in a pandemic. Just as we need an inclusive *we* to overcome a pandemic, we need an inclusive *we* that affirms the dignity and freedom of every human being to overcome the hierarchical privileges of caste.

INJURY AND REPAIR

I started this chapter by acknowledging that social and religious hierarchies of purity and impurity based on interpretations of Hindu teachings have inflicted physical suffering and indignities on millions of Dalits. I conclude by returning to this subject.

For marginalized communities, such as the Dalits, the Hindu tradition does not evoke gratitude. Those of us, however, who come from places of privilege and power within our traditions and who have never had our human dignity crushed by teachings and practices that proclaim our lesser worth, cannot speak of teachings of gratitude without addressing religiously justified injustice.

Religious traditions need to be especially attentive to the voices of those who experience the tradition as oppressive and unjust, and as denying them power and freedom. Such attention includes acknowledging those teachings, interpretations, and social structures that legitimize and perpetuate oppression; owning responsibility for them; and working with marginalized communities to overcome them. It also includes identifying and lifting up those teachings in the tradition that subvert and are antithetical to caste. Causing suffering to others (*hiṃsā*) and being indifferent to such suffering are the antithesis of what the Hindu tradition advocates as its highest ethical ideal of extending compassion and nonviolence (*ahiṃsā*).

CONCLUDING THOUGHT

One of my principal concerns in writing this chapter is to share Hindu resources that illumine the meaning and practice of gratitude. I believe teachings in the tradition deepen our understanding of gratitude and that, alongside those of other traditions, they enrich us all. At the same time, as with other traditions, I recognize that in describing such insights, I am speaking of religious ideals, and holding up such teachings without acknowledging the entrenched structural inequalities that promulgate such ideals is not satisfactory. Interdependence truthfully describes our human condition, but we cannot overlook that millions are involuntarily dependent on others and without the resources to exercise freedom.

In a similar way, gratitude is a beautiful way of being that flows from an awakening to the truth of our interdependent condition and a celebration of the gift of existence. Gratitude as a celebration, however, is difficult for those who are crushed, whose sense of self is devalued, and for whom daily life is a survival struggle. We must resist the manipulation of gratitude to legitimize the status quo. Consequently, gratitude cannot be commended in isolation without attentiveness to the specific social reality. Gratitude is most meaningful in a context where the dignity and sacred value of all human beings are affirmed and where each being enjoys freedom and access to the resources necessary for a joyful and fulfilled existence. We may commend gratitude without implying support for injustice.

Inequality, whether manifested in casteism or racism, is violence. Human beings are regarded as objects with instrumental value for those who enjoy power and privilege. But gratitude subverts inequality when we innately value and celebrate every life. Gratitude delights in the freedom and flourishing of every human being. It resists injustice and all that impedes the well-being of creation.

NOTES

1. Valmiki, *Joothan*, 48.
2. Valmiki, 154. *Savarnas* refers to members of the upper castes.
3. *Durlabhaṃ trayamevaitad devānugrahahetukam; / Manuṣyatvam mumukṣutvaṃ mahāpuruṣasraṃśrayaḥ*. See Dayananda Saraswati, *Talks on Vivekacūḍāmani*.
4. *Baḍe bhāga mānuṣa tanu pāvā/suradurlabha saba graṅthanhi gāvāa / Sādhana dhāma mokṣa kara dvāra/pāi na jehim paralokoka saṃvārā*. See "Uttarakāṇda," in *Sri Ramacaritamanasa*.
5. *Sukṛtám* also means a "virtuous action," suggesting that the bringing forth of human beings was a virtuous act on the part of the divine.
6. The point here is that the divine is always present in everything since creation is not outside but within the divine. There is nothing apart or separate from Brahman.
7. My translation.
8. See Ambedkar, *Riddles in Hinduism*, 171.
9. Tyagananda, *Walking the Walk*, 52.
10. Cited in Beckerlegge, *Swami Vivekananda's Legacy*, 94–95.
11. I am using dharma in one of its many meanings, cognizant that appeals to dharma are also made to justify the hierarchies of caste and patriarchy.
12. Again, I am reading *lokasamgraham* in a progressive way. It is also read more conservatively to justify the status quo.
13. For a concise summary, see Narayan, *The Ramayana*.
14. See "Sundarakāṇda," in *Rāmacaritamānas*.

BIBLIOGRAPHY

Some English translations of Sanskrit verses have been modified.

Ambedkar, B. R. *Riddles in Hinduism: The Annotated Critical Selection*. Edited by Kancha Ilaiah. New Delhi: Navayana Publishing, 2016.

Bhagavadgītā. Translated by Winthrop Sargeant. Albany: State University of New York Press, 1993.

Beckerlegge, Gwilym. *Swami Vivekananda's Legacy of Service: A Study of the Ramakrishna Math and Mission*. New Delhi: Oxford University Press, 2006.

Dayananda Saraswati, Swami. *Talks on Vivekacūḍāman.i* Rishikesh: Sri Gangadhareswar Trust, 1997.

Chāndogya Upaniṣad. Translated by Swami Swahananda. Madras: Sri Ramakrishna Math, 1975.

Eight Upaniṣads with the Commentary of Śaṅkarācārya. Translated by Swami Gambhirananda. 2 Volumes. "Īśa," "Kena," "Kaṭha," and "Taittirīya" in vol. 1; "Aitaraya," "Muṇḍaka," "Māṇḍūkya and Kārika," and "Praśna" in vol. 2. Calcutta: Advaita Ashrama, 1965–66.

Narayan, R. K. *The Ramayana*. New York: Penguin Classics, 2006.

Śaṅkara. *Vivekacūdāmaṇi*. Translated by Swami Madhavananda. Calcutta: Advaita Ashrama, 1978.

Tulasīdāsa, *Sri Ramacaritamanasa*. Translated by R.C. Prasad. Delhi: Motilal Banarsidass, 1991.

Tyagananda, Swami. *Walking the Walk*. Ludhiana: Chetna Parkashan, 2014.

Valmiki, Omprakash. *Joothan: An Untouchable's Life*. Translated by Arun Prabha Mukherjee. New York: Columbia University Press, 2003.

CHAPTER 7

Gratitude as a Revolutionary Act of Resistance

Edward Donalson III

THE AGE OF PANDEMIC AND THE ZONE OF NONBEING

I am a Black professor and administrator in a Catholic (Jesuit) university while serving as a bishop in the Pentecostal tradition in the sixteenth year of my episcopacy. I am unapologetically Black and unashamedly Christian among a myriad of other social identities that make up my lived reality on the margins of the dominating class. As a constructive theologian with a liberative lens, I find it is not enough to write about gratitude in a pandemic if by "the pandemic" one limits one's thinking to COVID-19. COVID, economic crisis, and racially motivated violence work in concert to create the palpable unrest and dis-ease that hang in the atmosphere and rest in the ethos. In crafting theo-logic, it is my goal, in the tradition of James Baldwin and fueled by a lifetime of study, engagement, and creative tension with movements for justice around the world, to develop a capacious, revolutionary theory and practice of lived resistance to capitalism, imperialism, classism, and all forms of oppression.[1] The work of public theology is foundational to my vocation both as a bishop and as a scholar.[2]

The longing for freedom and personhood amid an alien and racist surrounding culture uniquely prepares already injured and marginalized people for a robust conversation about resistance that is only made more complex and nuanced by the circumstances of a global health crisis. Matters of society and justice are never separate from religion as it is our religion (whatever form it may take) that compels us toward a more just and humane world. *Theo-logic is always political.* The pandemic age demands a robust theo-political interrogation to move humanity forward.

It is clear to me that humanity is always wrestling with the significance of religion. A constructive theologian sees the whole world as a canvas for theological engagement. They host dialogue between Scripture and situation with special attention to what it means for today. Viable religion is one that has a working reciprocity with the culture that produces it or with which it interacts.[3] To really understand what religion might offer in this present pandemic age, one must interrogate the age, the culture, and a religious response that is in active conversation with both. We need theo-logic(s) useful in a pandemic age, birthed out of a generative and robust analysis of the times, and a full understanding of the gift theo-logic brings to the commons. While religious expression takes many forms, this work will explore a particular religious response from the margins of society through the Christian tradition.

The dominant culture in North America has historically worked under a social contract of imperialist, anti-Black (white supremacist), capitalist cis-heteropatriarchy. These interlocking systems of oppression collude to marginalize people in a social caste system that centers cisgender heterosexual men who perceive themselves to be white in the imperialist project of capitalism. This project of marginalization in this pandemic age is promoted by a right-wing, evangelical fundamentalist, national civil religion that hijacks the name of Jesus and has nothing to do with the life and teaching of Jesus. This dehumanizing social contract is built on systems of practices, meanings, and values that provide legitimacy to the dominant society's arrangements and interests, forming an ideological hegemony almost impossible to see because of its cultural omnipresence.[4] This social contract allows the minority of people to minoritize the majority of people by placing a small group at the center of power and privilege. All of the interlocking systems of marginalization work together as a leviathan, terrorizing the majority imprisoned in a zone of nonbeing. Personhood and full engagement are eradicated by the absence of freedom for people existing under the constant threat of terror. Because they hold the limits and definitions of identity, the members of this small group create realities for others that they wish themselves to escape. To keep this social contract in place requires shared responsibility between the oppressed and the oppressor, as they are bound together within the same society, accepting the same criteria, sharing the same beliefs, and thereby depending on the same realities.[5]

Dominating culture in North America names itself white, which is the terrorizing standard of normativity used to create the radical other. Whiteness is culturally normative in that it becomes the standard against which all things are measured; that is, they are defined in relation or opposition to whiteness. In media and other cultural markers, minoritized people are portrayed as and viewed as exotic others in the most egregious pattern of paternalization and patronization.[6] Whiteness in this work is not a skin color, because the parameters of whiteness change over time; rather, whiteness is the social construct of power and domination rooted in anti-Blackness that serves to disinherit and marginalize those considered radically other. Race is not a concrete or static reality but an imaginative construct created in particular times and places by specific influences and impacts.

Whiteness is not a biological fact relegated to people of European descent, despite what popular opinion holds. In fact, whiteness is a way of being in the world, and seeing the world, that forms cognitive and affective structures able to seduce people into its habitation and its meaning making.[7] The history of North America has been a racialized project of creating the category of white, sorting some people into it, and assigning material benefits on the basis of excluding the non-white others.[8] We have learned to define people by what they are not in an effort to center the superiority of a particular group. Even the advent of the language "people of color" and "Black, Indigenous, and other people of color" (BIPOC) is a cultural device that centers whiteness as normative and lumps all people who are not considered white into one group of others. Whiteness is always an expression of anti-Blackness. Whiteness essentializes Blackness to maintain a master trope of purity, supremacy, and entitlement as a ubiquitous, fixed, unifying signifier that seems invisible.[9] Whiteness is a way to think of the world; it has its philosophical resonances and theological employments. It is a violent encounter and a way of life that is fundamentally about interdiction, the desired theft of the capacity to breathe.[10]

Race is not at all an ontological reality, but the pervasive nature of its social acceptance makes its effect ubiquitous. Racial exclusion was designed to protect the elite cisheteropatriarchy of North American whites. In the racial logic of the nation-state, immigrants and other non-white bodies were racialized as the antithesis of cisheteropatriarchal ideals. Race as an American institution is an invitation to power and privilege or excommunication and exclusion from that same power and privilege. The construct of race is built to identify proximity to power. As ethnicity and social construction were invented, racial exclusion and ethnic assimilation provided the genealogical context for sociology's inscriptions of race and sexuality as socially constructed.[11]

Whiteness as a project cannot be separated from the pursuit of capitalism. Race is an economic and political reality. While laissez-faire capitalism is a form of governance and is synonymous with power in the Western construct, it cannot be unmoored from the idea of money and the function of money in society. Marginalization results from the overarching system of powers that are characterized by oppressive political relations, biased race relations, patriarchal gender relations, unjust economic relations, and the use of violence of various forms to maintain them all as they currently exist.[12] The racialized caste system in North America is inextricable from the monetary foundation of a nation-state built on stolen land with the stolen labor of chattel slavery. To ensure financial security and prosperity, white male landowners perpetrated systemic injury of the majority. The sins of slavery and all its atrocities are a secondary consequence of imperialism and the capitalist enterprise. Baldwin rightly assessed that marginalized people are the victims (injured) of a system whose only fuel is greed, whose only God is profit.[13] The economic disparities and community impact of the present pandemic age clearly show the link between racial constructs and capitalism, as well as the proximity to morbidity this unholy alliance demands.

The policing system in the United States is a direct outgrowth of the slave patrols. Government-sanctioned violence against minoritized bodies in this current era is directly related to the economic foundations of the American experiment. Logics and functions of whiteness operate through socioeconomic legalities of enslavement, internment, incarceration, and redlining. These patterns of anti-Blackness and white supremacy repeat themselves globally, playing themselves out in a particular way in the socioeconomic realities of the United States.

Cisheteropatriarchy is a sociopolitical system that insists those assigned male gender at birth and continue throughout their lives in this identification while sexually and romantically engaging women are inherently superior to everyone else. These men expect to dominate, and everyone else is expected to be joyfully subordinate. Everyone else, especially women, is deemed weak, and these men are endowed with the right to dominate and rule over the weak through various forms of psychological terrorism and violence.[14] Since gender is the consideration of both sexual and cultural constructs that more often than not dictate normative behavior for the individual, cisheteropatriarchy works to privilege a particular group of men as the top tier of the American caste system.[15] Our centralized institutions and localized practices legitimate and privilege cisgender men and heterosexual relationships as fundamental and natural within our society, undergirding the sociopolitical power of cisheteropatriarchy. Governmental agencies have contributed to the continued marginalization of non-cisheteropatriarchy in minoritized communities through biased reports, such as the 1965 Moynihan Report, which produced in the public discourse the notion of the Black "Welfare Queen." This report also fed the idea that most underclass young Black men engage in reckless heterosexual behavior, and that led to their being viewed as irresponsible baby-making factories.[16]

The conditions of the age of pandemic work in concert with social power structures to create a condition of nonbeing. Oppression and the pandemic create a zone of nonbeing that is an extraordinarily sterile and arid region within which life is a virtual hell.[17] Mandatory social-distancing measures, racially specific police brutality, and the effects of poverty all work against the human impulse toward wholeness and freedom. Freedom often means possessing the ability to deal with the realities of one's situation so as not to be overcome by them.[18] Freedom, however, does not stop there; it is more than the ability to survive adversity. Freedom is the indispensable condition for the quest for human completion or the pursuit of one's highest self.[19] To be free is to be in a state where one names for oneself the realities of personhood and has the ability to manifest or actualize the very conditions one has named. Systems of marginalization lead to dehumanization (a state that is further intensified in the realities of a pandemic era) of both the oppressed and the oppressor.

The experience of power has no meaning aside from the other-than-self reference that sustains it. If the position of ascendancy is not acknowledged both tacitly and actively by those over whom ascendancy is exercised, then it falls flat.[20] In the American experiment particularly, the acceptance of white identity is always a debasing and dehumanizing enterprise in that it is a replacement identity whose sole purpose is claiming proximity to power over others.

The current political climate is permeated by a perverse reverse revenge fantasy. Whiteness shrouded in religious language imagines itself as the underdog while holding all the power; therefore, it fantasizes about cruelty in a way that justifies any and all expressions of marginalization and dehumanization. Clearly we have both national leadership and large segments of the general population willing to enact radical suffering and repackage it under the name of law and order, all in an effort to maintain power and privilege.[21] Evil is perpetuated by ordinary citizens and agents of the state alike in ways that refuse to be shocking because no matter how grotesque or bizarre, the injury has become commonplace.

We watch police kneel on the necks of Black men while life drains from Black human bodies, and the video clips circulate thousands of times an hour. It is a callousness that our genetic code embraces because we are descendants of people who sent postcards with pictures of lynchings. In this era of digital lynching, it is so common that any outcry against the mendacity of white supremacy is met with claims of reverse discrimination. The way that COVID vaccines are distributed in communities made up of the dominant culture juxtaposed to the availability of vaccines in marginalized communities reveals that infrastructure is designed to preserve the lives of those closest to power and privilege. The historical danger of this blatant violation of civility and human dignity is it ultimately leads to the devastation of crusades, witch trials, McCarthyism, and holocausts. These examples of collective sins are the result of slow responses to radical suffering.

Often radical suffering is not seen as collective sin because we have been so desensitized to the horrific atrocities of daily life that the marginalized endure that it is easy to pretend that suffering is always the result of one evil agent or bad apple. Sin is a complex phenomenon: It is communal as well as individual; it is bondage as well as guilt; it is the source of injustice and the lack of response to injustice.[22] The unchecked misuse of power will always unfold into collective sin. The human need for power over and the desire to bring another into a subservient role are abominations. People who have fallen victim to ableism, sexism, ageism, genderism, poverty, and all the other atrocities perpetuated by the imperialist, white supremacist, capitalist, heteropatriarchy may well be served by a fresh understanding of sin.[23] Sin and righteousness, once clearly opposites, are in this zone of nonbeing almost devoid of clarity. This religiously based movement afoot exemplifies a savage impulse that is contrary to human flourishing.

The American project of anti-Black, imperialist, capitalist cisheteropatriarchy wrapped in right-wing, evangelical fundamentalist, civil religion invites those on the underside of power and privilege into the practice of resistance discourse to reclaim their full humanity. Resistance discourse denotes terms, phrases, figures of speech, concepts, poetry, and songs that are common to a particular group of subjugated people, all of whom understand the elements of the discourse as calling them to resist in some way the oppression to which they are subjected.[24] Marginalized people, to enact the reclamation of personhood and the re-membering of their full humanity, cultivate and maintain strategies that circumnavigate the systems that collude to disassemble humanness. People who find themselves injured by institutionalized systems of domination face the dilemma of developing strategies that draw attention to one's plight in ways that merit regard without reinscribing a paradigm of victimization.[25]

THE REVOLUTIONARY ART OF GRATITUDE

As a vehicle of self-determination, gratitude functions as a subversive and transgressive agent by resisting the denial of full personhood that is perpetuated by the dominant culture. Adopting a sense of gratitude as an emotional, psychological, or spiritual lifestyle serves to militate against the feelings of insignificance that plague people for whom self-determination is diminished by structural erasure. Gratitude is a technology of self-assertion, summoning the agency to resist. The incomparable mystic, Howard Thurman, taught that the fight for selfhood is unending. There is the ever present need to stand alone, unsupported and unchallenged. To be sure of one's self, to be counted for one's self as one's self, is to experience aliveness in its most exciting dimension.[26]

Gratitude becomes a revolutionary act of resistance for marginalized people in that it is a vehicle for naming one's own truth. In the face of oppression, marginalized people must learn to love themselves. Gratitude demands emotional awareness, self-love, relational skills, and an assertive self-determination, empowering the individual or community to engage themselves as the subject. The experience and expression of gratitude free both the oppressed and the oppressor by removing the dynamic of soul bondage and disallowing the power dynamic that refuses personhood. Only the oppressed, by freeing themselves, can free the oppressor.[27] Gratitude affords those most dehumanized a mechanism of care, responsibility, respect, and self-knowledge, resulting in the self-love obfuscated by the societal norms of dehumanization.

The Jewish and Christian traditions share a sacred text from the prophet Isaiah: "And to help the sorrowing people of Jerusalem, I will give them a crown to replace their ashes, and the oil of gladness to replace their sorrow, and clothes of praise to replace their spirit of sadness. Then they will be called Trees of Goodness, trees planted by the Lord to show his greatness."[28] Prophetic praxis is behavior that engages countercultural practices on behalf of the least among us; in these religious traditions, gratitude becomes a weapon to reclaim personhood. As systems of domination work to truncate and/or erase marginalized lives, the prophet paints a picture of a preferred future by suggesting that gratitude become the source of power to animate personhood. This move of reconciliation is not to the status quo; rather, it is a reconciliation to the agency and personhood of self-awareness.

To those for whom the culture diminishes selfhood, the authority of selfhood comes from their claiming joy for themselves even as they exist in systems made to antagonize all experiences of joy. The pandemic age is filled with physical, intellectual, and psychic terror; gratitude targets each mechanism of terror directly through its ability to impact the entirety of one's personhood. Gratitude both personally and communally demands that self-critical analysis, which is the ground of being.

Gratitude holds both the oppressor and the oppressed accountable to recognize the full humanity of the marginalized and the inhumane behavior of the dominant culture. As systems are the collective product of individuals, gratitude serves to hold individuals responsible to be reconciled to the highest standards of human flourishing. Gratitude is not a work of neoliberal post-racial Utopianism; rather, it is grounded in an understanding of the fracture that must be healed in a humanity that has not committed to relationships of mutuality. Gratitude is then reconciliation—not the restoration of a broken social order but the reconciliation to full personhood for both the oppressed and the oppressor. While grief and lament have been the constant partners of minoritized life, gratitude has served to uplift the oppressed in ways that empowered survival and even flourishing. The gratitude of people most closely aligned with death has been the agent of resurrection, revolution, and reconciliation.

What people think and feel is rooted in their character, which is molded by the total configuration of their practice of life or, more precisely, by the socioeconomic and political structure of their society. Fear is the result in societies ruled by a powerful minority holding the masses in subjugation.[29] Gratitude dismisses fear and births responsibility. The human impulse is to care for that for which one is grateful. Responsibility in its true sense is an entirely voluntary act; it is the exercise of agency. To be responsible is to be able to respond based on one's internal capacity and willingness.[30]

To acknowledge and express gratitude, one must take responsibility for one's selfhood and emotions. The act of naming one's gratitude makes one responsible for one's thoughts and feelings. As a function of conviction, gratitude is a container of humanity. By "conviction" I mean an opinion rooted in personal character, in the total personality, that motivates one to action.[31] This responsibility while existing in the zone of nonbeing leads to a life-affirming self-awareness that those on the margins use as a witness to personhood in facing proximity to death. Those who are marginalized testify to the evils of marginalization, not simply by naming that which is inhumane but also by their act of gratitude in exposing the myth of their nonbeing.

AN INTERSECTIONAL THEO-LOGIC FOR A PANDEMIC WORLD

Within the Christian tradition is an emerging theo-logic that offers a glimpse into both the history of gratitude and the potential of gratitude as a revolutionary act of resistance. Intersectional theology is birthed from those on the margins and is rooted in the heritage of Pentecostalism, known for its joyous celebrations and exuberant worship. The term "intersectional" is borrowed from a Black feminist critique of antidiscrimination doctrine, feminist theory, and anti-racist politics originally authored by Kimberlé Crenshaw.[32] Her original work focused on the intersection of race and gender pertaining legally to the ways in which race and gender cause separate, yet compound, issues of marginalization. The work also lifts up the extreme and compound marginalization of race, sex, class, sexual orientation, age, and physical ability.

A Black female law professor, Crenshaw points out how the dominant conceptions of discrimination condition us to think about subordination as a disadvantage occurring along a single categorical axis. Identity theologies of liberation have heretofore been guilty of the same constructs without taking into consideration the ways in which multiply burdened intersectional realities might impact our words about God, the church, and the world. Intersectional theology takes this work and, in an interdisciplinary tradition, contextualizes its significance in the life of the church, the academy, and the marketplace. Intersectional theology is a radical work of resisting the terrors attached to the values of dominant society.

The embodiment of intersectional theology demands participation in politics, education, corporate and private business, nonprofits, and cultural production of all types.[33] Intersectional theology offers a counternarrative to other systematic theologies that center and sanction heteronormativity, which is tightly interwoven with colonialism and the silencing of non-Euro, non-modern, non-capitalist others.[34]

Intersectional theology takes seriously a Pentecostal perspective in that it is rooted in the experience of Acts 2. It invites the church to be the place where all people hear collectively the good news and hear it in a language they can both understand and receive. Since the areas of sex, race, and class are all factors in Pentecostalism, the powerful use of language as an instrument of freedom is a revolutionary message of good news.

The dominant culture has used language to subordinate the majority, but Pentecostalism upends the norm, making language accessible to all. Pentecostalism is a strategy of exercising the voice and promoting representation in such a way that it foretells movements such as Black Power and #BlackLivesMatter. Pentecostalism grounds intersectional theology in that it provides potential for both personal expressions and rich community life. Intersectional theology holds that all genders are filled with God's spirit and that ageism has no place in the beloved community. This theology relishes difference, seeing it as foundational to the work of the Spirit in the world. By understanding that the realm of God is present in unity, the underlying theo-logic of intersectional theology implicates exclusion and inequality as contrary to Gospel narrative. One cannot claim to be Pentecostal and traffic in division or dehumanization, since the very origins of Pentecostalism are found in the unity of diverse people. Imperialist, white supremacist, capitalist heteropatriarchy sits in total opposition to the liberating message of Pentecost, which is an open invitation of full personhood into total embodied fellowship with the divine.

The pneumatological roots of intersectional theology spring from a Pentecostal principle grounded in the capacity to begin or to demand a new beginning. Trusting fully the narrative of Acts 2, 6, and 15, the principal characteristic of the first followers of "The Way" is that they relied on the Spirit to continue to inspire them with new ways of being a community until the community of Judaism, which had been their incubator, could no longer contain them as a religio-social home. The idea of new ways of being also serves as a resistance narrative within the zone of nonbeing formed in the pandemic era. A fresh understanding of the breath of the divine empowers those on the margins to claim for themselves a breathing living identity. To breathe, for those on the margins, is to offer a critical performative intervention into the Western juridical apparatus of violent control, repression, and premature death.[35]

Intersectional theology takes the creation story seriously both as the *ruach* (Spirit) is present in creation and in God's act of breathing and animating humans. This animating makes the creativity of the Spirit an intricate part of a fully human being. Spirit is the origin of everything; it is first cause (Genesis 1:2). This universal life and energy finds an outlet in and through all that is energized.[36] The pandemic age has been marked by the slogan "I Can't Breathe" in response to the cries of Black bodies under police assault, but this cry extends to the millions of lives impacted by COVID-19, a virus that converts the mortal shell into a death trap so constricted by the disease that it cannot secure the necessary air required to sustain life. Gratitude acts as an internal ventilator for those crushed under the weight of dehumanization; it opens the psycho-spiritual airways to allow the soul to flourish.

Intersectional theology centers the Jesus who is incarcerated and dies in a government-sanctioned execution. Intersectionality casts Jesus in his lived reality as a practicing Jewish insurgent living in a territory controlled by Roman political, military, and economic forces. Insurgency is necessitated by the marginalization of the embodiment of Jesus. Jesus was and remains marked by sex, gender, and sexuality: Through preaching and practice, in living and behavior, Jesus performed masculinity in ways that opposed patriarchal expressions of maleness. The embodied Jesus, not fully vested in the performance of masculinity, bows to wash the feet of disciples for whom he will die hours later. From the posture culturally assumed by women as foot washers, Jesus rises to become a spiritual midwife in a garden of prayer.

Betrayal will lead to bodily crucifixion, where the plea of theodicy will arise as a cry of lament. There the forsaken body of Jesus, experiencing social alienation and estrangement for its resistance to a culture of dominance, will die a subjugated objectification of the projected fears of those in power.[37] In the Christian tradition, Jesus stands in for all those who are victimized by the conditions of marginalization. The very fact that Jesus in full hypostatic union represents the divine interruption of power and privilege offers all those who live on the underside of power a glimpse of their own divinity. In the exemplar Jesus and in the narrative of his life, we find the message of reclamation of personhood as much as we find the understanding of systems of evil. His body at resurrection (Mark 16; Matt. 28; Luke 24; John 20–21) is not contained by space and time, and yet does not remove itself from them. The followers of this insurgent move from his execution to his triumph in resurrection, and from there to Pentecost.

Pentecostalism, then, as a root of intersectional theology with its celebratory worship style, is ground zero for gratitude as a revolutionary act of resistance. For Pentecostal people, gratitude and celebration are synonymous. Gratitude serves to give voice to a people's longing and struggle for freedom to be in community amid alien surroundings and a culture that constantly seeks to dehumanize those in the zone of nonbeing. A theo-logic and worship style rooted in an Africanized spirituality and cultural past acts as a true source of authority along with Scriptures and the tradition of Protestantism in service to the struggle for freedom in the face of anti-Black, imperialist, capitalist cisheteropatriarchy. Internal agency is at the core of intersectional theology rooted in the Pentecostal tradition, and this agency is grounded in the choice of gratitude in the face of injury. From the inception of the Pentecostal tradition, it has been anti-racist, anti-sexist (particularly in its earliest forms), and pro-equity. These sociological postures could be seen not just in the theology of the preaching but also in the praxis. There in the Azusa Street Mission (the birthplace of modern Pentecostalism), the color line was nonexistent. This movement was minority led, and many of the organizations birthed from that initial experience were founded as organizations with full representation of all races. In the joyful expression of gratitude characterized by a new iteration of the African ring dance, gender and race lost consequence. Gratitude was responsible for an egalitarianism unique to Pentecostalism.

Gratitude in this present age is a revolutionary act of resistance that offers all members of society the opportunity to stand as individual souls responsible for their respective personhood. It takes away the power of oppressive systems and deadly viruses to create a zone of nonbeing. Because gratitude is contrary to the social construct that presently grips our society, it serves as a weapon in the struggle against the injuries of class oppression, racism, and sexism. Gratitude is the response of those who choose power for themselves. For those who have been marginalized by the minority, gratitude is the more difficult path of standing up to injustice as it is a tool of rage rather than the sublimation of it. The mendacity and violence that have become normative in the pandemic age are overtaken by the identification of truth as necessary to engage gratitude, for gratitude can never come from falsehood. In a society that is entirely hostile and, by its nature, seems determined to cut down so many, it becomes almost impossible to directly distinguish a real injury from a fancied one.[38]

Gratitude makes one at once both a truth-telling witness and a survivor. Disallowing despair to wrestle life away from those on the underside of power and privilege, gratitude is triumph over dehumanization. Freedom to reject the terror of the pandemic age by willfully engaging gratitude is the consequence of naming what one is grateful for and allowing that gratitude to serve as true north. Gratitude is power to the people.

NOTES

1. Mullen, *James Baldwin*, xiii.
2. Cone, in *Black Theology and Black Power*, taught that the task of the theologian is to revise and criticize the language of the church. I submit that criticizing the language of the church is unhelpful for both the church and the commons. What I find useful is the work of critique, which holds a different posture and allows the theologian to think with the church rather than against it. It is also useful to name public theology as engaging society in gospel values. In this light, we see the work of public theology as the

theologian in conversation with the commons to bring fresh insight and theo-logic to bear on the questions of a particular epoch.

3. Townes, *In a Blaze of Glory*, 19.
4. Sanders and Yarber, *Microagressions in Ministry*, 13.
5. Baldwin, *Notes of a Native Son*, 21.
6. Delgado and Stefancic, *Critical Race Theory*, 84.
7. Jennings, *After Whiteness*, 9.
8. Fletcher, *Sin of White Supremacy*, 3.
9. Johnson, *Appropriating Blackness*, 4.
10. Crawley, *Blackpentecostal Breath*, 6.
11. Ferguson, "Race-ing Homonormativity," in Johnson and Henderson, *Black Queer Studies*, 54–55.
12. Wink, *Powers That Be*, 39.
13. Glaude, *Begin Again*, 94.
14. hooks, *Will to Change*, 18.
15. The impact of cisheteropatriarchy is reflected in the ascendancy of Donald J. Trump to the presidency of the United States in 2016. The scope and realities of the pandemic age would be a completely different conversation were it not for the response and mismanagement of the forty-fifth president. A man known for unremorseful and blatant sexism, racism, and nationalism was in office during the first wave of COVID-19 and intentionally delayed public awareness for political cachet. This era is marked by the leadership of plutocrats and oligarchs emboldened by a president who represents the worst of their narcissistic interests. For many marginalized people in the United States, this presidency triggered a post-traumatic stress disorder–induced crisis.
16. Johnson and Henderson, *Black Queer Studies* 40–41.
17. Fanon, *Black Skin, White Masks*, xii.
18. Thurman, *For the Inward Journey*, 1984.
19. Freire, *Pedagogy of the Oppressed*, 47.
20. Thurman, *Jesus and the Disinherited*, 62.
21. Delay, *Against*, 106–7.
22. Farley, *Tragic Vision*, 119.
23. Donalson, *#BlackLivesMatter Movement*, 83.
24. Hendricks, *Universe Bends toward Justice*, 7–8.
25. hooks, *Killing Rage*, 58.
26. Thurman, *For the Inward Journey*, 60.
27. Freire, *Pedagogy of the Oppressed*, 56.
28. Isaiah 61:3, New Century Version.
29. Fromm, *Psychoanalysis & Religion*, 52.
30. Fromm, *Art of Loving*, 25.
31. Fromm, *On Being Human*, 39.
32. Crenshaw, "Demarginalizing the Intersection."
33. I offer excerpts from *#BlackLivesMatter Movement*, which I wrote in response to the theological significance of the #BlackLivesMatter movement and was released in the early parts of the shutdown of COVID-19. This work is in the long history of Black protest writing and speaks to oppression and socioeconomic subjugation of minoritized people. It seeks to impact the discourse of Black common sense. Since common sense in the Black community is a direct result of the Black Church and Black Academy

in concert with other institutions, this work speaks from the nexus of ideological formation within the Black community. It hopes to extend the welcome table for the most marginalized and invites us to interrogate the ways we talk about ourselves, our siblings, and all of God's beloved.

34. Crawley, *Blackpentecostal Breath*, 14.
35. Crawley, 34.
36. Holmes, *Science of Mind*, 35.
37. Donalson, *#BlackLivesMatter Movement*, 81.
38. Baldwin, *Fire Next Time*, 93–94.

BIBLIOGRAPHY

Baldwin, James. *The Fire Next Time*. New York: Dell Publishing, 1963.

———. *Notes of a Native Son*. Boston: Beacon Press, 1955.

Cone, James H. *Black Theology and Black Power*. Maryknoll NY: Orbis, 1997.

Crawley, Ashon T. *Blackpentecostal Breath: The Aesthetics of Possibility*. New York: Fordham Press, 2017.

Crenshaw, Kimberlé. "Demarginalizing the Intersection of Race and Sex: A Black Feminist Critique of Antidiscrimination Doctrine, Feminist Theory and Antiracist Politics." *University of Chicago Legal Forum* 1 (1989): 139–68.

Delay, Tad. *Against: What Does the White Evangelical Want?* Eugene: Cascade Books, 2019.

Delgado, Richard, and Jean Stefancic. *Critical Race Theory: An Introduction*. New York: New York University Press, 2012.

Donalson, Edward, III. *The #BlackLivesMatter Movement: Toward an Intersectional Theology*. Eugene: Cascade Books, 2021.

Fanon, Frantz. *Black Skin, White Masks*. New York: Grove Press, 1952.

Farley, Wendy. *Tragic Vision and Divine Compassion: A Contemporary Theodicy*. Louisville KY: Westminster John Knox Press, 1990.

Ferguson, Roderick A. "Race-ing Homonormativity: Citizenship, Sociology, and Gay Identity." In *Black Queer Studies*, edited by E. Patrick Johnson and Mae G. Henderson, 54–55. Durham NC: Duke University Press, 2005.

Fletcher, Jeannine Hill. *The Sin of White Supremacy: Christianity, Racism, & Religious Diversity in America*. Maryknoll NY: Orbis Books, 2017.

Freire, Paulo. *Pedagogy of the Oppressed*. New York: Bloomsbury, 1970.

Fromm, Erich. *The Art of Loving*. New York: Continuum, 1956.

———. *Psychoanalysis & Religion*. New Haven CT: Yale University Press, 1950.

———. *On Being Human*. New York: Continuum, 1994.

Glaude, Eddie S. *Begin Again: James Baldwin's America and Its Urgent Lessons for Our Own*. New York: Crown, 2020.

Hendricks, Obery M., Jr. *The Universe Bends toward Justice: Radical Reflections on the Bible, the Church, and the Body Politic*. Maryknoll NY: Orbis, 2011.

Holmes, Ernest. *The Science of Mind*. New York: G. P. Putnam's Sons, 1938.

hooks, bell. *Killing Rage*. New York: Henry Holt, 1995.

———. *The Will to Change: Men, Masculinity, and Love*. New York: Washington Square Press, 2004.

Jennings, Willie James. *After Whiteness: An Education in Belonging.* Grand Rapids: William B. Eerdmans Publishing, 2020.

Johnson, E. Patrick. *Appropriating Blackness: Performance and the Politics of Authenticity.* Durham NC: Duke University Press, 2003.

Johnson, E. Patrick, and Mae G. Henderson, eds. *Black Queer Studies: A Critical Anthology.* Durham NC: Duke University Press, 2005.

Lightsey, Pamela R. *Our Lives Matter: A Womanist Queer Theology.* Eugene: Pickwick Publications, 2015.

Mullen, Bill V. *James Baldwin Living in Fire.* London: Pluto Press, 2019.

Sanders, Cody J., and Angela Yarber. *Microagressions in Ministry: Confronting the Hidden Violence of Everyday Church.* Louisville KY: Westminster John Knox Press, 2019.

Thurman, Howard. *For the Inward Journey.* Richmond IN: Friends United Press, 1984.

———. *Jesus and the Disinherited.* Boston: Beacon Press, 1976.

Townes, Emily. *In a Blaze of Glory: Womanist Spirituality as Social Witness.* Nashville: Abingdon Press, 1995.

West, Cornel. *Prophesy Deliverance: An Afro-American Revolutionary Chrisitianity.* Louisville KY: Westminster John Knox Press, 1982.

Wink, Walter. *The Powers That Be: Theology for a New Millennium.* New York: Galilee Doubleday, 1998.

CHAPTER 8

Marked by 2020

Disorientation and Reorientation in a Pandemic Age

Jaisy A. Joseph

Roman Catholic priest Fr. Mark-David Janus, CSP, wrote these words for his 2020 Palm Sunday homily just days after surviving the COVID-19 virus:

> Sunday was well, happy, triumphant.
> Thursday night, we gathered for Passover.
> The next night, he was dead, buried by strangers.
> Over and done in five short days . . .
> But now . . .
> People are sick and die, in less time.
> The matriarch of a large Toms River Italian family
> Dying without knowing two sons died before her.
> Within the week, a New York physician dying in her husband's arms,
> Nurses across the street making gowns of hefty bags . . .
> Everyone out of work—no rent, no food, no hugs, no future . . .
> It all happened within a week to all of us . . .
> Milan, China, Spain, New York, everywhere.
> No time to prepare, to react, to grieve, to think of any future.
> This world ends quickly—even for Jesus . . .
> The speed of our surprise, suffering, grief,
> Is shared by the swiftly Crucified.[1]

In his private quarantined Mass during the first wave of the global pandemic, he prepared for "a Holy Week unlike any other, a Holy Week so dangerous people could not go to church to pray."[2] Overwhelmed with gratitude for having survived the virus, he was struck anew by the time line of Jesus's last days. The Gospel accounts reveal how quickly the world shifted for Jesus, who was hailed with palm leaves on a Sunday and crucified five days later. This alarming shift from joy to grief also caught Jesus's closest followers off guard. Two thousand years later, the abrupt hiatus of daily life likewise disoriented billions as they tried to make sense of the swift changes catalyzed by a deadly virus.

The year 2020, however, not only marked global consciousness with our vulnerability before Mother Nature but also revealed that other viruses remain dormant, erupting from time to time with a ferocity that reveals their surreptitious presence all along. In his October 2020 encyclical, *Fratelli tutti*, Pope Francis likened "racism" to "a virus that quickly mutates and, instead of disappearing, goes into hiding, and lurks in waiting."[3] The rise in anti-Asian hate crimes and the tragic murder of George Floyd during the initial months of lockdown stunned the world, interrupting pre-pandemic certainties of social progress. While the COVID-19 virus awakened a level of socioeconomic uncertainty previously unknown by our generation, our differing responses to this uncertainty in the United States have also revealed our current and historical capacity to wound one another along racialized lines. For James F. Keenan, SJ, "the call to recognize Black Lives Matter in the middle of a pandemic is a call to recognize the original sin of the US."[4] Resisting any rush to closure that ignores our vulnerability before each other, we in the United States must embrace a narrative of persistence that is capable of embracing both the disorientation away from pre-pandemic certainties secured by logics of domination and a reorientation to what remains—the truth of our profound interrelatedness.

The first part of my analysis of disorientation and reorientation turns to the Gospel of John to explore the resurrection encounter of Thomas the Apostle with the crucified-and-risen Jesus, providing an example from sacred scriptures of this dynamic amid trauma. I then explore how the uncertainty of 2020 was experienced by those on the margins in the United States, giving particular attention to the xenophobic scapegoating of Asian Americans and the racist police brutality against African Americans. Finally, I argue for how a resistance to fear through a recognition of mutual vulnerability invites us to reorient ourselves to the wounds that remain once the cloud of uncertainty has passed.

TURNING TO SACRED SCRIPTURES

Often nicknamed "doubting Thomas," Thomas the Apostle expressed his disbelief without hesitation after being told that Jesus Christ had risen from the dead: "Unless I see in his hands the print of the nails, and place my finger in the mark of the nails, and place my hand in his side, I will not believe" (John 20:25). When considered from the perspective of Holy Saturday, however, his reaction reveals far more than mere doubt. His words reveal complete disillusionment with what he had once held certain: Jesus was supposed to be the Messiah who would free the Jewish people from Roman oppression. Thomas, like other apostles, left everything behind for three years to follow Jesus as a disciple and to learn how he might participate in the liberation of his people. Thomas's need for proof of Jesus's resurrection after Good Friday reveals a broken spirit unable to make sense of the tragic turn of events that led to the Crucifixion. The cross, M. Shawn Copeland reminds us, is the

> supreme Roman penalty . . . intended to intimidate by example and subdue by spectacle; it was high state theatrical violence. Crucifixion called for the public display of a naked victim in some prominent place—at a crossroads, in an amphitheater, on high ground. Often the condemned was flogged, then made to carry a crossbeam through the streets to the place of execution. The victim's hands and feet were bound or nailed to the wood. If, after this torment, the victim were still alive, he could expect to die by suffocation.[5]

The swift shift from breaking Passover bread with Jesus the night before to hearing that he had taken his last breath on the cross the following day as an accused insurrectionist and blasphemer left Thomas completely disoriented about the purpose and meaning of following Jesus.

Thomas's disillusionment was also accompanied by guilt and shame. Only a few chapters earlier, the Gospel of John records how, when Jesus was willing to risk his life to return to Judea after Lazarus's death, Thomas boldly exclaimed, "Let us also go, that we may die with him" (John 11:16). Thomas was ready to put his life on the line to accompany the person he believed was the Messiah of his people. Yet when Jesus needed his friend in his most dire hour of need, Thomas feared for his own life and abandoned the one he had followed so closely for three years. The need to see the print of the nails in Jesus's hands and the wound in his side is both a profound recognition of the intense suffering that Jesus endured and an implicit regret that he did nothing to stop this violence. Through his silence and cowardice, he participated in his friend's torture.

Yet when Thomas encountered the crucified-and-risen Jesus nearly a week after the other apostles, he did not experience the event as Jesus seeking vengeance. Before inviting Thomas to examine the marks of crucifixion on his wounded body, Jesus's first words were "peace be with you" (John 20:26). In the logic of human reciprocity, Thomas knew the natural consequences of his actions deserved punishment. In fact, all that he had endured in the days since he broke bread with Jesus had produced anything but peace. This experience of being granted interior peace, however, resulted from the logic of divine gratuitousness that extended beyond any resolution that Thomas could construct for himself.[6] This peace came from being forgiven by the one he had betrayed. In the presence of these wounds, Thomas was simply left with awe and gratitude—"My Lord and My God!" (John 20:28). Roberto S. Goizueta notes that while Jesus did not demand justice or recompense from those who betrayed him, he did require memory. The need to remember leads to repentance. He notes that the "still-visible wounds on Jesus' glorified body represent the inerasable memories of suffering that forever remain a part of the resurrection. Even the Victim's offer of forgiveness cannot wish the wounds away. Thus, the offer of mercy can be received only if and when the wounds are acknowledged, responsibility is accepted, and behavior is transformed: My Lord and My God!"[7]

Here we see that Jesus does not promise a restoration of pre-crucifixion assumptions or "certainties" but rather invites his closest followers to be reoriented to the wounds that forever remain a part of his glorified body. Through these wounds, they are awakened to the long-persistent temptation of humans to turn against their own in moments of uncertainty. Once Thomas and the other apostles acknowledge these wounds and accept their responsibility in bringing them into existence, the wounds themselves are transformed from a source of pain to the promise of redeemed relationality. In this moment of conversion, Thomas was given a second chance at being in right relationship with Jesus, and it is this persistent hope that he shared as good news to all he met thereafter.

UNCERTAINTY AND DISORIENTATION IN A PANDEMIC AGE

By April 2020, approximately half of the world's population, or 3.9 billion people in more than ninety countries and territories, experienced some form of lockdown.[8] In response to the growing anxiety gripping the globe,

Pope Francis delivered an unprecedented urbi et orbi blessing before "an almost ghostly [but televised] St. Peter's Square."[9] Sitting alone in the rain before a crucifix, Pope Francis reflected on how this pandemic "exposes our vulnerability and uncovers those false and superfluous certainties around which we have constructed our daily schedules, our projects, our habits and priorities. . . . In this storm, the façade of those stereotypes with which we camouflaged our egos, always worrying about our image, has fallen away, uncovering once more that (blessed) common belonging, of which we cannot be deprived: our belonging as brothers and sisters."[10]

Like Thomas, the sudden stripping of our pre-pandemic routines left us disoriented in a world that now took its cues from an unknown, unpredictable virus. Religious ethicist Vincent W. Lloyd describes how this "present moment carries with it a level of uncertainty that few of us have ever known . . . economic uncertainty an order of magnitude greater than the Great Recession, social and political uncertainty as institutions strain and fail to respond, and existential uncertainty as we each confront unexpected, uncontrollable sickness and death."[11] While many exemplified Pope Francis's words by going to heroic lengths to save the lives of those whom they never knew, others compromised efforts at solidarity by refusing to recognize our shared belonging as brothers and sisters.

In many ways, the lockdown was "a solidarity that [was] neither sought after, nor wanted, but it [was] lived" amid the disorientation of the unknown. Andrea Vicini, SJ, believes that "uncertainty paralyzes many because it reduces and inhibits the ability to control and act. Uncertain, one becomes powerless."[12] In the false attempt to regain control and power, some deny our common belonging by looking to scapegoats for immediate catharsis. Drawing further from historian, philosopher, and literary critic René Girard (1923–2015), Vicini argues how the minoritized other "becomes responsible in an exclusive way. 'We' are the victims. . . . Since the 'others' are the cause of what we suffer, by eliminating and marginalizing them, we believe we can remove all evil from us, concentrating what is negative in them, in those we have turned into scapegoats and are ready to sacrifice for our own good."[13]

In the United States, the surge in anti-Asian discrimination and hate crimes during the pandemic revealed the pervasiveness of this false attempt at regaining power and control. Despite tracing the genesis of COVID-19 in the United States to travelers from Europe and within the country, many scapegoated Asian Americans "as the embodiment of China and potential carriers of COVID-19."[14] From March 19, 2020, to June 30, 2021, the organization Stop AAPI Hate recorded over nine thousand incident reports.[15] For example, one Asian American man was sitting outside a Mountain View,

California restaurant when a white woman approached him, spat on him, and told him to "go back where you came from." In Queens, New York, a fifty-two-year-old Asian woman was thrown to the pavement outside of a bakery, reflecting a surprising pattern of attacking the elderly.[16] In Midland, Texas, a nineteen-year-old man was charged with attempted murder after stabbing a Burmese American father and his two children outside of a Sam's Club because he thought they were Chinese and spreading the virus.[17]

Early on, the Trump administration and certain media outlets insisted on using charged terms such as "Wuhan virus," "China plague," and "kung flu"; that only exacerbated violence against Asian Americans. Those of Asian heritage had to deal with not only the general uncertainty of the pandemic but also the constant anxiety of random victimization at the hands of those seeking false control of the situation. Russell Jeung, a professor of Asian American studies at San Francisco State University and the cofounder of Stop AAPI Hate, told the news channel MSNBC that Trump's language had "racialized the virus . . . with deadly consequences."[18] As early as March 27, 2020, the FBI released a statement warning that the growing association of the spread of the coronavirus with China and Asian Americans was leading to a rampant rise in anti-Asian hate crimes.[19]

Unfortunately, regardless of ethnicity or generational status, Asians in the United States have long been scapegoated as being the other throughout US history, making them highly vulnerable during moments of heightened economic and sociopolitical uncertainty. Hannah Tessler, Meera Choi, and Grace Kao argue that "these hate crimes and other incidents of bias have historical roots that have placed Asians outside the boundaries of whiteness and American citizenship."[20] During the late nineteenth and early twentieth centuries, fear of Asians in America was expressed as "yellow peril" by associating their unwanted presence with drugs (opium) and disease (typhoid). This fear led to the Chinese Exclusion Act of 1882, the first immigration ban in the United States to target a specific ethnic group.[21] Within a context of white supremacy, COVID-19 has only bolstered the "perpetual foreigner" stereotype to reinforce the bias that white bodies are clean and pure, and non-white bodies are unclean and dangerous. Leading Asian American historian Erika Lee argues that "the pandemic has revived and fed upon existing racist, anti-immigrant narratives that are part of the United States' long history of xenophobia and racism," revealing the truly mythical nature of Asians as "model minorities."[22] As an irrational fear of all considered "foreign," xenophobia "is a form of racism that has functioned alongside slavery, settler colonialism, conquest, segregation, and white supremacy as a function of institutionalized discrimination that has shaped so much of American history."[23]

Each of these abuses that results from the irrational fear of the other expresses a desire for false forms of control and power in response to uncertainty, revealing deep wounds within US history that can no longer be camouflaged by pre-pandemic routines. Like Vicini, Lloyd warns that fear often follows uncertainty, but he goes further in naming how the "flow of fear from uncertainty" only appears "natural from the perspective of privilege, the unspoken condition of liberalism and whiteness."[24] For many in the United States, uncertainty is not the obvious cause of existential fear but a part of daily life. In many ways, the "tsunami of uncertainty brought by the pandemic is but a somewhat larger-than-ordinary wave."[25] The tragic murder of George Floyd on May 25, 2020, only two months into lockdown, revealed how many African Americans in this country live with constant uncertainty, whether there is a pandemic or not. Through social media, the United States and the world witnessed "an unarmed 46-year-old African American man [be] brutally killed . . . by a white police officer who knelt on his neck for [nine minutes and twenty-nine seconds], despite being restrained, despite the urgent requests of onlookers, despite his repeated desperate pleas: 'I can't breathe.'"[26] This senseless murder, along with those of Breonna Taylor, Ahmaud Arbery, and countless others, forced the American public to face the heightened uncertainty that marginalized peoples experience daily due to entrenched, institutionalized racism and anti-Blackness that serve white stability.

Mourning the loss of George Floyd to police brutality, Bryan Massingale wept in deep prayer as the season of Pentecost neared. He implored, "Come, Holy Spirit," until he realized the key to understanding this moment of racial reckoning was not in Minneapolis, where Floyd was murdered, but rather in an incident that took place that same day, nearly twelve hundred miles away in New York. On Memorial Day 2020, Christian Cooper decided to go to Central Park for bird-watching. Noticing that Amy Cooper's (no relation) dog was unleashed, he requested that she comply with posted signs that asked for dogs to be leashed in public parks. In a video that went viral, she is seen calling 911 and saying, "There's a man, an African American, he has a bicycle helmet. He is recording me and threatening me and my dog. . . . I'm being threatened by a man in the Ramble [a wooded area of Central Park]. Please send the cops immediately!"[27] Amy Cooper, a white woman, called the police because a Black man asked her to comply with park rules.

Massingale argues that the key to understanding this painful moment lies in the fact that Amy Cooper knew what she was doing, and so do the rest of us. He then lays out a detailed list of twenty assumptions that reveal the wounded nature of our relationships with one another in this country. I have selected a few of these assumptions for our consideration:

- She assumed that she would have the presumption of innocence.
- She assumed that Christian, the Black man, would have a presumption of guilt.
- She assumed that the frame of "black rapist" versus "white damsel in distress" would be clearly understood by everyone: the police, the press, and the public.
- She assumed a Black man had no right to tell her what to do.
- She assumed Christian Cooper could and would understand all of the above. (And she was right. He clearly knew what was at stake; that is why he had the presence of mind to record what happened.)[28]

These assumptions, these pre-pandemic "certainties," provide the only framework by which her lies and actions can make sense. The fundamental lie, the original sin of America, at the heart of this fraught encounter between two Coopers in Central Park is that white lives matter more than Black lives. For Massingale, that Black lives matter less than white lives is "the basic assumption that links Christian Cooper with COVID-19, Breonna Taylor, Ahmaud Arbery, [and] George Floyd."[29]

The disorientation and uncertainty of the pandemic era are not solely about health and economic concerns. This era is marked by a number of social injuries that force the American public to face a difficult truth: "The only reason for the persistence of [xenophobia and] racism is because white people benefit from it."[30] Amid the disorientation that grips the world during the COVID-19 pandemic, the cries of Asian Americans and African Americans in the United States present only two examples of numerous marginalized communities holding out their hands and exposing their sides, begging the rest of America to witness these generational wounds that result from false attempts at power and control in the face of uncertainty. These wounds cry out for memory within a narrative that persists with the hope of being in right relationship to one another in this country.

REORIENTATION TO THE WOUNDS THAT REMAIN

In his article "Rethinking Humanity's Progress in Light of COVID-19," James Keenan argues how the increase in commerce, transportation, medicine, technology, and globalization during the past century gave us the impression of human progress and interconnectedness. The pandemic, however, has interrupted the status quo and "found us lacking" by laying "bare astonishing inequities" along racial, ethnic, and class lines. In America, he argues, "COVID-19 has exposed our shame."[31] As a country, we remain marked by the injuries of 2020 in which financial and pandemic uncertainty exposed a new generation to the underlying violence of our relationships, exemplified in the scapegoating of Asian Americans and police brutality against African Americans. The cries of these communities compel us toward a collective examination of conscience in the United States and a conversion to mutual vulnerability as the only way forward.

In Greek philosophy, conscience is the name of that deep moral sense whose pangs within an individual awaken them to the disconnect between what is and what should be. Thomas the Apostle experienced these deep pangs of conscience in the days following the Crucifixion of Jesus. His profound disillusionment in the aftermath of trauma could not provide him with the interior peace that he needed to return to his former life. The pangs of conscience, if listened to, become the threshold for a new receptivity to truth. For Keenan, however, the collective conscience of the American public remains "pathetically ineffective" because the lies of "manifest destiny" and the "turn to slavery so corrupted the Christian conscience that it was left without its capacity for courageous vigilance, hospitable solidarity, and honest sense of remorse." In previous waves of economic and sociopolitical uncertainty throughout US history, the dominant culture became dominant as those with power began stealing land, lives, and labor from marginalized populations to secure their own generational wealth and stability *over* and *against* others. By accommodating the sins of xenophobia and racism, the American conscience is paralyzed by COVID-19 uncertainties because "we cannot tell right from wrong."[32]

Yet if we return to the last great racial reckoning in this country, Catholic writer and Trappist monk Thomas Merton stands as a clear example of a white American Catholic whose eyes were opened from blindness. Responding to Dr. Martin Luther King Jr.'s 1963 "Letter from Birmingham Jail," Merton acknowledged the racial wounds that cried out for recognition in his time through his "Letters to White Liberals."[33] Understanding his time as one of profound Kairos, through which the spiritual dimensions of Black nonviolent protest sought to reach the hearts of all Americans who had internalized whiteness as superior, Merton uses the baptismal imagery of dying to one's old self to highlight the conversion that is needed in the United States. He argues that "in all literal truth, if they 'heard' the message of the Negro . . . they would cease to be the people they were. They would 'die' to everything which was familiar and secure. They would die to their past, to their society with its prejudices and its inertia, to false beliefs, and go over to the side of the Negroes."[34]

Merton appeals to the basic Christian call of discipleship that begins at baptism. Like Thomas the Apostle, who left all behind to follow Jesus, Merton is specifically asking white Christians to understand that they must leave their old self constructed from the false certainties of racial superiority and put on a new self, one rooted in the Gospel. Merton goes further to develop what this specific call to conversion meant in 1963, and it still bears resonance for our time. The "radical challenge" of Black protest

> is a source of uneasiness and to all whites attached to their security. If they are forced to listen to what the Negro is trying to say, the whites may have to admit that their prosperity is rooted to some extent in injustice and in sin. And, in consequence, this might lead to a complete re-examination of the political motives behind all our current policies, domestic and foreign, with the possible admission that we are wrong. Such an admission might, in fact be so disastrous that its effects would dislocate our whole economy and ruin the country. These are not things that are consciously admitted, but they are confusedly present in our minds. They account for the passionate and mindless desperation with which we plunge this way and that, trying to evade the implications of present crisis.[35]

Like Keenan, Merton is acutely aware of how the majority of white American Christians have been able to avoid the pangs of conscience for so long. Yet it is precisely the nonviolent presentation of these generational wounds and the requirement for accurate memory that interrupt the cycles of violence through a constant appeal to conscience. Like the misunderstanding of Thomas the Apostle prior to his encounter with the resurrected Jesus, the logic of human reciprocity suggests retaliation and vengeance as the expected intention of Black protest. Yet the nonviolent character of most demonstrations both in 1963 and today reveals a deeply spiritual begging to be recognized as brothers and sisters whose lives matter with equal dignity. Merton understood this then and remains a prophetic voice for America today.

"Merton," Massingale argues, "took the time to actually read Black thinkers and writers. And not just the ones that make white people comfortable. He read Malcolm X. And Martin Luther King. And James Baldwin. He read them not to refute their arguments, but to be informed by them. He read them with an openness to being seared by what they had to say, with an openness to being converted to new ways of thinking and acting."[36] Merton's openness to conversion is rooted in his vulnerability before the wounded other. Vulnerability avoids emotional shortcuts that secure one's stability by stealing that of the other. A recognition of mutual vulnerability amid deep uncertainty appears to be the only way for Americans to interrupt generational cycles of violence.

Keenan also argues for mutual vulnerability as an antidote to violence amid uncertainty in a pandemic age. As Vincent Lloyd expressed earlier, fear as an obvious outcome to uncertainty only appears natural to those with privilege. For those without privilege, uncertainty is simply the condition of life that leads to a desire for community.[37] To need another is not a sign of weakness. Keenan, however, draws from Judith Butler to argue that vulnerability is not simply about being in need. Those of the dominant culture often misunderstand, thinking that to respond to those in need, one must first be invulnerable and give from their excess as charity; rather, vulnerability is the defining feature of our human nature. To be invulnerable, therefore, is to be inhuman.

To be vulnerable is also to be available to the other. In Christian belief, when God became human, it was not as an expression of dominance but as an expression of vulnerability throughout, from beginning to end. God became available to us as Emmanuel, "God with us," from the vulnerability of the manger in Bethlehem to the cross on Golgotha. To be vulnerable is also to be a neighbor, as in the narrative of the Good Samaritan. When the priest and the Levite walked past the beaten man lying half dead on the side of the road, they remained invulnerable—and therefore inhuman—to the display of human suffering before them. It was the "one who showed mercy," the Samaritan, who was capable of authentic human response in mutual vulnerability.

Rooted in the thought of Emmanuel Levinas and Hannah Arendt, Butler argues that the foundational human capacity for mutual vulnerability is expressed this way: "You call upon me, and I answer. But if I answer, it was only because I was already answerable; that is, this susceptibility and vulnerability constitutes me at the most fundamental level and is there, we might say, prior to any deliberate decision to answer the call. In other words, one has to be already capable of receiving the call before actually answering it. In this sense, ethical responsibility presupposes ethical responsiveness."[38]

Through his vulnerability to the words and wounds of the crucified-and-risen Jesus, Thomas the Apostle experienced a deep conversion of conscience from his pre-crucifixion certainties. Merton, during the civil rights era of the

1960s, likewise made himself vulnerable to the truths of the Black experience in America as a call to living out his baptismal promise more deeply. Today, the wounds of xenophobic scapegoating and racist police brutality amid pandemic uncertainty beg the American conscience, clouded by white supremacist thinking, to become open to mutual vulnerability. As a country, we have been undeniably marked by the medical and social injuries of 2020, both of which are captured by the phrase "I can't breathe." Nonetheless, this very phrase becomes an opportunity for our country to be reoriented to the wounds that remain. Through these wounds, we are awakened to the long-persistent temptation of humans to turn against each other in moments of uncertainty. By allowing these wounds to become our new starting point, may we begin the work of healing. Once the wounds are acknowledged and responsibility is taken, the wounds themselves are transformed from a source of pain in US history to the promise of right relationality.

NOTES

1. Janus, "Experiencing Covid-19," in Kasper and Augustine, *Christian Response to COVID-19*, 76–77.
2. Janus, 75.
3. Francis, *Fratelli tutti*, § 97.
4. Keenan, "Rethinking Humanity's Progress," 732.
5. Copeland, *Knowing Christ Crucified*, 115.
6. This reading of Thomas the Apostle's encounter with the resurrected Jesus is grounded in the mimetic insights of James Alison. For more on his approach, please refer to Alison, *Knowing Jesus*.
7. Goizueta, "Preferential Option," in Lassalle-Klein, *Jesus of Galilee*, 179.
8. Sandford, "Coronavirus."
9. Kasper, "COVID-19 as Disruption," 3.
10. Francis, *Extraordinary Moment of Prayer*.
11. Lloyd, "COVID and Religious Ethics," 350–51.
12. Vicini, "Life in the Time."
13. Vicini.
14. Tessler, Choi, and Kao, "Anxiety of Being Asian American," 637.
15. Yellow Horse et al., "Stop AAPI Hate." The acronym stands for Asian American and Pacific Islander.
16. Joshua Chaffin, "Asian Americans Suffer Surge of Covid-Era Hate Crimes," *Financial Times Limited*, March 18, 2021.
17. Tessler, Choi, and Kao, "Anxiety of Being Asian American," 639.
18. Chaffin, "Asian Americans."
19. Margolin, "FBI Warns."
20. Tessler, Choi, and Kao, "Anxiety of Being Asian American," 638.
21. Lee, "America First," 3.

22. Lee, "COVID through the Eyes of Historians."
23. Lee, "America First," 5.
24. Lloyd, "COVID and Religious Ethics," 351.
25. Lloyd.
26. Massingale, "What to Do," 9.
27. Massingale, 9.
28. Massingale, 9.
29. Massingale, 9.
30. Munch, "'Worship of a False God.'"
31. Keenan, "Rethinking Humanity's Progress," 716–17.
32. Keenan, 731.
33. "Liberal" is not a reference to partisan politics but to any white person who believes in the dignity of all human persons.
34. Merton, "Letters to a White Liberal," 505.
35. Merton, 505.
36. Feuerherd, "Thomas Merton's Writings."
37. Lloyd, "COVID-19 and Religious Ethics," 350–51.
38. Butler, "Precarious Life," 142.

BIBLIOGRAPHY

Alison, James. *Knowing Jesus*. London: SPCK Publishing, 2012.

Butler, Judith. "Precarious Life, Vulnerability, and the Ethics of Cohabitation." *The Journal of Speculative Philosophy* 26, no. 2 (2012): 134–51.

Copeland, M. Shawn. *Knowing Christ Crucified: The Witness of African American Religious Experience*. Maryknoll NY: Orbis Books, 2018.

Feuerherd, Peter. "Thomas Merton's Writings on Race Still Resonate: 'Letters to a White Liberal' Gains Renewed Attention in 2020." *National Catholic Reporter* 57, no. 7 (January 8, 2021).

Francis. *Extraordinary Moment of Prayer*. Sagrato of St Peter's Basilica, March 27, 2020. https://www.vatican.va/content/francesco/en/homilies/2020/documents/papa-francesco_20200327_omelia-epidemia.html.

———. *Fratelli tutti* [On Fraternity and Social Friendship]. Encyclical letter, October 3, 2020, § 97. https://www.vatican.va/content/francesco/en/encyclicals/documents/papa-francesco_20201003_enciclica-fratelli-tutti.html.

Goizueta, Roberto S. "The Preferential Option for the Poor: Christ and the Logic of Gratuity." In *Jesus of Galilee: Contextual Christology for the 21st Century*, edited by Robert Lasalle-Klein, 175–86. Mahwah NJ: Orbis Books, 2011.

Janus, Mark-David, CSP. "Experiencing Covid-19 in New York City." In *A Christian Response to COVID-19*, edited by Walter Kasper and George Augustine, 71–80. Mahwah NJ: Paulist Press, 2020.

Kasper, Walter. "COVID-19 as Disruption, Upheaval, and New Beginnings." In *A Christian Response to COVID-19*, edited by Walter Kasper and George Augustine, 1–21. Mahwah NJ: Paulist Press, 2020.

Keenan, James F., SJ. "Rethinking Humanity's Progress in Light of Covid-19." *Asian Horizons* 14, no. 3 (2020): 713–35.

Lee, Erika. "America First, Immigrants Last: American Xenophobia Then and Now." *The Journal of the Gilded Age and Progressive Era* 19 (2020): 3–18.

———. "COVID through the Eyes of Historians: Erika Lee." University of Minnesota, August 18, 2020. https://cla.umn.edu/history/story/covid-through-eyes-historians-erika-lee.

Lloyd, Vincent W. "COVID-19 and Religious Ethics." *Journal of Religious Ethics* 48, no. 3 (2020): 349–87.

Margolin, Josh. "FBI Warns of Potential Surge in Hate Crimes against Asian Americans amid Coronavirus." *ABC News*, March 27, 2020. https://abcnews.go.com/US/fbi-warns-potential-surge-hate-crimes-asianamerican/story?id=69831920.

Massingale, Bryan, SJ. "What to Do about White Privilege? Amy Cooper Knew Exactly What She Was Doing. We All Do. And That's the Problem." *National Catholic Reporter* 56, no. 18 (June 12–25, 2020).

Merton, Thomas. "Letters to a White Liberal." *Blackfriars* 44, no. 522 (1963): 503–16.

Munch, Regina. "'Worship of a False God': An Interview with Bryan Massingale." *Commonweal* 47, no. 7 (December 27, 2020). https://www.commonwealmagazine.org/worship-false-god.

Sandford, Alasdair. "Coronavirus: Half of Humanity on Lockdown in 90 Countries." *euronews*. April 3, 2020. https://www.euronews.com/2020/04/02/coronavirus-in-europe-spain-s-death-toll-hits-10-000-after-record-950-new-deaths-in-24-hou.

Tessler, Hannah, Meera Choi, and Grace Kao. "The Anxiety of Being Asian American: Hate Crimes and Negative Biases during the COVID-19 Pandemic." *American Journal of Criminal Justice* 45 (2020): 636–46.

Vicini, Andrea, SJ. "Life in the Time of Coronavirus." *La Civiltà Cattolica*, March 30, 2020. https://www.laciviltacattolica.com/life-in-the-time-of-coronavirus/.

Yellow Horse, Aggie J., Russell Jeung, Richard Lim, Boaz Tang, Megan Im, Lauryn Higashiyama, Layla Schweng, and Mikayla Chen. "Stop AAPI Hate National Report: 3/19/20–6/30/21." https://stopaapihate.org/wp-content/uploads/2021/08/Stop-AAPI-Hate-Report-National-v2-210830.pdf.

CHAPTER 9

Trauma, Post-traumatic Growth, and Gratitude in the Time of the COVID-19 Pandemic

Kristi A. Lee

Intellectual and spiritual leaders across time have agreed on what seems to be a truth of human existence: We suffer. While there are many aspects to the experience of being a human, suffering appears to be part of the human condition. In the professional spheres of mental health counseling, psychology, social work, and other human-focused disciplines, we call this suffering *trauma*. The word "trauma" is used colloquially, sometimes lightly or in humor; however, in the world of mental health care, the word "trauma" is always meaningful and often heavy. It can mean damage, pain, and wounding. Sometimes it means destruction—of life, of beliefs, of innocence, of dreams. Trauma is never neutral.

Trauma has many manifestations; it can be an individual, acute experience or a collective, chronic experience. The effects of trauma can be diffuse across individuals or entire communities and can be shared across generations. Difficult and painful experiences do not always result in trauma, however. It is unclear exactly why, given similar experiences, one person will become traumatized, and another person will not. However, a traumatic experience does not have to define a person's life.

As much as suffering appears to be a part of the human condition, so is healing. People can recover and go on to thrive after a traumatic experience;

recovery and thriving are part of a process called *post-traumatic growth.*[1] In this chapter, I review the current understanding of trauma and some of its manifestations, as well as discuss the path of healing and thriving after trauma. Then I introduce gratitude as a simple and accessible practice that can promote growth and healing. These concepts are highly relevant at this time of collective human experience of the COVID-19 pandemic and a pandemic age, and can assist with the development of a new, *post-pandemic* narrative.

TRAUMA AS PSYCHIC INJURY

The most common understanding of trauma is as a specific and terrible incident, a one-time acute event, that one person experiences. Judith Herman, a foundational contributor to the understanding of trauma, describes these events as "extraordinary, not because they occur rarely, but rather because they overwhelm the ordinary human adaptations to life. Unlike commonplace misfortunes, traumatic events generally involve threats to life or bodily integrity, or a close personal encounter with violence and death. They confront human beings with the extremities of helplessness and terror and evoke the responses of catastrophe."[2] In teaching my students about working with people in clinical mental health counseling, I refer to this type of experience as "trauma with a capital T." While not an exhaustive list, these types of traumas include serious accidents, physical or sexual assaults, acute illnesses or hospitalizations, and other life-threatening events.

Mental health practitioners and society at large now widely understand that a direct traumatic experience can significantly impact an individual. In addition, there is growing awareness that trauma can diffuse from the immediate victim to others around them. The impacts of trauma can ripple out from the direct victim to affect others through close association or identification.[3] In addition, people in helping roles, including counselors, psychologists, and other health providers, can become traumatized in the course of *their* work with traumatized people. Exposure to traumatic stories through direct work with victims can cause a trauma response in those who are seeking to provide assistance and support. Various terms have been used to name this type of trauma including "secondary trauma" and "vicarious trauma."[4]

Lesser well known are other types of trauma that can diffuse through families over time. Diffusion of this order is referred to as *generational trauma.*[5] This type of trauma may be experienced when the effects of traumatic experiences are transmitted across generations in a family or in a community. Research on the mechanisms of transmission of generational trauma is growing, and researchers increasingly believe there are biological, epigenetic, and behavioral methods through which younger generations are impacted by the trauma that their parents, grandparents, or even older generations experienced.

While trauma can be experienced at an individual level, it can also be experienced collectively by a group of people who share an experience or identity.[6] An examination of human history shows how specific communities or identity groups have been targeted for violence, deprivation, and genocide. While the motivation for this type of cruelty is difficult to understand, the experience of collective trauma for the targeted community or identity groups is real and can be devastating. A town struck by a powerful hurricane, tornado, or tsunami can be collectively traumatized by the loss of life, livelihoods, and homes. Natural disasters tend to be confined to a region or geographical area whose inhabitants can bond together in their shared experience of collective trauma.

While trauma is often thought of as caused by a single, extraordinary event, trauma can also be chronic and pervasive. This latter type of trauma is often referred to with a lowercase T, but it does not insinuate these traumas are less impactful or devastating, as chronic trauma can be more or less intense in any one moment. In fact, accumulating research demonstrates the ongoing nature of chronic trauma can create compounding impacts on an individual's life. In a hierarchical society such as that in the United States, where privilege is assigned based on race, the ubiquitous presence of individual acts of discrimination can traumatize people.[7] Furthermore, the systemic nature of racism embedded in all aspects of society can traumatize communities. Any group or person that experiences discrimination and systemic exclusion from society can become traumatized by the accumulation of seemingly small incidents that cumulatively result in a major impact.

Clearly identifying the impact of trauma, whether acute or chronic, can be difficult because the intensity and manifestation of trauma vary as widely as the humans who experience it. People who experience trauma can have physical, psychological, relational, spiritual, and existential sequela. The two concepts of post-traumatic stress and post-traumatic stress disorder improve our understanding of trauma and its aftermath.

POST-TRAUMATIC STRESS

Humans have evolved to have specific reactions to trauma that researchers have termed "post-traumatic stress."[8] While an in-depth discussion of the psychological and physiological expressions of post-traumatic stress is beyond the scope of this chapter, it is useful to know that certain responses to a traumatic experience are adaptive and protective. The human species has survived to the modern day partly because of what is commonly known as the *flight, fight, or freeze* response. When a traumatic threat is in the environment, the human brain and body mobilize for protection with increased heart and breathing rates, spikes in adrenaline, pupil dilation, muscle tension, and increased vigilance and fear, among other changes.[9] These rapid physiological changes can be uncomfortable, but they are normal and natural. Without this highly evolved alert and protection system, the human species likely would not have survived to today.

For most people who experience an acute trauma, their post-traumatic stress response will fade over time, and they will return to pre-trauma homeostasis. The process of recovery from post-traumatic stress can be supported through counseling, social support, and a return to physical and psychological safety. However, a small percentage of traumatized people struggle to recover, and their symptoms do not decrease. When the intensity and persistence of symptoms significantly interfere with daily living, a diagnosis of post-traumatic stress disorder may be warranted.

POST-TRAUMATIC STRESS DISORDER

When a person's response to trauma is long-lasting and of a level of intensity that interferes with aspects of daily life, it can become *post-traumatic stress disorder* (PTSD). The *Diagnostic and Statistical Manual of Mental Disorders,* the text that names and describes diagnostic criteria for mental health disorders, defines PTSD as "the development of characteristic symptoms following exposure to one or more traumatic events."[10] Symptoms can include intense emotional reactions, avoidance of stimuli that are associated with the traumatic event, negative memory or cognitive changes, hypervigilance, and sleep disturbances, among others.

Post-traumatic stress and a diagnosis of PTSD are distinguished by the difference in the intensity, frequency, and severity of symptoms. When people can no longer function at work, in relationships, or at home, a diagnosis of PTSD can be warranted and helpful. While debate about the utility and implications of mental health diagnoses remains unsettled, receiving a diagnosis of PTSD can help people understand their experience. In addition, a diagnosis can assist counselors in providing effective treatment to help the traumatized person recover from their psychological, spiritual, or existential wounds.[11] Indeed, people can and do heal from PTSD. Counselors and medical practitioners use multiple evidence-based practices to assist people in their journey to healing and then thriving: cognitive behavioral therapy, eye movement desensitization reprocessing therapy, animal-assisted interventions, and psychotropic medication.[12]

Unfortunately, many people who experience trauma do not receive mental health care from a counselor in their healing journey.[13] In the United States, there are many complex reasons for the lack of access to mental health care, including the limits on health insurance coverage, the high cost of mental health care, and the social stigma against seeking counseling. In addition, there are not enough counselors with historically marginalized identities who likely could better serve their own communities. Traditional counseling practices were often developed by and for a white, middle- and upper-class, Christian majority, and they can have limited utility for people with other identities. The lack of both counselors with marginalized identities and counseling practices that are culturally responsive is extremely problematic, especially given the chronic trauma that people with marginalized identities often live with every day.[14] The lack of mental health care resources is unfortunate. As human society emerges from the COVID-19 pandemic, the need for mental health care will likely increase for years to come.

While all too brief, the preceding presentation of trauma and its manifestations provides context for understanding what the entire human community has experienced since the onset of the COVID-19 pandemic in early 2020. As we have moved through the years since the pandemic began, many have experienced multilayered traumas that have been individual, acute, collective, and chronic, and sometimes all at the same moment. For communities or people who live with chronic trauma or generational trauma, incidents of acute trauma can be more severe as multilayered impacts compound. As the chronic medical emergency of the pandemic wanes, the pandemic's effects on mental health will become more visible.

Focusing on recovering from trauma will be essential for healing in our pandemic age. Seeing a qualified counselor who provides "expert companionship" in the healing process is certainly helpful but not the only way people can recover from trauma.[15] Religious traditions have practices for responding to trauma that provide comfort and support, and help people see meaning in their suffering. What counseling practices and religious traditions hold in common is the conviction that we can grow beyond trauma, that life continues and can be made whole again.

POST-TRAUMATIC GROWTH AS RESTORATION

While suffering through trauma seems to be an undeniable part of the human condition, so does healing. Humans have an incredible capacity to heal and to grow through trauma and loss, not only to survive difficulty, but also to move beyond survival to thriving. This process of *post-traumatic growth* (PTG) is defined as "positive psychological changes after struggling with a traumatic life event."[16]

Before beginning a discussion on post-traumatic growth, it is important to note that even when an individual experiences post-traumatic growth, this does not mean that the traumatizing event or events were welcomed or needed. Growth after a traumatic experience "does not equate to an absence of distress."[17] Preventing trauma from occurring in the first place is always preferable and is better for mental health outcomes overall. Efforts to prevent trauma are particularly important for communities and individuals who experience chronic and generational trauma that can make them more susceptible to negative impacts of acute trauma. Additionally, focusing on or attempting to move a person toward post-traumatic growth too quickly risks invalidating distress. People need time to experience and process the grief, terror, and loss that trauma causes and elicits. This process should not be rushed. However, when the conditions for healing and support are present and the timing is right, people and communities can heal through trauma and can go on to thrive. The conceptual framework of post-traumatic growth provides a structure for understanding how healing and thriving become possible.

ELEMENTS OF POST-TRAUMATIC GROWTH

Viktor Frankl, a doctor of neurology and psychiatry, was imprisoned in the Auschwitz-Birkenau concentration camp during the Holocaust. Most of his family and loved ones were murdered by the Nazis. Given the extreme degradation and evil he and millions of others experienced at the hands of the Nazis, it almost defies comprehension that Frankl emerged with a powerful and peaceful understanding of trauma and the human experience. A foundational tenet of his theory is that "when we are no longer able to change a situation, we are challenged to change ourselves."[18] Traumatic experiences are never asked for; trauma is something that *happens to* a person. It is reassuring to know that, according to Frankl, "suffering ceases to be suffering at the moment it finds a meaning"[19] Healing, even transformation, is possible after trauma.

One of the negative impacts of trauma can be a "shattered world view."[20] An intact and meaningful life narrative can be rebuilt, and the study of post-traumatic growth can illuminate the path forward. Richard Tedeschi and L. Calhoun's research with survivors of trauma identifies five domains of post-traumatic growth through factor analysis of the Posttraumatic Growth Inventory.[21] Representing areas where PTG can occur for a person who experienced trauma, these domains are relating to others, personal strength, appreciation for life, new possibilities, and spiritual and existential change.[22]

RELATING TO OTHERS

In experiencing and recovering from a traumatic experience, positive changes in relationships and relating to others may occur. According to Richard Tedeschi and Bret Moore, people report that "relationships have a deeper emotional quality" where connections are stronger.[23] Surviving and healing from trauma often necessitate sharing the experience with others, who may include friends, family members, counselors, or others who have had similar experiences. When received with empathy and compassion, sharing the traumatic experience can result in meaningful connections, deeper respect, and the vulnerability that is required for stronger relationships. Social support appears to be an important source of growth and provides a sense of comfort to survivors.[24]

PERSONAL STRENGTH

In the immediate aftermath of an acute traumatic experience or in the daily experience of chronic trauma, survival is the focus. When a person comes to understand that they have survived the event or events, a sense of personal strength can emerge.[25] This may be characterized by the difference between the two terms "victim" and "survivor." There is a qualitative difference in the meaning of these terms, and their use can signal something about the recovery and healing process. Moving from seeing oneself as a victim to a survivor may indicate self-reliance, courage, and new confidence that any challenge can be faced. *Healing* means carrying forward a sense of personal strength into whatever comes next.

APPRECIATION OF LIFE

Having endured the loss, terror, or pain of a traumatic experience, survivors may develop a new sense of gratitude or an appreciation for life that might have been missing. This shift of focus from trauma to appreciation appears to emerge from a reflective state where a reconsideration of what is valuable, is important, and was previously overlooked occurs. Things that formerly might have been taken for granted become more important, and gratitude grows from the relief of survival.[26] Gratitude practices may support the emergence of this domain of PTG and are discussed below.

NEW POSSIBILITIES

Trauma often is characterized by some type of loss. This loss can be physical or material in nature, such as the loss of life, ability, or property, and it can be psychological or existential, such as the loss of a belief in a fundamentally safe world or the destruction of a planned-for future. Whatever its nature, the loss has the potential to destroy a person's understanding of their life in a way that may never be regained. For a person to recover from such loss, new paths and possibilities must be embraced. New ways of living that may never have occurred to the person previously can be equally or even more fulfilling than the lost path.[27]

SPIRITUAL AND EXISTENTIAL CHANGE

When a person's worldview is shaken or destroyed by a traumatic experience, deep existential or spiritual questions can emerge. People with a faith tradition may begin to doubt their previously held beliefs, and those with no faith tradition may find themselves reconsidering that stance. Questions of the meaning and purpose of life are often reexamined; seeking to understand "how the divine is part of their lives" is common.[28] What can arise from these explorations of one's soul and purpose is a deep understanding of forgiveness, spirituality, and existential meaning.

People who demonstrate post-traumatic growth in one or more of these areas have better outcomes in physical health, mental health, and other domains. The COVID-19 pandemic has been a collective, chronic, and acute trauma; therefore, seeking ways to promote post-traumatic growth is essential as we collectively emerge from the pandemic.

FACILITATING AND PROMOTING PTG

In summary, post-traumatic growth can be encouraged in many ways. Again, it is important to note that rushing to seek post-traumatic growth does not facilitate that growth. People need time to grieve, to feel their emotions, and to regain a sense of stability in life functioning. This process cannot and should not be rushed. When it is time, post-traumatic growth can be facilitated with the assistance of "expert companionship," those who can guide the process of healing.[29] Cognitive-behavioral, existential, narrative, and interpersonal approaches can be used to facilitate post-traumatic growth. Education about trauma and healing can help traumatized individuals understand and make meaning of their experiences. However, achieving post-traumatic growth does not mean returning to life as it was before the trauma because trauma often destroys a person's understanding of the world. Instead, the goal of supporting post-traumatic growth is to help a person construct a new worldview and narrative that incorporates the struggle of the trauma and the strength they have found in surviving and overcoming it.

GRATITUDE AS A TOOL TO PROMOTE POST-TRAUMATIC GROWTH

Certainly, working with a professional counselor as an expert guide can provide important assistance in the process of healing from trauma and moving toward thriving through post-traumatic growth. However, one of the disparities laid bare during the COVID-19 pandemic was the inaccessibility of mental health care for most people in the United States. Further, people with historically marginalized identities can find it difficult to find counselors who share their identities or who use culturally responsive and responsible practices. These problems need to be remedied if we are to address the mental health crisis that is emerging as the physical threat of COVID-19 wanes. Until sufficient and high-quality mental health services are available for all who would like to access them, other tools are needed to help people heal and thrive after trauma. One relatively simple option that can be used by anyone is the *practice of gratitude.*

In a relatively new area of scholarship, gratitude has been shown to be "positively associated with psychological well-being and post-traumatic growth" in adult participants who had lost parents as children.[30] Intentionally focusing on what a person is grateful for was shown to reduce intrusive rumination and to have a positive impact on post-traumatic growth.[31] For women with blood cancer, for example, a practice of gratitude correlated significantly with post-traumatic growth.[32] These findings are just a few from the many studies that are showing the power of gratitude in finding healing and growth after trauma.

Promoting gratitude practices is a simple, accessible, and yet powerful way for anyone to engage their own healing and growth process. People can find and use strategies that work for them to enhance a sense of gratitude. While not meant to be an exhaustive list, researchers have identified the following strategies as useful in cultivating and expressing gratitude:

- Recording things for which one is grateful in a journal
- Sharing gratitude for a person verbally or in writing
- Pausing each day to identify things for which to be grateful for ("count your blessings")
- If part of a religious or spiritual tradition, expressing gratitude through prayer or meditation[33]

While less research has focused on collective practices of gratitude, communities can adopt gratitude practices to support collective healing and growth. Leaders of organizations, congregations, or other community groups can work to set a culture where gratitude is regularly shared for the people, places, and experiences of life. Community-based gratitude practices could help to promote post-traumatic growth and should be considered as an important element in helping community members emerge from the collective trauma of the COVID-19 pandemic.

CONCLUSION

As the world community begins to unwind from the COVID-19 pandemic, many of us will carry lingering impacts of traumatic experiences. Some of us will have endured acute trauma layered upon chronic, generational traumas.

Understanding the experience of trauma, and the hope for healing through post-traumatic growth, is essential to finding our way into a post-pandemic world. Embracing gratitude for what life is now is a path toward healing and thriving again.

NOTES

1. R. G. Tedeschi and L. G. Calhoun, "Posttraumatic Growth: Conceptual Foundations and Empirical Evidence," *Psychological Inquiry* 15, no. 1 (2004): 1–18.
2. Judith Herman, *Trauma and Recovery: The Aftermath of Violence from Domestic Abuse to Political Terror* (New York: Basic Books, 1992), 33.
3. K. A. Lee et al., *The Ripple Effect of Hate Crimes: Diffused Hate Crime Victimization and Trauma*, presentation at the International Network of Hate Studies Conference, Seattle, 2020.
4. N. Whitfield and D. Kanter, "Helpers in Distress: Preventing Secondary Trauma," *Reclaiming Children and Youth* 22, no. 4 (2014): 59–61; and T. Foreman et al., "The Impact of Trauma Exposure: Vicarious Traumatization and Posttraumatic Growth among Counselor Trainees," *Journal of Counselor Practice* 11, no. 2 (2020): 21–43.
5. M. Doucet and M. Rovers, "General Trauma, Attachment, and Spiritual/Religious Interventions," *Journal of Loss and Trauma* 15, no. 93 (2010): 93–102, https://doi.org/10.1080/15325020903373078.
6. G. Hirschberger, "Collective Trauma and the Social Construction of Meaning," *Frontiers in Psychology* 9 (2018): 1–14, https://doi.org/10.3389/fpsyg.2018.01441.
7. K. L. Nadal, *Microaggressions and Traumatic Stress: Theory, Research, and Clinical Treatment* (Washington DC: American Psychological Association, 2018).
8. S. Joseph, *What Doesn't Kill Us: The New Psychology of Posttraumatic Growth* (New York: Basic Books, 2011).
9. Joseph.
10. "Trauma and Stressor Related Disorders," in *Diagnostic and Statistical Manual of Mental Disorders (DSM-5)*, 5th ed., edited by the American Psychiatric Association (Washington DC: American Psychiatric Association, 2013): 274.
11. J. Sareen, "Posttraumatic Stress Disorder in Adults: Impact, Comorbidity, Risk Factors, and Treatment," *Canadian Journal of Psychiatry* 59, no. 9 (2014): 460–67, https://doi.org/10.1177/070674371405900902.
12. W. Brown et al., "A Critical Review of Negative Affect and the Application of CBT for PTSD," *Trauma, Violence, & Abuse* 19, no. 2 (2018): 176–94; and A. Valiente-Gómez et al., "EMDR beyond PTSD: A Systematic Literature Review," *Frontiers in Psychology* 8 (2017): 1–10.
13. Sareen, "Posttraumatic Stress Disorder."
14. Nadal, *Microaggressions and Traumatic Stress.*
15. R. G. Tedeschi and B. A. Moore, "Posttraumatic Growth as an Integrative Therapeutic Philosophy," *Journal of Psychotherapy Integration* 31, no. 2 (2020): 9.
16. Z. Asgari and A. Naghavi, "Explaining Post-Traumatic Growth: Thematic Synthesis of Qualitative Research," *Iranian Journal of Psychiatry and Clinical Psychology* 25, no. 2 (2019): 222–35, https://doi.org/10.32598/ijpcp.25.2.222.

17. M. Brooks et al., "I Get Knocked Down, but I Get Up Again: A Qualitative Exploration of Posttraumatic Growth after Multiple Traumas," *Traumatology* 27, no. 3 (2021): 1.
18. V. E. Frankl, *Man's Search for Meaning: An Introduction to Logotherapy* (New York: Simon & Schuster, 1984), 117.
19. Frankl, 117.
20. Brooks et al., "I Get Knocked Down," 1.
21. R. G. Tedeschi and L. G. Calhoun, "The Posttraumatic Growth Inventory: Measuring the Positive Legacy of Trauma," *Journal of Trauma Stress* 9 (1996): 455–71.
22. Tedeschi and Moore, "Posttraumatic Growth."
23. Tedeschi and Moore, 2.
24. Brooks et al., "I Get Knocked Down," 1.
25. Tedeschi and Moore, "Posttraumatic Growth," 1.
26. Tedeschi and Moore, 1.
27. Tedeschi and Moore, 3.
28. Tedeschi and Moore, 3.
29. Tedeschi and Moore, 4.
30. N. Green and K. McGovern, "Gratitude, Psychological Well-Being, and Perceptions of Posttraumatic Growth in Adults Who Lost a Parent in Childhood," *Death Studies* 41, no. 7 (2017): 442, http://dx.doi.org/10.1080/07481187.2017.1296505.
31. E. Kim and S. Bae, "Gratitude Moderates the Mediating Effect of Deliberate Rumination on the Relationship between Intrusive Rumination and Post-Traumatic Growth," *Frontiers in Psychology* 10 (2019), https://doi.org/10.3389/fpsyg.2019.02665.
32. S. Mousavi, M. Goodarzi, and S. Taghavi, "Prediction of Post-Traumatic Growth Based on Gratitude and Perceived Social Support in Women with Blood Cancer," *Quarterly Journal of Health Psychology* 8, no. 30 (2019): 39–53, https://doi.org/10.30473/hpj.2019.40332.4008.
33. R. A. Sansone and L. A. Sansone, "Gratitude and Well-Being: The Benefits of Appreciation," *Psychiatry* 7, no. 11 (2010): 18–22.

CHAPTER 10

Traumatic Ontology

COVID-19—Epochal, Societal, and Personal Transformation

Douglas F. Peduti, SJ

Near the end of World War II, Maurice Merleau-Ponty, reflecting upon the human condition, exhorted us "not to forget 'the experience of unreason,' that is, to think (sensibly) about what is experienced as, and is perhaps doomed to remain, strictly speaking, non-sense."[1] Merleau-Ponty was, of course, referring to the trauma inflicted by global war and the atrocities of the Holocaust. While World War II had a different cause and intensity of trauma than our current pandemic, Merleau-Ponty's advice is, nevertheless, apposite advice for us today: We cannot ignore "experience[s] of unreason" as we seek to glean the meaning of our pandemic age.

Specifically, this chapter reflects on the trifold relationship of gratitude, injury, and repair in a pandemic age. COVID-19 is our era's *longue durée* (long term) of trauma. As such, I argue that, as an experience of trauma, we must investigate the pandemic's inflictions both visible and invisible to make some sense of an experience that wounds more deeply than what physical effects reveal. Only then can we begin to find some solace in repairing our livelihoods and proffering gratitude in its wake. I call this traumatic ontology, or a study of "being in trauma."[2] This analysis encompasses the whole person and community over time. In the final assessment, traumatic ontology reveals avenues of insight and healing that can assist us as we undergo the pandemic, insights that contribute to the repairing of the underlying flaws of our communities at the deep levels that the pandemic rendered visible. We also need more time than the current moment to narrate any meaningful story that can heal and reveal new insights regarding how to dwell in a healthy human community. This is a cautious narrative of hope.

Every narrative arises from a particular voice or group. I write in the Jesuit Catholic tradition, one that emphasizes justice in the service of faith. One distinctive aspect of Jesuit education at all levels is its emphasis on teaching "the whole person": mind, body, and spirit. The objective of teaching whole persons to become men and women for others, as the Jesuit motto counsels, is rooted in the fundamental gospel principle to hear the call of the poor and the suffering, and to honor its obligation to address the pain that is easily overlooked by those who live in comfort. Describing the gospel principle in stronger terms, Hilary Jerome Scarsella claims, "The discipline of Christian theology is itself a response to trauma. Without the traumatic event of Jesus's crucifixion and the rupturing belief that the one who was killed rose again from the grave, Christian theology as we know it would not have come into being."[3] More precisely, to be authentic, Christianity redresses trauma.

Hence, I have chosen to develop traumatic ontology—that is, being in trauma—first, to determine a way of understanding our current age; secondly, to assist in its repair; and ultimately, to find a source of gratitude. We need to reflect on our feelings of loss and our patterns of thoughts, and to ponder anew on what is most valuable; otherwise, the injury will only continue its hold on us. Gratitude can arise from a newfound understanding of the human spirit and from repairing the systemic cracks that make our institutions unfair.

INJURY

Dylan Trigg defines trauma as "*the wound of experience*."[4] Trauma is a wound that defies conscious control. Cathy Caruth argues that trauma gives itself to consciousness in a way that indicates that the malaise persists *by* its ability to defy a conscious rendering: Something in life is *missing*.[5] Trigg further describes trauma in these terms: It is "the body's ability to conceal the past from the present, characterized by indirection and discontinuity."[6] Given these parameters, I argue that for us to educate the whole person, we must direct our attention to this non-sense, this disjunction between the mind, body, and spirit.

Can we make sense of non-sense? The question has become ever more urgent during our recent turmoil from the COVID-19 pandemic. Loss, desire, bodily reaction, reflection, belief, and hope—all are part of a complex mix that the pandemic has roiled anew. In the face of the pandemic, we naturally look for solutions to the virus, but as it perdures, it also focuses our attention on the very way we live. In many ways, our way of life does not make sense.

One question should help our reflection: What type of person do I want to be, and correlatively, what type of people do we wish to be? So *prima facie*, an openness to the future as one of hopeful possibility seems paramount as a way to begin the journey of making life sensible. Certainly, amid the pandemic, we hope to experience someday, perhaps even today, gratitude and repair, even when any hope still seems rather dim and untenable. Thus, envisioning a possible future is the first step in moving toward healing.

Yet non-sense clouds future prospects. We still often feel weighed down by the pandemic's injurious effects. Thus, let us then place our attention on what is most pressing, the present injury. What is the pain? How do we feel it? How is our life disrupted, ruptured, or lost? Unmistakably, the cost of human lives weighs heaviest; as of today, the death toll seems overwhelming, even to the point of numbness. The World Health Organization, as of October 20, 2024, reported that world deaths exceed 7,070,128, with 776,546,006 documented cases.[7] Many sources estimate that number undercounts by a million hidden deaths and cases. As obviously troubling as those numbers appear, more wounds are still unaccounted for, even unimagined; long-term effects are still pending. Beyond the physical and biological harm, we have yet to determine demographic effects: increased poverty, mass dislocation, disenfranchisement, inequality, and psychological impairment due to isolation. If one were to describe the felt pain of COVID-19 now, by all accounts, it could be described accurately as a trauma.

Trauma has been applied loosely to many types of maladies. More narrowly, the American Psychiatric Association defines trauma in the *Diagnostic and Statistical Manual of Mental Disorders* (*DSM-5*) with the following terms: It requires "actual or threatened death, serious injury, or sexual violence."[8] Stressful events not involving an immediate threat to life or physical injury, such as psychosocial stressors, are excluded. For this reason, events such as divorce or job loss are not considered traumatic by this definition. To combat this etiologically narrow definition, Carol North and others have argued that we must reassess trauma, relying less on theory and more on actual case studies of patients who exhibit intrusive memories, avoidance and numbing, and hyperarousal.[9] From their perspective, trauma is a persistent negative emotional state that includes fear, horror, anger, guilt, or shame. Markedly diminished interest or participation in significant activities also accompanies it. The corollary to trauma is post-traumatic stress disorder, which is defined as persistent, distorted cognitions about the cause or consequences of the traumatic event(s) that led the individual to blame themselves or others. As it extends its reach, our current pandemic arguably relates to most, if not all, of these criteria.

But official criteria are not what concerns us in our everyday lives (except, of course, those who need a diagnosis for medical and financial support). For the most part, the pandemic concerns us as it burdens our lives and our relationships. We feel numb, anxious, and exhausted. At times pandemic constraints may be felt by some as mere inconveniences, but the long-term effects of even minor inconveniences build into a compounded malaise. Loneliness sets in and develops anxieties and anger into neuroses. Our usual ways of socializing and self-care are impeded or prohibited. Our emotional lives become threadbare, our relationships frayed, and our community fragmented. Whether we develop physical symptoms or not, as family members, caregivers, first responders, and even casual consumers, we are all affected.

Because we are social creatures, we are placed at a further disadvantage in isolation; one needs to look only at the way isolation has affected our politics. Usual quirkiness and distrust of authority and institutions have become exaggerated. Short-term effects develop into acute, long-term problems. Politics compound the physical and social into unmanageable national and world events of crises. Even science and truth, which were once consoling common ground in our era, are now questioned. Conspiracy theories and disinformation undermine what science seems to dictate to anyone with common sense. For example, vaccine resistance partly lies in a moral, religious concern about using stem cells for its testing; yet only one brand of vaccine uses these cells for testing. This claim is further inaccurate, at best, for the cells used are no longer cells from aborted fetuses but from the human embryonic stem cell (HESC) line, with the NL-HESC1, first derived in the Netherlands, thousands of cell generations later. Such stem cells are used in research to cure diabetes, Parkinson's disease, and myocardial infarction or cardiac failure. Furthermore, if such a principle would be held fast, then shouldn't the hundred or so everyday products, such as aspirin, ibuprofen, and cosmetics that commonly used such testing for decades also be abandoned? But these counterarguments are simply ignored; reason is defied. It seems natural that we dismiss conspiracists as cranks, but ignoring them only exacerbates public unrest. Rather than dismiss these persons as arbitrarily political or peculiarly crazy, we should view their struggles as part of the complex event called COVID-19. Denial seems a pervasive coping method both at the individual and communal levels, becoming even more pervasive in this pandemic. Politics and denial of reality, too, are part of the non-sense of trauma.

Denial of reality at its extreme threshold can lead to derealization, or a mental state where people feel detached from their surroundings, where people and objects seem unreal.[10] E. C. Hunter, M. Sierra, and A. S. David suggest that 70 percent of the population experiences such derealization; if this is even remotely true, it will have a large influence on the way the community is envisioned and the way it operates.[11] Their claim implies that about 30 percent of the population will not experience derealization. This minority could try to persuade skeptics via reason and science; however, according to "derealized people," reason and science are not helpful, for reason always already appears to be part of the conspiracy. Instead of dismissing their concerns as outlandish, we must build a bridge of dialogue. Only then can we fairly address the concerns of the pandemic. Yet the avenue to dialogue in its current state still eludes us. Can we learn to dialogue by including non-sense as part of the regular discussion?

Not only does the pandemic take its toll on our social interactions but also, more problematically, it impinges more acutely on the marginalized. Percentages of death are remarkably higher for persons of color. The Yale School of Medicine published an article as early as September 2020 on the way the pandemic has affected various groups in the United States. Black, Hispanic, American Indian, and Alaskan Native people in the United States continue to suffer an outsize share of sickness and death in the ongoing COVID-19 pandemic. Ohioan Blacks (13 percent of the state's population) represent 31.8 percent of its hospitalizations, Virginian Hispanics make up 9.6 percent of the state's population but account for 36.2 percent of all COVID-19 hospitalizations, and Arizona's Indigenous population accounts for 4 percent of the population but comprise 15.7 percent of COVID-19 hospitalizations.[12] Only Asian Americans seem not to follow this pattern. Most telling, the Centers for Disease Control and Prevention (CDC) released a study examining outbreaks of COVID-19 from March to June 2020 in Utah workplaces. The study reported that workers who identified as Hispanic, Black, American Indian or Alaskan Native, Asian, Native Hawaiian or other Pacific Islander, two or more races, or any race other than white accounted for 73 percent of COVID-19 cases even though the totality of all people who identify as such consists of only 24 percent of all workers in the state. As Dr. Carolyn M. Mazure, the director of Women's Health Research at Yale, assessed the situation: "People of color are significantly less likely to have work that can be done remotely during this pandemic." She underscores the problem: "The greater risk this entails is one of the many reasons why people of color are suffering greater negative outcomes of this disease, including greater health risks stemming from decades of disparity in access to equitable resources including health care. As we confront COVID-19, we must remedy the systemic inequities that continue to exist in our society."[13]

Thus, it should be clear that the injury is overwhelming. Whether speaking of mortality, long-term physical illness, and psychological malady at the level of an individual or of economic distress in families, marginalized groups, or communities, we have located untold injury that is only beginning to seep into our awareness. In short, we are in a state of trauma from many trajectories. Just think of the early days of the virus in March 2020: Though we were quite fearful of its virulency, we applauded our health care workers with welcoming encouragement, clanging pots and pans; then we hunkered down, worked remotely, and rarely was there even the slightest attempt to revive our spirits psychologically. The promise of vaccines and their haphazard, sporadic delivery did little to revive hope. Booster shots and the infection rate versus the virulency of new variants shifted regularly. Consequently, we live in a constant state of wariness. And now we are impatient at the slightest inconvenience. Truly, we are exhausted in mind, body, and spirit.

Even if or when the pandemic comes under our control and its viral effects have diminished greatly, we are still left with its aftereffects: the toll of grieving our lost loved ones, the fatigue of long COVID, the failures of our government to protect us, and the callousness of some neighbors who downplay our pain. The pandemic and its isolation have taken a personal and social toll. The felt injury is clear: We are traumatized.

Many have characterized our present age as *the* age of trauma. For instance, Vincenzo Di Nicola characterizes our situation today in these questions: "Why is our experience constructed this way in our time and why has trauma become the emblematic experience of contemporary life to the point that we may invoke the epithet 'the age of trauma'?"[14] He argues that even before the pandemic, we were living in an age of anxiety. We live from one crisis to the next. Thus, the dilemma needs more than a cursory, albeit much-needed, epidemiological analysis. We need to understand why we live in constant crisis mode.

Having looked squarely at the enormity of the injury, what can one now dare to say of repair and gratitude? How do we leave constant crises and proceed to dwell in peace? While physically, the repair is less speedy than hoped, there are physical signs and daily accounts of increasing vaccinations and lessening strains. Biologically our medical profession has inspired us with its outstanding research, though not all appreciate its intervention with equal measure. What could repair possibly look like in such a multifaceted problem? How do we move toward gratitude that is more than mere lip service?

Looking into the face of the damage with clear eyes is the best approach, I argue. Again, we cannot simply move on and try to bury the pain that places it in the past. The pain doesn't simply dissipate with time; rather, the feelings of loss need reckoning, for they affect our thought patterns and ways of coping in the world. Instead, reflecting upon loss can lead us to reevaluate what we cherish most. In either event, the pandemic's long arm will determine who we are as a people and persons for generations, not unlike what the Holocaust or the attacks of September 11, 2001, did decades ago. Furthermore, trauma is engrained in the fiber of our bodies, is stored in our subconscious, and will imperceptibly influence our decisions for years. We live in an epoch of trauma.

With so much at stake, a more thorough investigation that employs several helpful resources is demanded. All areas of study are needed to unravel our dilemma. Epidemiologists and social workers, yes, but also psychologists, psychoanalysts, philosophers, and theologians are needed. Already they are all busy attempting to understand and treat trauma in all its variations, whether narrowly or broadly conceived. To place this overarching dilemma into a richer context, Richard Polt has coined the phrase "traumatic ontology" to capture the entire experience, wherewith we must each discover the appropriating events of emergency in our own lives and communities.[15] By "events," Polt intends events that surround us and affect us in ways both obvious and hidden. By "appropriating," Polt cautions us that we must respond in some authentic way; otherwise, we will be affected in detrimental ways. This does not mean that we can control every aspect of the traumatic event, but we must engage it if we are to find some aspect of understanding or coping. As we see, traumatic ontology is not only a search for the causes of the trauma but also a way forward toward aspects of repair.

These aspects are most challenging with trauma, for we try to avoid pain and submerge injuries; by definition, the primary difficulty of trauma is that we avoid its effects vigorously. Thus, we need to look closely at our own weaknesses. As another way of envisioning this scenario, Di Nicola describes trauma as a metaphor akin to Achilles' spear that both wounded and healed Telephus of Mysia in the *Iliad* and to the ancient Greek term φάρμᾰκον, or *phármakon,* a word meaning "poison" and "medicine," from which our English word "pharmacy" derives.[16] It is our hope that the poison of this traumatic experience will also give us an antidote in the form of more than a viral vaccine *and* a healthier way of living, for now we know what we missed so badly during isolation—a healthy community. We can now reevaluate our values and rebuild accordingly.

Though we do this with eyes still unable to see clearly, we must, nevertheless, begin to look at the untold effects of trauma. Psychiatrists and psychologists have argued about the parameters and treatment of personal and social trauma. Funding is necessary. But more than funding, Dr. Sandra Bloom encourages us to design a culture that removes the personal stigma of trauma, for we have not yet understood the way it affects our everyday cognitive functioning.[17] Stigma is an unnecessary added layer of complication and social burden; its removal will necessitate our approach to mental health care. Funding alone will not resolve the problem. Treating a person exhibiting mental "abnormalities," mutatis mutandis, is no different from treating someone with a broken leg. Here, society can change its attitudes toward individuals.

REPAIR

But how can society repair itself? Judith Herman outlines the harmful effects incurred from social upheavals, such as the Holocaust; she cautions us to investigate the hidden cultural wounds they cause, such as increased crime. We tend to submerge these hidden effects of trauma, to silence the inner voices so that they not only impair us now but for generations to come.[18] For example, news outlets shocked us with the report on September 27, 2021, that murders spiked in 2020. National Public Radio's Ryan Lucas reported that across the nation, in large cities and small towns, "[t]he data shows 21,570 homicides in the U.S. in 2020, which is a staggering 4,901 more than in 2019."[19] This is the highest it has been for twenty-five years. This rate continued in 2021 and has only recently dropped in large cities except for Washington, DC.[20] The tally makes clear—in concrete terms—just how violent the last years were. The overall violent crime rate, which includes murder, assault, robbery, and rape, inched up to around 5 percent, while property crimes continued their long-running decline and dropped 8 percent from 2019.[21] Asked to speculate on the causes, Lucas responded that thus far, all we have are correlations: the pandemic, the rise in firearms permits (much of the violence was driven by firearms, with nearly 77 percent of murders being committed with some sort of firearm), and the protests against police brutality. Etiology is still uncertain, but we are seeing more clearly underlying stressors that became more intense during the pandemic. Facing these stressors isn't easy, but in a positive manner, they show us avenues in which we must travel. Resolutely addressing gun violence is no longer avoidable.

Stressors are compounded in surprising ways. Donna Orange, a professor of psychology at New York University, documents that trauma often destroys memory.[22] Discussing the effects of trauma demands that we talk through the pain, yet ironically the psyche buries the pain. What are we to do? Lest we give in to despair, Françoise Davoine and Jean-Max Gaudillière bolster our hearts, for they argue, recrafting a phrase from Ludwig Wittgenstein's *Tractatus*: "Whereof one cannot speak thereof one *cannot* stay silent."[23] Where does the repair occur? In the very recounting of the countless injuries, the narrative begins to apply its balm. In the very act of seeing the violence, we become resolute to end it. In other words, the poison is also the medicine. In the words of Elie Wiesel on another traumatic event: "Never shall I forget these things, even if I am condemned to live as long as God Himself. Never."[24] The painful recounting of the injury is in itself part of the repair. Recounting can lead to resolve, and resolve can lead to positive action; inaction only leads to malaise.

But recounting the multiple injuries incurred alone is not the only necessary solution; timing is key as well. Psychoanalyst Robert Stolorow, drawing from the death of his wife, counsels that we need patience with ourselves and our inadequacies to better approach the trauma. He writes, "Painful emotional states become unbearable when they cannot find a context of emotional understanding—what I came to call a 'relational home'—in which they can be shared and held."[25] A relational home needs trust and a comforting ear to convey that which is most troubling to recount. This takes time and loving friends and family—all of whom are hurt in similar yet discrete ways. Trust, comfort, loving friends, and family are the ties that bind us together as a compassionate society.

From the preceding paragraphs, we cannot overemphasize this fact: As *personal* as trauma is, it is also *social*. Our institutions, too, need fresh eyes to reimagine our world in healthier ways. Political, social, philosophical, ethical, and legal theories need readjustment to correlate to our newfound needs. In this vein, we look for healthier social institutions. We take advice from philosophers, anthropologists, and sociologists. Hannah Arendt, familiar with trauma, discusses it in terms of new foundations of thinking. She argues that trauma evokes "philosophical shock," the very shock or wonder (*thaumazein*) that is at the origin of thinking and philosophy.[26] She understands that the shock of injury is related to the philosophical concept of wonder and thinking anew. Her enormously influential work *The Origins of Totalitarianism* presciently labors over the ways individual fears lead to communal ills.

Implicitly, she argues that we need to dispel fear and replace it with trusting relationships.

The relationship between individuals and society is unmistakable. Giles Deleuze discusses the way the subject is constituted through society; as François Zourabichvili explains, Deleuze understands the relationship as a matter of "affirming the relation of exteriority that links thought to what it thinks."[27] In other words, our interior life is never divorced from how we view the outside world. Conversely, the outside world is always infiltrating our interior life. Similarly, Catriona Mackenzie argues for relational models of autonomy and self that include self-conception, body image, and points of view of race, family, class, and other values.[28] As such, the person is socially situated. To wit, how we see the world, our point of view, and the way we conceive ourselves as persons are mirror images that are judged according to what matters most to ourselves. Reimagining oneself is, at the same time, reimaging society and vice versa. Reimaging or rethinking with compassion replaces distrust and fear with care and hope; we reimagine who we are.

Rethinking our lives as encountering our world with compassion at its heart will spark new thoughts of living more healthfully, possibly even more ethically. While never easy or simple, rethinking our dwelling is nonetheless quite valuable. Here, we shall rely upon Martin Heidegger's concept of dwelling and living in balance with ourselves and nature.[29] Heidegger weaves a circular narrative that clarifies: Dwelling rightly leads us to think rightly and thus to build rightly. Thinking rightly permits us to build rightly and to dwell rightly. Building rightly allows us to dwell rightly and to think rightly. Dwelling, for Heidegger, is relational living with nature, with ourselves, and with others. It is beyond mere coping or existing; it is always co-relational. But more intimate than relatedness, we are intertwined as individuals being with others. Society and individuals are coextensive. Any healing (or injury) that may occur is rooted in our (lack of) interdependence. Hence, the community's repair is of paramount concern.

Finally, François Raffoul, following Jean-Luc Marion, delineates the ways traumatic events are saturated phenomena that, at times, flood more experience into us than we can handle.[30] The saturated phenomenon is unbearable; that is, it has a super abundance of quality. Events such as trauma overwhelm the senses. It is natural to shut down, avoid the pain, and move on, but reflecting on the saturated experience will help articulate the overall experience. Such articulation of what is beyond our senses, making sense of non-sense is halting at first, involving coining words, reworking our vocabulary, and even reworking what is real and what is a false reality. Yet articulating and forging through non-sense is the only way toward understanding our livelihood in new ways of healthy living.

For a better understanding of this saturated experience, authors of diversity help pinpoint overwhelming problems and redirect our institutions toward repair. Accordingly, George Yancy unravels the complexity of the white gaze and the Black experience.[31] In his famous teaching story, "The Elevator," he textures the experiences of a large Black man and a frail white woman who clutches her handbag in the elevator as its doors close on the two of them. It simply is not sufficient to recognize the differing perspectives, Black versus white; rather, students are asked to embody the experiences and discuss their rendition of the story with each other. The ensuing dialogue binds the diverse students together into a multilayered account that is its own healing in its interrelatedness. Relational repair is necessary.

But more than relational repair is required. Ethical responses that inform new codes of conduct are crucial. Judith Butler reimagines our ethical stance of nonviolence.[32] Recounting Rev. Martin Luther King Jr. and Mahatma Gandhi, she explains that nonviolence is not simply a strategy but also a broader struggle for social equality. Nonviolence is not a passive practice that surfaces from a calm interior; rather, it appreciates the more violent side of our nature and holds this in tandem with our better tendencies. This poised ambivalence is a reality check. It sees clearly and yet acts rightly while holding both sides, injury and repair, together. Butler envisions the poison as part of the cure. Our ethical codes must reflect our truer nature and not simply be codes against transgressions; they must also include ideals to strive toward a positive future.

Acting rightly isn't simply asserting the mind over the body or controlling psychological drives. The whole person needs repair, the whole community needs attention, and our ethics need reworking to reflect a broader notion than individual rights set as paramount; otherwise, trauma and inequality become the new normal as we ethically look for ways that benefit us and ours. Ethics needs to engage not mere conduct but also compassion. Tina Chanter helps us to see the abyss between the extremes of conduct and compassion, of aesthetic and representational regimes (feelings and politics) that lead to trauma becoming the new normal. Segregating our feelings and aesthetic concerns from thought processes is part of the divide that leads to trauma. Chanter counsels us, as whole persons in a community, to a reintegration of siloed camps within ourselves as well as in the community. Reminiscent of Nietzsche, she argues for the cooperation of these psychic and social tendencies. Building bridges is key.[33] But debates widen the gap, and politics places us into camps. What are we to do?

Two examples can help us learn how to diminish these obstacles. The first is employing heroes. For example, Mahatma Gandhi tried in differing ways with mixed results to combat the oppression of the Raj: education and law, court battles, community activism, protests, sit-ins, and rallies. Again, these efforts had varying degrees of success. Not until he was a beloved national and international hero and threatened his own existence with a hunger strike was he able to bring the opposing forces into a movement of positive change. This is not to advocate hunger strikes but to illustrate that in extraordinary times when people cannot listen to one another because they are preoccupied with defending their camps, we need to find a way to help us listen. The mere thought of losing an esteemed person helped India and Britain reevaluate their positions and work toward a more just society. Listening occurred on the social register through Gandhi's insight and sacrifice because he was an esteemed hero, and his loss would have been unimaginably devastating.

The second example recounts listening at the personal register. Recently, several of us were at the lunch table. Our immigrant cook, masked for her own and our protection against COVID-19, asked us about our vaccination status. Nearly all were vaccinated, were boostered, and wore masks in public places, according to the recommendation of the CDC. But one, a young seminarian, did not believe the policy advocated was to his liking; in fact, thinking the policy was politically motivated, he thus refused to abide by its directives. Previously, each of us had tried to discuss this with him, to no avail. Our cook attempted to discuss the issue further at that lunch, only to be dismissed by the seminarian as being overly emotional. (I heard in his tone that he found her not too intelligent, evidenced by her broken English.) She broke into tears, explaining that she had nearly lost her husband to COVID-19. Only after a harrowing week of hospitalization did he begin to recover. She left the room quite distraught. Then the seminarian explained to us (rather incoherently) that his decision was personal and that Wall Street would disagree with her assessment of what is fitting for our nation. Even his bishop said the seminarian's decision was not merely personal and that his decisions can and do affect others adversely. Authority elicited no change. The seminarian looked at a third person at the lunch, who, without a full sentence, blurted out, "But her tears!" Then managing a full sentence, he said to the seminarian, "How does your response look in any way like the compassion of our God?" It finally dawned on the seminarian; later, he apologized to the cook and scheduled his vaccination. He now wears a mask in public places. Surprisingly, when emotion was tied to fundamental compassion, the seminarian changed his stance. This personal encounter initiated change.

In both instances, usual accounts of reason and persuasion alone aren't particularly helpful for transformation. Facts, debates, studies, and data seem counterproductive. What seems to work varies; it is always different in each situation. But change does seem to emerge spontaneously; it comprises emotions, fundamental principles, and the whole person, not simply reason.

In addition to these two ways that break through the impasse, the cry of the poor ultimately rings true. People of color and minorities are disproportionately the voices of the poor. Authors of diversity and stories of vulnerable people assist in repairing our political and social institutions. To hear these people's stories, we must engage them face-to-face. With their eyes, we experience their plight. In experiencing their plight, we are more apt to be moved toward compassionate actions.

Professionals of every stripe, who hear the voice of the marginalized and the vulnerable, are needed. Philosophers, psychologists, and sociologists, in their own way and in their respective fields of concern, must also be heeded; for as complex as trauma is, we need a complex set of answers. The narrow specialty of one area does not suffice. As Nietzsche counsels, we must engage all perspectives. The more eyes the better the perspective. Still, the voices that address the poor and marginalized sectors need easier access to share their concerns, for the poor and the vulnerable carry the heft of the burden.

THE IMPORTANCE OF NARRATIVE

Our last area of investigation involves this previous notion of saturated experience, of excess beyond our experiences. For a better understanding, theologians and poets attempt to narrate our story as one of repair. Placing the event in terms of meaning is also part of the repair. A narrative of growth and repair helps place our lives as a journey that is slow but one of healthy growth. Theologians are of particular help here. Shelly Rambo applies systematic and constructive theology to interpret contemporary issues of trauma. She places our current dilemma in relation to biblical stories that help to situate our problems in terms of a greater narrative of well-being.[34] Similarly, Scarsella focuses on trauma in terms of the brokenness of the Crucifixion.[35] In another approach, Marcia Mount Shoop focuses on the body instead of the intellectualization of narrative, as the body teaches us much of what we need to learn about trauma.[36] Poets, such as the American poet and activist Amanda Gorman, focus on traumatic issues of oppression, feminism, race, and marginalization, as well as on the African diaspora, in words that are not simply elegant but that also move us toward active healing practices. Lastly,

Pope Francis opens our eyes to our responsibility to the most vulnerable, including immigrants, and to our environment.[37] These theologians, religious thinkers, and poets attempt to negotiate this saturated experience and transform it into an enlightened one that compels us to act in healing ways. Narrative has a healing balm that gives any struggle long-term meaning and purpose beyond mere physical management.

More than empty fanciful words giving us false hope, narratives offer something more substantial. As we learned earlier, since trauma blurs memory and ties the body to triggered actions, healing requires recalling the words of our past and the places we inhabited to assist the recovered memories. This reconnects body to spirit. As difficult and painful as revisiting injury is, allowing another's assistance not only can ease the trauma but also builds relationships and ties communities together. Relationships forge trauma into an experience of trust, forging success over helplessness and turning unconscious recurring actions into helpful habits. Trigg invests heavily in this reworking of memory, bodily placement, and trust. Since our bodily identity is shaped through being touched by the past, he argues, holding onto the place of trauma can be itself the source of reattaching the body to the psyche and mind.[38] In the paradox of danger lies the saving grace.[39] Abiding with this danger, however, can only occur in a trusting relationship.

Thus, we see how theologians and poets, together with social activists, philosophers, politicians, psychologists, and psychoanalysts, will proffer helpful ways to understand trauma and fully engage ourselves in our traumatic event. Our era might very well be characterized as being an epoch of trauma or the epoch that faced it squarely. If we can bear our burden with others, we can begin to undergo our transforming repair both personally and as a community. Only then, with time, can we broach the words of gratitude wherein we offer a blessing instead of a curse, embrace dedication instead of isolation, and shape preservation instead of devastation. In perhaps all too facile phrasing, traumatic ontology argues that our way of being in trauma is also our way of being in health. From this, we can see a ray of hope through the fog of injury; from this, we can allow gratitude to surface. Just as trauma is remarkable in its resistance to integration, we must hold it fast and allow it to cauterize the wound. These are easy words; yet with courage, we can manage it, and with assistance from many trusted resources over time, we can thrive. Only then can we live in harmony together. This living is dwelling rightly wherein the mind, body, and spirit can thrive and become stronger, even during this vulnerable pandemic. Sometimes grief is what binds us together most strongly and fairly. Alternatively, trauma will warp us into persons and communities that further wound and traumatize.

Merleau-Ponty is correct: We cannot reason ourselves through non-sense. He is also quite correct that striving for meaning is in itself the essence of the journey toward recovery, making sense of the non-sense. Perhaps now, more than in any previous era, we will be able to reclaim ourselves as inter-dependent persons in community: our minds, bodies, and spirits, whole persons dwelling together, healing our fractured world by truly listening to the poorest of the poor. Transformation can occur at the individual, societal, or epochal registers if we try to make sense of the non-sense—that is, if we listen and respond to more than mere argument and reason, and instead engage the whole person and persons, and think *sensibly*. As we revisit our injuries, let us take bold measures to repair while we cautiously hope, for in our danger lies our saving grace.

NOTES

1. I am grateful to Tamsin Jones for this reference from Merleau-Ponty. Jones, "Can Victims Make Sense," 847.
2. I borrow this phrase from Richard Polt, *Time and Trauma*. See below for a detailed discussion.
3. Scarsella, "Trauma and Theology," in Boynton and Capretto, *Trauma and Transcendence*, 256.
4. Trigg, *Memory of Place*, 239. Emphasis in original.
5. Caruth, *Unclaimed Experience*, 62.
6. Trigg, *Memory of Place*, 282.
7. WHO, "COVID-19 Dashboard."
8. American Psychiatric Association, *Diagnostic and Statistical Manual*, 271.
9. North et al., "Toward Validation."
10. The most common event that can trigger derealization is emotional abuse or neglect at a young age. The experience prompts the child to detach from their surroundings as a way to manage the trauma, such is the severity of the disorder. For particular symptoms and diagnosis, see Hunter, Charlton, and David, "Depersonalisation and Derealisation."
11. Hunter, Sierra, and David, "Epidemiology of Depersonalization."
12. Harrison, "People of Color Suffer."
13. Harrison.
14. Di Nicola, "Two Trauma Communities," in Boynton and Capretto, *Trauma and Transcendence*, 18.
15. Polt, *Time and Trauma*, 7.
16. Di Nicola, "Two Trauma Communities," in Boynton and Capretto, *Trauma and Transcendence*, 23.
17. Bloom, " Elephant in the Room," in Bergo and Golden, *Trauma Controversy*, 147–48.

18. Herman, "Crime and Memory," in Bergo and Golden, *Trauma Controversy*, 130.
19. Ryan Lucas, "FBI Data Shows an Unprecedented Spike in Murders Nationwide in 2020," All Things Considered, NPR, September 27, 2021, https://www.npr.org/2021/09/27/1040904770/fbi-data-murder-increase-2020.
20. World Bank, "U.S. Murder/Homicide Rate."
21. Lucas, "FBI Data."
22. Orange, "Traumatized by Transcendence," in Boynton and Capretto, *Trauma and Transcendence*, 71.
23. Davoine and Gaudillière, *History beyond Trauma*, 13. See Wittgenstein, *Tractatus Logico-Philosophicus*, 85. My emphasis.
24. Wiesel, *Night*, 34.
25. Stolorow, "Phenomenological-Contextualism," in Boynton and Capretto, *Trauma and Transcendence*, 54.
26. Arendt, "What Is Existential Philosophy?," in *Essays in Understanding*.
27. Zourabichvili, *Deleuze*, 51. See also Deleuze, *Empiricism and Subjectivity*, 98–99.
28. Mackenzie, "Imagining Oneself Otherwise," in Mackenzie and Stoljar, *Relational Autonomy*, 124–26.
29. Heidegger, "Building Dwelling Thinking," in *Poetry, Language, Thought*.
30. Raffoul, *Thinking the Event*, 98.
31. Yancy, "Elevator Effect," in *Black Bodies, White Gazes*.
32. Butler, *Force of Non-Violence*.
33. Chanter, "Artful Politics of Trauma," in Boynton and Capretto, *Trauma and Transcendence*, 121.
34. Rambo, *Spirit and Trauma*.
35. Scarsella, "Trauma and Theology," in Boynton and Capretto, *Trauma and Transcendence*, 256.
36. Shoop, "Body-Wise," in Boynton and Capretto, *Trauma and Transcendence*, 240.
37. Francis, *Laudato si'*, §§104–8.
38. Trigg, *Memory of Place*, 27.
39. This phrase is a rendering from Heidegger and his reflection on Hölderlin's poem "Patmos," in "Question Concerning Technology," in *Question Concerning Technology*.

BIBLIOGRAPHY

American Psychiatric Association. *Diagnostic and Statistical Manual of Mental Disorders* (*DSM-5*). 5th ed. Washington DC: American Psychiatric Association, 2013.

Arendt, Hannah. "What Is Existential Philosophy?" In *Essays in Understanding, 1930–1954: Formation, Exile, and Totalitarianism*, edited and translated by Jerome Kohn, 163–87. New York: Harcourt, Brace, 1994.

Bloom, Sandra L. "An Elephant in the Room: The Impact of Traumatic Stress on Individuals and Groups." In *The Trauma Controversy: Philosophical and Interdisciplinary Dialogues*, edited by Bettina Bergo and Kristen Brown Golden, ch. 8. Albany: State University of New York Press, 2009.

Boynton, Eric, and Peter Capretto, eds. *Trauma and Transcendence: Suffering and the Limits of Theory*. New York: Fordham Press, 2018.

Butler, Judith. *The Force of Non-Violence: An Ethico-Political Bind.* London: Verso, 2020.

Caruth, Cathy. *Unclaimed Experience: Trauma, Narrative, and History*. Baltimore: Johns Hopkins University Press, 1996.

Chanter, Tina. "The Artful Politics of Trauma: Rancière's Critique of Lyotard." In Boynton and Capretto, *Trauma and Transcendence*, ch. 6.

Davoine, Françoise, and Jean-Max Gaudillière. *History beyond Trauma: Whereof One Cannot Speak, Thereof One Cannot Stay Silent.* New York: Other Press, 2004.

Deleuze, Giles. *Empiricism and Subjectivity: An Essay on Hume's Theory of Human Nature.* Translated by Constantin Boundas. New York: Columbia University Press, 1991.

Di Nicola, Vincenzo. "Two Trauma Communities: A Philosophical Archaeology of Cultural and Clinical Trauma Theories." In Boynton and Capretto, *Trauma and Transcendence*, ch. 1.

Harrison, Rick. "Health Notes: People of Color Suffer Disproportionate Impact of COVID-19 Pandemic." Yale School of Medicine, September 2, 2020. https://medicine.yale.edu/news-article/health-notes-people-of-color-suffer-disproportionate-impact-of-covid-19-pandemic/.

Heidegger, Martin. "Building Dwelling Thinking." In *Poetry, Language, Thought*, 145–61. Translated by Albert Hofstadter. New York: Harper and Row, 1975.

———. "The Question Concerning Technology." In *The Question Concerning Technology and Other Essays*, 4–35. Translated by and William Lovett. New York: Harper & Row, 1977.

Herman, Judith Lewis. "Crime and Memory." In *The Trauma Controversy: Philosophical and Interdisciplinary Dialogues*, edited by Bettina Bergo and Kristen Brown Golden, ch. 7. Albany: State University of New York Press, 2009.

Hunter, Elaine C., Jane Charlton, and Anthony S. David. "Depersonalisation and Derealisation: Assessment and Management." *British Medical Journal* 356 (2017). https://www.jstor.org/stable/26949815.

Hunter, E. C., M. Sierra, and A. S. David. "The Epidemiology of Depersonalization and Derealization: A Systematic Review." *Social Psychiatry and Psychiatric Epidemiology* 39, no. 1 (January 2004): 9–18. https://doi.org/10.1007/s00127-004-0701-4.

Jones, Tamsin. "Can Victims Make Sense of Trauma?" *Philosophy Today* 65, no. 4 (Fall 2021): 847–61. https://doi.org 10.5840/philtoday202183423.

Mackenzie, Catriona. "Imagining Oneself Otherwise." In *Relational Autonomy: Feminist Perspectives on Autonomy, Agency, and the Social Self*, edited by Catriona Mackenzie and Natalie Stoljar, 124–26. Oxford: Oxford University Press, 2000.

Merleau-Ponty, Maurice. *Sense and Non-Sense*. Evanston IL: Northwestern University Press, 1971.

North, Carol, Alina M. Suris, Miriam Davis, and Rebecca Pringle Smith. "Toward Validation of the Diagnosis of Posttraumatic Stress Disorder." *American Journal of Psychiatry* 166, no. 1 (January 2009): 34–41. https://doi.org/10.1176/appi.ajp.2008.08050644.

Orange, Donna. "Traumatized by Transcendence: My Other's Keeper." In Boynton and Capretto, *Trauma and Transcendence*, ch. 3.

Polt, Richard F. H. *Time and Trauma: Thinking through Heidegger in the Thirties*. New York: Rowman & Littlefield, 2019.

Raffoul, François. *Thinking the Event*. Bloomington: Indiana University Press, 2020.

Rambo, Shelly. *Spirit and Trauma: A Theology of Remaining*. Louisville KY: Westminster John Knox Press, 2010.

Scarsella, Hilary Jerome. "Trauma and Theology: Prospects and Limits in Light of the Cross." In Boynton and Capretto, *Trauma and Transcendence*, ch. 12.

Shoop, Marcia Mount. "Body-Wise: Re-Fleshing Christian Spiritual Practice in Trauma's Wake." In Boynton and Capretto, *Trauma and Transcendence*, ch. 11.

Simeon, Daphne, and Jeffrey Abugel. *Feeling Unreal: Depersonalization Disorder and the Loss of the Self.* Oxford: Oxford University Press, 2006.

Stolorow, Robert D. "Phenomenological-Contextualism All the Way Down: An Existential and Ethical Perspective on Emotional Trauma." In Boynton and Capretto, *Trauma and Transcendence*, ch. 2.

Trigg, Dylan. *The Memory of Place: A Phenomenology of the Uncanny.* Athens: Ohio University Press, 2012.

———. "The Uncanny." In *The Routledge Handbook of Phenomenology of Emotion*, edited by Thomas Szanto and Hilge Landweer, ch. 47. London: Routledge, 2020.

Wiesel Elie. *Night.* Translated and edited by Marion Wiesel. New York: Hill and Wang, 2006.

Wittgenstein, Ludwig. *Tractatus Logico-Philosophicus.* Translated by Gilles-Gaston Granger. New York: Harcourt, Brace, 2012.

World Bank. "U.S. Murder/Homicide Rate 1960–2024." Accessed January 6, 2024. https://www.macrotrends.net/countries/USA/united-states/murder-homicide-rate.

World Health Organization. "WHO COVID-19 Dashboard." Accessed October 20, 2024. https://data.who.int/dashboards/covid19/deaths?n=c.

Yancy, George. "The Elevator Effect: Black Bodies/White Bodies." In *Black Bodies, White Gazes: The Continuing Significance of Race in America*, 17–50. 2nd ed. Lanham MD: Rowman & Littlefield, 2017.

Zourabichvili, François. *Deleuze, a Philosophy of the Event: Together with the Vocabulary of Deleuze.* Edinburgh: Edinburgh University Press, 2012.

CHAPTER 11

Our Pandemic Age, Relationships, and Forgetting

Michael Reid Trice

In October 2019 the first seeds were planted for a collaborative, interdisciplinary, and interreligious project titled "Gratitude to God, Sacred Texts, Injury, and Restoration," to be hosted by the Center for Ecumenical and Interreligious Engagement (CEIE) at Seattle University. In its original pre-COVID form, the project's director would ask scholars to research and write on what religious traditions teach about the relationship between the human and the divine when life is personally and societally painful. How are rituals restorative, and which stories assist in times of adversity? What sacred texts locate human experience in gratitude, even in what appears to be an ambivalent, if not unjust, universe?

Once scholars met in April 2021, a bit more than a year after the World Health Organization declared COVID-19 a global pandemic, a fourth term was added to the project to clarify our moment, a "pandemic age." The addition was a response to the worldwide human experience of being inundated with injury and death brought on by the virus. As well, the circumstances of the pandemic revealed qualities of contagia seemingly culturally incurable and socially intractable, such as systemic racism, xenophobia, ethnoreligious nationalism, misogyny, and casteism. Through the viral pandemic, awareness increased of other epidemic states and contributed to the scholars' changing "restoration" to "repair" in the project's title. The scholars agreed to this further change because, given the scale of suffering and death through the COVID virus, and the uneven impact of the virus upon Black and Brown bodies, *repairing* what was broken felt historically more honest than *restoration,* a term that whitewashed the history of structural racism in the American experience. The previously added phrase "pandemic age" grew in importance as a context for the scholars' writing.

"Pandemic age," signaled to scholar and reader alike that the project was not undertaken in a normal time. Instead, the emergence of COVID-19 marked a time of significant uncertainty in the world with uneven degrees of personal threat, loss, and death. A pandemic is not a univocal experience for an individual or the entire population, and over a three-year period, it became many experiences for an individual person. Even with people's different experiences of a pandemic across time, broadly shared characteristics emerged, such as fatigue, loss, and under-metabolized grief, as well as differing renditions—including financial, relational, or literal—of the grave. People reported feeling disproportionately estranged both from others and from their own sense of the world. Life was interrupted by an unexpected private and public trauma, the consequences of which were moments of personal and societal incoherence, a marker of significant traumatic impact. Indeed, as Kristi Lee forecasts in chapter 9, the psychological, spiritual, and existential dissonance will be evident for years to come through the steep incline of post-COVID psychiatric and other forms of clinical and medical care needs within society.

A pandemic age is a time of crisis. It is not reduceable to a viral pandemic, although the abrupt shock of COVID-19 caused society to recognize numerous corollary epidemic situations. True to point, some of the scholars involved in the project named the epidemic states early on as pivotal to the project and wrote about them for their contributions to this volume.

Throughout the project, scholars pointed to at least two features of crisis in our pandemic age. What follows in this chapter is a religious studies assessment of these two features and how religious worldviews share goals to *prevent* and to *heal* crises even amid a pandemic age. The aim of these pages is neither causal nor correlative. I do not argue that if humans cared more for nature and one another then the viral pandemic would not have taken place. Instead, I invite the reader to consider what religious worldviews have long said about two common features of personal and societal crises, including what religions' suggestions are about how crises of this kind may be prevented and even healed. The teachings hold true for endemics whose viral epidemiology is biological (such as COVID-19) or systemic (such as structural racism). The last claim—that is, to heal—suggests to us that how we finally come through our pandemic age, the poly-crisis of our time, is not predetermined and that religious worldviews also offer humanity actionable choices that require our moral and collective agency.

A first feature of our pandemic age is an overwhelming public response of psychological, existential, and cognitive incoherence and estrangement. Dislocation of this magnitude develops when assumptions about how the world works—what is calculable, reasonable, sustainable, or meaningful—are no longer verifiable or match evidence external to us. How ironic, Douglas Peduti suggests to us, that we exist today more than ever in a technologically sophisticated time unlike any before, and yet the structures that normally render life calculable, manageable, and reasonable seem unable to provide a sustainable and coherent, unified narrative that reassures people they are safe in a physical, natural environment undergoing severe change. In the first four months of 2020, the COVID-19 virus killed twice as many people in the United States (over 130,000) as the total accounted deaths of US servicemen and women through the Vietnam War (58,000). By 2023, 1.1 million people in the United States had perished due to COVID-19, and nearly 7 million died around the world. Today, we see clinical depression, heightened suicidal ideation, and hospitalization at soberingly young ages, and we also witness a rise in domestic violence, gun violence, and mass shootings.[1] Society is enduring a precipitous rise in separatist tensions evident in hate speech and public displays of planned violence, both domestic and abroad, *and* a concurrent growth in the resurgence of ideological identity groups around the world. At the very least, humanity is responding to prolonged stress, exhibiting behavior expected of populations that feel uncertain and unsafe, with millions of people projecting these emotions onto the world around them.[2]

Two further examples of incoherence are identified in this volume. The first is a grown disconnection from many of the established truths of democratic governance, such that they are no longer self-evident and so unable convincingly to adjudicate societal normative values and public conduct based upon a shared vision of communal well-being. In chapter 4, James Spickard details the historical emergence of national and ideological trends in the spirit of the American experience to the present day. He is careful to underscore the threat to civil liberties that are heightened in the COVID-19 pandemic. This careful historical work is necessary if we are to understand why these truths are not providing a convincing corrective to many of the stark ideological divisions growing around us.

The second incoherence is that the enduring authoritative, religious truths that informed a constitutive sense of well-being essential to flourishing societies are less trusted now as new, aberrant, religious nationalist movements emerge in the world.[3] A case in point is how the Christian moral imperative to care for the marginalized has been transformed into an imperative to ameliorate the self-declared suffering of the white patriot within Christian nationalism. For Edward Donalson, the too easy dislocation of those at the margins is part of the epidemic quality of systemic injuries that relegates the marginalized to what sociologists term moral "death zones." Death zones encompass entire peoples in the world who are displaced into inhabitable geographic spaces and so rendered unable to foster opportunities for viable lives or livelihoods. Adding the perspectival distance of a millennia, Nathanael Vette helps the reader to see how a whole community—in this case, the Jewish community of Ezra 4—was marginalized, misinterpreted, and then scapegoated for centuries. He reveals how scapegoating has an epidemic quality in that a marginalized community will be transvalued into a cultural pollutant for reasons that are historically forgotten and incoherent in the present. Yet incoherence, with its estrangement and displacement, has lasting impact and implications for individuals and society today and even long into the future.

The scholars in this study identify a second feature of our pandemic age as a struggle with impermanence and finitude. They agree that humans construct calculable, meaningful, coherent worlds that feel safe and serve their interests, *and* that we mistake our temporary control for comprehensive power and agency. In chapter 5, Susan Abraham interrogates our post-modern hubris and frenetic self-distraction through self-exploitation.

The viral pandemic age reminded human beings of the limits of assumed control and the nature of impermanence; we are finite and limited. Mona Siddiqui writes in chapter 1 that the virus "has forced us to acknowledge the lack of human control and finitude."[4] Patricia O'Connell Killen, in chapter 2, notes how the experience of COVID-19 shook every "material, psychic, social, and spiritual" dimension of our lives, rupturing the ruse of impermeability like the magma blasting off the northern face of a mountain. Using the violent eruption of Mount St. Helens in 1980 as her prism for the impact of COVID-19, Killen says we are "unable to weave a fabric of coherent meaning to what humanity and the earth are undergoing."

Our age, marked by incoherence, estrangement, and a struggle with the limits of finitude, is an age of tragic existence; yet these same features also invite consideration of a religious worldview's core spiritual truths that are intended to help *prevent* and *heal* human crises, including the crisis of a pandemic age.

Religious worldviews often opt for the strength of relationships that hold a meaningful universe intact. Love that does justice, truth from a heart of deeper unity, an understanding of personal suffering, meditative ritual, and kindness toward others—all are motifs on the theme of *relationship* in religious worldviews. Humans endure deep loneliness, injustices are entrenched in society, and enculturated biases repress whole communities, and no simple appeal to *relationship* mitigates these hardships or realities. The chapters also reveal what we likewise know: Absent relationships of understanding, strategic empathy, or a commitment to structural repair, trustful dialogue, and retrieving dangerous memories, there is little hope for healing.

Religions attest to two kinds of relationships: a relationship to others in the world around us and a relationship to the transcendent (to the divine, to God, or to mystery). A relationship to and within the world creates neighbors and neighborliness, which aids in refining shared values, moral codes of conduct, stories, customs, traditions, and cosmologies. They help render the world meaningful, calculable, and safe to a degree that communities can plan and aspire for the horizon of a future together. In agrarian terms, communities sow with the prudent expectation of harvesting together; the season of growth in between provides a resource of security and hope. Religious worldviews also teach how a relationship to the transcendent may provide balance to human existence. Consider the Christian Orthodox concept of kenosis, a personal practice of surrendering one's own ambition in favor of a listening form of discernment or meditative technique. Most often, practices such as kenosis are understood as a way of being wakeful to the infinite while aware that being finite limits one from knowing mystery in any complete form.

Religious traditions feature rich and varied explanations of the relationship to the transcendent, ranging from the Brahman ontology of the self to the Sunyata, or the void accounted for in Jain, Hindu, and Buddhist philosophy. In most of these accounts, reference to the transcendent mystery of the cosmos is to a subjective presence or cosmological deity. Religious worldviews remind human beings there is something untamed and wild in transcendent mystery that produces wonder and *awe*, a specific dimension of reverence that is only partially comprehended. For instance, Genesis 1:1 assures the listener that infinite mystery is everywhere before and after the beginning of time: "Darkness rules over the surface of the deep."[5] Religious worldviews bear in common how human beings—our relationships and our lives, our joys and distortions, and our hopes and failures—exist within a boundary situation of finitude, circumscribed by untamed mystery that precedes our coming and going, and is not under our control.[6]

Taken together, these two essential relationships tell us about much more than moral codes and the limits of finitude. Religious worldviews reveal both how relationships require self-transcendence and how individual narcissism leads to existential, psychological, and spiritual pain. For *this* individual, the true value and needs of others become less noticeable or recognizable; the systemic endemics within society also become less noticeable. Indeed, whole societies learn to endure injustices all around, granting them a moral sheen of permissibility or normalcy. A personal trauma or societal crisis, such as COVID-19, disrupts this dynamic. It awakens a recognition of others that may thereafter awaken empathy and, later, one day help explain some of the intractable sources of human isolation.

Religious worldviews exhibit a preferential option for strong interpersonal relationships and a connection to mystery; in so doing, they open a creative possibility for interpreting our personal and social lives, and the fragile riot of life amid all the things over which we have little, if any, control.[7] In addition, religions ask human beings to transcend themselves to understand not only individual and social relationships but also, if we are fortunate, the long history of human relationality that predates all of us.[8]

Humans have used grave goods for just over 100,000 years; for four thousand generations, those in our line of DNA have gathered and practiced ritual events of some proto-religious or religious communal significance. Across time, space, and culture, human beings never stopped the practice. Examples include a handprint stenciled in pigment blown through hollow bones, or gods chiseled into rock, or names spoken aloud or written in text. Today we inherit eons of relationship with one another and with mystery. Sometimes God is a sparrow hewn into a stone or spoken as the image of a whirlwind. Our forebears learned about failure through a flood, about resilience through a swarm, and about a community's rebirth through breath permeating dry bones strewn on a desert floor. Innumerable crises are averted, or succumbed to, in heeding or avoiding relationships.

One final word on the wisdom of religious worldviews regarding relationships: Religious worldviews will speak of two essential relationships, not in a binary way, but in a unified, seamless manner such that the experience of the transcendent, or of mystery, is both in and beyond the world. The finite and infinite never fully exhaust each other, either; so within the finite, uncontrollable beat of human life is a deep, abiding sense of infinite co-creation. Perhaps the truths of a religious response to crisis are best articulated by poets, artists, songwriters, and every person with a care to believe that there is, *after all*, a core mystery that requires deep inquiry and valuation by us and, *second*, that relationships matter, along with a sense of empathetic connection and a spark of gratitude for the lives of others around us . . . and even a surprising sense of gratitude to the universe for the immensity of it all.[9]

Relationships are critical to this study. Equally important are the essential themes of forgetting and forgetfulness. Forgetting the value of others is a persistent human propensity to which we succumb often enough to cause dire problems. Religious worldviews, which emphasize relationships as essential to assisting human beings with respect to personal and societal crises, also place prohibitions against forgetting one's sibling for the same reason.[10] The moral proximity of others as strangers or siblings differs across religious cosmologies. Illuminative on this point is the Buddhist precept that the entire universe is contained in a singular human subject, as the ocean is contained in a drop of water or all life within a sibling. Religious worldviews suggest the distance between negligence and murder is the forgetting of the two core truths of one's relationship to others and to the transcendent.

Sacred canons are replete with prohibitions against murder, often with divine recrimination and consequences for forgetfulness that will involve social exile of the offender. In the case of God's condemnation of Cain's murder of Abel, the earth serves as a whistleblower: "Your brother's blood is crying to me from the ground."[11]

In oppressive systems, no deus ex machina or similar dramatic contrivance saves the day of the neglected and forgotten. In their unique ways, the scholars of this study responded to oppressive organizational structures. The chapters unmask how systemic injustice breeds forgetfulness and buries human beings by creating incoherence. Douglas Peduti clarifies how we cannot have absolute certainty over "non-sense," and Susan Abraham takes up the current theme of "burnout society" and the postmodern attempt to escape the system through social media, radical solipsism, or the self-achievement society in which we become "entrepreneurs of ourselves."[12] They are responding to a form of forgetfulness that pervades human creation and organization of systems.

This is of particular concern because everything human beings organize, with an intention that it will last, fits into a system. Systems are resilient, are self-perpetuating, and become both less nimble and more hierarchical with age. They also exhibit tendencies toward the uneven distribution of equity, generating long-term marginalization. Systems are coherent, linear human constructions in a nonlinear natural universe that aim to be precise and yet *always* miss the mark; consequently, systems are constructed in such a manner as to conceal weaknesses. They are armed with self-protective mechanisms in the present and are provided with predictive abilities for minding their own best interests in the future. To endure, systems require an internal grammar of compliance, or "bounded rationality," for determining rational choices now that will protect the systems tomorrow. Bounded rationality is what allows flagrant injustices to disappear within a system: The unsheltered, the hungry, the disposed, and the beaten are all part of a manageable minority, while societal racism, casteism, misogyny, or genocide are all present within overlapping systems in ways so long enculturated and assumed as to be invisible. While not all systems are bad, when they are—as when they elicit fear and inordinate self-protection in times of societal stress or the crisis of a pandemic—they can be a horror. Scholars note how, throughout the viral pandemic, global indexes revealed the rise of hate groups and nationalist ideologies; the emergence of old discriminatory tropes targeted at Asian Americans, Jews, Hindus, Sikhs, and Muslims; and the forging of common cause among groups that exist at the fringes of dominant systems.

Even though systems are resilient, when suffering becomes intolerable in society, human beings have difficulty squaring linear responses with their experience of the world. For example, police brutality does not align with constitutional democracy, the death of children is incongruent with the story of a loving God, and so on. Given a large enough impact, such as that of a pandemic, allegiance to former truths weaken, and a spiritual crisis ensues. Leaders who are promoting a healthier vision of a religious worldview will of necessity reject oppressive systems or risk losing trust.[13]

Forgetting one's neighbor either in our everyday relationships or through failing to experience their needs concealed within unfair systems requires a response, and religious worldviews aim to do so in the manner clarified above. Remembering and caring for one's neighbor is essential to a healthy life, and it requires a world where one's self and the neighbor are not forgotten or concealed but instead included in a larger story of importance that makes use of transcendence, mystery, and the wonder and awe of the cosmos around us.

In a spiritual crisis, human beings have two basic options to respond: *give up* or *give in*. The first option, to give up, would be to accept positions such as those of psychotherapist Francis Weller, who writes that we exist in a "death-dealing, nature-consuming, hell-bent-on-our-collective-demise society"—a defeatist acceptance of struggle that, Weller says, will become an "apprenticeship with sorrow."[14] Many may feel like giving up in the face of great odds. For instance, global crises are such today that a new term, "polycrisis," is used to categorize the plurality of what the World Economic Forum calls the top ten risks facing the world today. The quantitative amassing of crises into an epidemic cluster introduces new emanations of disequilibrium and estrangement. We live at an axis of systemic ruptures with no unidirectional means of solving the incoherence and pain of our time. Scholars signal concern for irresolvable tensions in their chapters. They agree we have entered a new age, and yet we have never considered giving up. Religious worldviews also do not have a language of surrender; even martyrdom is giving in *toward* something.

The second option in a spiritual crisis, to give in, is to follow the direction of the project's scholars, beginning with Kristi Lee's understanding of trauma and with Patricia O'Connell Killen's reflections on injury caused by a volcanic blast: "The mountain says that recovery does not come from outside, but from within. It is what is left behind that matters."[15] If there is a shared learning from the scholars' work in this volume, it is that the whole effort toward healing comes from surprising places and often at the site of injury. The work therefore must start from within, which requires giving and recommitting ourselves. Life, rebirth, repair from trauma, and all forms of healing will emerge first from the sites of war and wound, where the localized stories began amid pain and loss. The form of giving *in* required is the surrender of oneself through relationship by observing, witnessing, listening, learning, and responding to the experiences of others.

Our juridical structures, economic systems, means of access to general resources, vast wealth disparities, massive inadequacies in medical care, continued genocide, pitted sovereignties, childhood predation and human trafficking, and global pockets of hunger and starvation—all are signals that we constructed a world that thrives on deficit forms of relationship spending, or forgetting.

What is left behind, what matters, is something none of us can control. What matters is the life of another. The new normal is already clear, if nongovernmental organizations, universities, philanthropic agencies, and additional agencies are correct: We are in a crisis within crises. Amid so much that is unknown, our future direction is also unmistakable: The only way forward is to *give in* to relationships with one another and, in so doing, to seek deeper cause in the world that requires our mutual fidelity, faith, and trust.

NOTES

1. According to the World Health Organization, depression—or that "gray drizzle of horror," as William Styron refers to it—is the leading global cause of disability, from which more than 300 million people of all ages suffer. In the United States, these numbers are rising among the young.
2. The American Psychological Association reported in 2022 that around the world, the COVID-19 pandemic led to an increase in loneliness, which "constitutes a risk of premature mortality and mental and physical health."
3. Ernest Becker, *The Denial of Death* (London: Free Press, 1973), 33.
4. Siddiqui provided an insightful keynote presentation for the Conference on Gratitude, Injury, and Repair in a Pandemic Age that provided the basis for her chapter.
5. Human identity enters the cosmos through the mystery of the deep, and our classic Western narratives reveal we are resilient and fragile, heroic, and tragic, and born into relationships from the womb. Our project remains in the religious creation narrative of the Hebrew tradition, in clarifying what theologians understand as a *primary* spiritual relationship typified in the phrase *imago Dei* (Gen 1:26–27), which seeks to know and be known by the darkness first.
6. Rudolph Otto understood this relationship as the *mysterium tremendum et fascinans*, experienced first as awe and wonder at the mystery of the cosmos and what he believed to be experienced with some similitude across religions and cultures. Theologians and philosophers have long pondered the proximal height and depth of what can be known between the first mover and the human moved, and always in ways supersaturated in relationship.
7. See Hans Blumenberg, *Shipwreck with Spectator: Paradigm of a Metaphor for Existence* (London: MIT Press, 1997) for one of the more stirring existential metaphors for the realities of finitude.
8. See Alexei V. Nesteruk, *The Sense of the Universe: Philosophical Explication of Theological Commitment in Modern Cosmology* (Minneapolis: Fortress Press, 2015), 469–80. Nesteruk's "saturated universe" helps the reader understand one's relationship or proximity to the immensity of the universe as a phenomenon and not mere ideation.
9. Martin Heidegger was asked in his final interview (*Der Spiegel*) if he believed in God. He replied that he believed in "the god of the poets." It wasn't the first time that philosophers and theologians at the close of their careers felt that all they could say about the noumenal was little more than, "Straw," which was indeed Thomas Aquinas's own assessment of his own theology.
10. Our forgetfulness brings harmful consequences in the form of additional spiritual injuriousness, to which religious and wisdom traditions also attest. These include accounts of fratricide, often taking place after creation itself, as is the case with the Hebrew story of Cain's slaying his brother Abel. The Mesopotamian epic *Gilgamesh* reveals all homicide to be an act of fratricide, in which murder is the boundary of forgetting a fundamental truth, and *simplest* equation, about the nature of the human being's relationship to others.
11. John of the Cross, *Dark Night of the Soul* (New York: Image, 1990, 104–05). A sixteenth-century priest, Saint John also reflects upon the trial of Job and this point of distance from God in the cosmos.

12. See Abraham's chapter 5, "On Not Letting a Pandemic Go to Waste: Theory for the Sick and Dying." Abraham quotes Korean-German philosopher Byung-Chul Han's *The Burnout Society*. See also Martin Heidegger, *The Question Concerning Technology and Other Essays*, ed. William Lovitt (London: Harper Touchbooks, 1977), 5. "The current conception of technology . . . can therefore be allied with the instrumental or anthropological definition of technology. . . . Technology conditions every attempt to bring man into the right relation to technology."
13. See Donella H. Meadows, *Thinking in Systems*, ed. Diana Write (White River Junction VT: Chelsea Green Publishing, 2008). This text is still the standard in master of business administration programs around the United States and a primer for systems thinkers.
14. Francis Weller, *The Wild Edge of Sorrow* (Berkeley: North Atlantic Books, 2015), 137.
15. Killen is citing Robin Kimmerer, "On the Ridge," in *In the Blast Zone: Catastrophe and Renewal on Mount St. Helens*, ed. Charles Goodrich, Kathleen Dean Moore, and Frederick J. Swanson (Corvallis: Oregon State University Press, 2008), 44, 43, 45, 46.

CONTRIBUTORS

Susan Abraham is the professor of theology and postcolonial cultures, the vice president of academic affairs, and the dean of faculty at the Pacific School of Religion, Berkeley, California. She is the author of *Blessed Are Those Who Mourn: Depression, Anxiety and Pain on the Path of an Incarnational Spirituality* (Marymount Press, 2020) and *Identity, Ethics, and Nonviolence in Postcolonial Theory: A Rahnerian Theological Assessment* (Palgrave Macmillan, 2007). She is also the coeditor of *Frontiers in Catholic Feminist Theology: Shoulder to Shoulder* (Fortress, 2009). She is president of the Board of Editors of *Concilium* and the current vice president of the Catholic Theological Society of America.

Edward Donalson III is the director of doctor of ministry program for the School of Theology and Ministry of Seattle University, Washington. A professor, author, thought coach, and multimedia personality, the Right Reverend Donalson is a visionary with a dynamic message of empowerment. Born in Philadelphia, Pennsylvania, and cultivated in Seattle as a bicoastal youth, he developed a heart for diversity and an ability to navigate all socioeconomic, educational, and ethnic spheres. Traveling nationally as a guest lecturer, workshop clinician, and preacher since 1996, he is a constructive theologian with a liberative lens. His scholarship centers intersectional theology as an emerging discipline.

Jaisy A. Joseph is an assistant professor of theology and religious studies at Villanova University, Pennsylvania. With interests primarily in ecclesiology and theological anthropology, her main areas of research involve understandings of unity and difference in the Catholic Church, how these definitions have shifted over the centuries, and how erroneous expressions have wounded the bonds of communion between different peoples.

Patricia O'Connell Killen is professor of religion, emerita, and a faculty research fellow in the Division of Humanities at Pacific Lutheran University,

Tacoma, Washington. A historian and theologian, Killen's scholarship focuses on Christianity in North America, religion and spirituality in the Pacific Northwest, and mission and identity in faith-inspired higher education. She is the coeditor of *Religion at the Edge: Nature, Spirituality, and Secularity in the Pacific Northwest* (University of British Columbia Press, 2022) and of *The Future of Catholicism in America* (Columbia University Press, 2019).

Kristi A. Lee is an associate professor of clinical mental health counseling at Seattle University, Washington. In her role, she teaches a human development course using service learning and has collaborated on over seventy community-based projects with students and community partners. Kristi is the director of the Academic Service-Learning Faculty Fellows Program, which trains faculty in the pedagogy of service learning. In addition, she serves on the leadership team of the Seattle University ADVANCE program, working to bring equity to faculty promotion guidelines for women and faculty of color.

Douglas F. Peduti, SJ, is a professor of philosophy and scholar in residence of the Simon Silverman Phenomenology Center at Duquesne University, Pittsburgh, Pennsylvania. Born and raised on a farm in the Pittsburgh area, Peduti enjoys hiking in the great outdoors and the spiritual strength that it implicitly shelters. Interested in religious life, he entered the Jesuits in 1983 and was ordained as a Jesuit priest in 1996. His academic and ministerial focus is on bridging the religious, cultural, and linguistic depths of the human spirit and experience.

Anantanand Rambachan is professor emeritus of religion at Saint Olaf College, Northfield, Minnesota. He was also a visiting professor at the Academy for the Study of World Religions at the University of Hamburg, Germany (2013–17). His books include *Pathways to Hindu-Christian Dialogue* (Fortress Press, 2022); *Essays in Hindu Theology* (Fortress Press, 2019); *A Hindu Theology of Liberation: Not-Two Is Not One* (SUNY Press, 2015); *The Advaita Worldview: God, World, and Humanity* (SUNY Press, 2006); *The Limits of Scripture: Vivekananda's Reinterpretation of the Authority of the Vedas* (University of Hawaii Press, 1994); and *Accomplishing the Accomplished: The Vedas as a Source of Valid Knowledge in Śankara* (University of Hawaii Press, 1991).

Mona Siddiqui, OBE, holds a chair in Islamic and interreligious studies at the University of Edinburgh. She contributes widely to the media and public debates on religion and society. Her research areas are primarily in the field of Islamic jurisprudence (*fiqh*) and ethics and Christian-Muslim relations. Among her publications are *Human Struggle* (Cambridge University Press, 2021); *Hospitality in Islam: Welcoming in God's Name* (Yale University Press, 2015); *Christians, Muslims and Jesus* (Yale University Press, 2013); and *The Good Muslim: Reflections on Classical Islamic Law and Theology* (Cambridge University Press, 2012). She is a fellow of the American Academy of Arts and Sciences and a fellow of the Royal Society of Edinburgh.

James Spickard recently retired after thirty-one years of teaching at the University of Redlands, Redlands, California. Most of his courses were in sociology and anthropology, particularly social theory, the sociology of religion, social inequality, the American class system, international development, and social science research design. He also taught in the programs of religious studies, environmental studies, and visual/media studies.

Michael Reid Trice is the Spehar-Halligan Professor and founding director of the Center for Ecumenical and Interreligious Engagement (CEIE) at Seattle University, Washington, and the founder of Religica Theolab, a popular virtual and multimedia platform. Trice also adopted into the CEIE platform *The Interfaith Observer*, an online popular journal and substantial archive of firsthand accounts that promotes cultural, religious, indigenous, and values-based fluencies around the world. Trice's first book, *Encountering Cruelty: The Fracture of the Human Heart* (Brill, 2011), won the humanities award at Loyola University, Chicago. Trice participated on a Vatican dicastery ecology interreligious advisory committee through the Parliament of the World's Religions, served as a fellow at the Science for Seminaries program of the American Association for the Advancement of Science and at the Shalom Hartman Institute in Jerusalem, and is coeditor of a forthcoming volume on leadership and creative innovation through an Ignatian lens (Georgetown University Press, 2026).

Nathanael Vette is Teaching Fellow in New Testament and Christian Origins at the School of Divinity, University of Edinburgh. His research focuses on varieties of Jewish and Christian experience within the Roman empire in the early centuries CE, particularly between the two Great Revolts (70–130 CE). He is the coeditor with Mona Siddiqui of *A Theology of Gratitude: Christian and Muslim Perspectives* (Cambridge University Press, 2022) and the author of *Writing with Scripture: Scripturalized Narrative in the Gospel of Mark* (Bloomsbury, 2022).

INDEX

Abraham, Susan, 179
affect, 81–83
age of pandemic, 114–120
AIDS/HIV pandemic, 76, 79, 81, 83, 85
Aitareya Upaniṣad, 99
Albanese, Catherine, 20
algophobia, 88
alt-right, 52, 66, 68
Ambedkar, B. R., 101
American Psychological Association, 182n2
anti-Blackness, 116, 117
appreciation of life, 150
Aquinas, Thomas, 90
Arendt, Hannah, 90, 139, 163–164
avidyā (ignorance), 99
Azusa Street Mission, 125

Babylonian exile and Jews experience, analogy between, 36–37
Bageant, Joe, 61
Baldwin, James, 114, 117, 138
Barber, Stephen M., 79
Bellah, Robert, 53–54, 65–67
  on civil religion, 54–59
Benjamin, Walter, 89
Bhagavadgītā, 99–101, 104, 105
Biden, Joe, 15, 62
biopolitics, 87
Black Death of 1347–51, 20
Black Lives Matter movement, 11, 123, 126–127n33, 130
Black Theology and Black Power (Cone), 125–126n2
Bonaventure, Saint, 76, 78
Boston Tea Party, 55, 64
boundary experiences, 9, 19–22, 24
bounded rationality, 180
Bradford, William, 56
Brooks, David, 67–68
Burnout Society, The (Han), 87
Butler, Judith, 139, 165

Calhoun, John C., 56
Calhoun, L., 149
care for the soul, 14–15
Caruth, Cathy, 156
caste, 97–98, 105, 107, 108, 111, 115, 117
  dismantling, 101–102
casteism, 112, 173, 180
cataclysm, 9, 19, 20, 22, 24, 27, 32
CDC. *See* Centers for Disease Control and Prevention (CDC)
CEIE. *See* Center for Ecumenical and Interreligious Engagement (CEIE), Seattle University
Center for Ecumenical and Interreligious Engagement (CEIE), Seattle University, 3–4
  "Gratitude to God, Sacred Texts, Injury and Restoration," 1, 173
Centers for Disease Control and Prevention (CDC), 159, 166
Chandogya Upaniṣad, 100

change, 25
Chanter, Tina, 165
Chinese Exclusion Act of 1882, 134
Choi, Meera, 134
Christian Century, The, 6
cisheteropatriarchy, 117, 118, 126n15
  capitalist, 115, 119, 124
  elite, 116
civil religion, 52–68
"Civil Religion in America." (Bellah), 53
Clark, David L., 79
Coates, Ta-Nehisi, 62
cognitive dissonance, 23
Colasurdo, Christine, 22
common good, 105–106
compassion, 44, 102, 110, 111, 149, 164–166
Cone, James H., 125–126n2
conspiracy theories, 158
Constitution of the United States, 55–57
  Article 1, section 9, clause 1, 69n22
Copeland, M. Shawn, 131
coping, 11, 158, 161, 164
courage, 15, 63, 77, 149, 168
Cox, Karen, 60
creation, 18, 25–28, 30, 55, 88, 99, 107, 108, 112, 123, 179, 182n5
Crenshaw, Kimberlé, 122
"Crisis of Freedom, The" (Han), 87
Crockett, Davy, 59

David, A. S., 159
Davoine, Françoise, 163
decentering, 19, 20
Declaration of Independence, 55
Deer Hunting with Jesus (Bageant), 61
dehumanization, 118, 120, 123–125
Deleuze, Giles, 164
denial, 23, 27, 28, 101, 120, 158–159
destruction, 11, 16, 20, 23–28, 30, 31, 35, 36, 39–43, 46, 48, 143, 150
dhanyavād, 108
dharma, 104–105
Diagnostic and Statistical Manual of Mental Disorders (DSM-5), 146, 157
Didion, Joan, 66
dignity, 97–98
Di Nicola, Vincenzo, 160, 161
discrimination, 11, 62, 122, 145
  anti-Asian, 133
  institutionalized, 134
  reverse, 12, 119
dislocation, 8, 175, 176
  of gratitude, 9, 18–32
disorientation, 6, 22, 132–136
divine-human unity, 101–102
divine is joy (*raso vai sah*), 100
divine virtue, gratitude as, 106–108
Donalson, Edward, 12, 176
Dred Scott decision, 57
dualism, 99
dwelling, 164

Eckhart, Meister, 90
Edsall, Thomas, 62, 63
"Elevator, The" (Yancy), 165
Emancipation Proclamation, 57
Emerson, Ralph Waldo, 14
equality, 52, 53, 55–58
  racial, 11
  social, 165. *See also* inequality
extraordinary boundaries, 20

Fight Club, 60
"First White President, The" (Coates), 62
fiscus Iudaicus (Jewish tax), 36–37
Floyd, George, murder of, 11–12, 13, 130, 135–136
Foucault, Michel, 84, 87
Francis, Pope, 133, 168
Frankl, Viktor, 148
Franklin, Benjamin, 53, 55
Franklin, Jerry F., 25, 26
Friedman, Milton, 66

Galston, William, 61
Gandhi, Mahatma, 166
Garrett-Akinsanya, BraVada, 11–12
Gaudillière, Jean-Max, 163
generational trauma, 144–145, 147, 148, 152
generosity, 15, 21, 99, 101, 108
gift of human existence, 98–101
Gilgamesh, 182n10
Girard, René, 133
Godfather, The, 60
Goodrich, Charles, 24
Gorman, Amanda, 167
Gorski, Philip, 55–56, 69n18
gratitude, 1, 5–16, 66–68, 81
  and common good, 105–106
  destabilization of, 22–24
  and dharma, 104–105
  and dignity, 97–98
  dislocating, 9, 18–20, 31–32
  as divine virtue, 106–108
  and gift of human existence, 98–101
  and interdependence, 102–104
  and lessons of pandemic, 109–111
  and post-traumatic growth, 151–152
  relocated, 28–31
  as revolutionary act of resistance, 114–125
  and yajña, 104–105. See also *individual entries*
"Gratitude, Injury, and Repair in a Pandemic Age," 52
grief, 9, 10, 12, 15, 16, 25, 84, 91, 93, 121, 130, 148, 168–169, 174
Gunfighter Nation (Slotkin), 60

Han, Byung-Chul, 77, 78, 86–94
hate, 12, 36, 37, 48, 80, 97, 98, 109
  crimes, 130, 133, 134
  groups, 188
  speech, 110
Heidegger, Martin, 164, 182n9
Henry Luce Foundation, 4n1
Herman, Judith, 162
High Noon, 60
Hinduism, 97–112
Hirshfield, Jane, 19
Hochschild, Arlie, 61
Homolar, Alexandra, 62
hope, 6, 14–16, 21, 27, 53, 66–68, 77, 83, 86, 92, 132, 136, 153, 156, 157, 160
humility, 15, 24, 102, 106
Hunter, E. C., 159

idiotism, 92
Ignatius of Loyola, 4
illegal slave trade, 69n23
imagination, 15–16
incarnation (*avatāra*), 99, 106
Independence Day, 60
inequality, 67, 101, 112, 123, 157, 165
  caste, 108
  economic, 66
  global, 10
  health, 13
  political, 66
  racial, 13
  social, 66
  of social institutions, 11
  structural, 108, 111. *See also* equality
inhumanity, 97
injury, 5–16, 111, 156–162
  Jews among gentiles and, 35–48
  as rupture, 7–8
injustice, 11, 68, 98, 102, 106, 111, 112, 119, 125, 138, 177, 178, 180
  class, 67
  climate, 67
  racial, 3, 67
  structural, 3, 32
  systemic, 179
interdependence, 102–104
intersectional theo-logic, for pandemic world, 122–125

In the Blast Zone: Catastrophe and Renewal on Mount St. Helens (Moore), 22
isolation, 9, 112, 157, 158, 160, 162, 168, 178
Itinerarium (Bonaventure), 78

Jackson, Andrew, 56
Janus, Mark-David, 129
Jayagopal, Sathish, 13
Jefferson, Thomas, 53, 57
Jeffries, Stuart, 87
Jews among gentiles, and injury, 35–48
  70 C.E. to 135 C.E., 40–42
  164 B.C.E. to 135 C.E., 37–40
  after 135 C.E., 42–46
  moral injuries, 46–47
  moral repair in pandemic age, 47–48
Johnson, Lyndon, 53
Joothan: An Untouchable's Life (Valmiki), 97–98
Joseph, Jaisy, 6
Judaism, 37, 39–42, 46, 49n10, 123

Kafka, Franz, 91
kāmadhuk, 103
Kant, Immanuel, 30
Kao, Grace, 134
Keenan, James F., 130, 136–137, 139
Kennedy, John F., 54, 55
kenosis, 177
Kierkegaard, Søren, 6
Kimmerer, Robin Wall, 23, 24, 26, 27, 30
King, Martin Luther, Jr., 137, 138, 165
Kruse, Kevin, 61

laissez-faire capitalism, 117
Lee, Erika, 134
Lee, Kristi, 174
Le Guin, Ursula, 23, 24, 27, 30, 31
"Letter from Birmingham Jail" (King), 137
"Letters to White Liberals" (King), 137
Levinas, Emmanuel, 139
liberalism, 78, 135
libertarianism: Christian, 61, 62
  leftist, 78
Lincoln, Abraham, 53–54, 65, 68, 69n23, 69, 70n25
  on capital punishment against slave trader, 57
  on declaration limited equality to whites, 56–57
  Gettysburg Address, 58
Lind, Michael, 66
Lisbon earthquake of 1755, 20
Lischer, Richard, 6
Lloyd, Vincent W., 133, 135, 139
lockdown, 6–11, 130, 132, 133, 135
Löfflmann, Georg, 62
lokasaṁgraham, 103, 105, 106
loneliness, 11, 158, 177, 182n2
Lowell, Robert, 58
Lucas, Ryan, 162

Mackenzie, Catriona, 164
Malcolm X, 138
marginalization, 46, 115, 117, 118, 122, 124, 167, 180
Marion, Jean-Luc: 164
Marx, Karl, 87
masochism, 92
Massingale, Bryan, 135–136, 138–139
Mazure, Carolyn M., 159–160
McNulty, Tim, 25
McVeigh, Timothy, 60
Merleau-Ponty, Maurice, 155, 169
Merton, Thomas, 137–140
Moore, Kathleen Dean, 18, 23–24, 31
Moore, Thomas, 14–15
Morrison, Toni, 16
Mount St. Helens, volcanic eruption in, 8–9, 18–32
  boundary experiences, 19–22

gratitude, destabilizing, 22–24
Moynihan Report of 1965, 118
Myrdal, Gunnar, 62

Nagpaul, Chaand, 13
narrative, importance of, 167–169
National Health Service (NHS), 13
neoliberalism, 87
new life, 23, 24, 28, 30, 31
NHS. *See* National Health Service (NHS)
Niebuhr, Reinhold, 69–70n25
Nietzsche, Friedrich, 90, 91, 165, 167
Nixon, Richard: second inaugural address, 58
nonbeing, zone of, 114–121
non-dual (*advaita*), 100
nonviolence (*ahiṃsā*), 111, 165
North, Carol, 157
North America: culture of, 115, 116
racialized caste system, 117

Oakes, James, 69n23
Omicron, 15
oppression, 12, 32, 44, 53, 59, 83, 98, 102, 105, 110, 111, 114, 115, 117–121, 126–127n33, 179, 180
class, 125
of the Raj, 166
Roman, 131
systemic, 78, 82
Orange, Donna, 163
ordinary boundaries, 20
Origins of Totalitarianism, The (Arendt), 163–164
O'Toole, Fintan, 65
"Yeats Test" for direness, 52–53
Otto, Rudolph, 182n6

paganism, 37
Palliative Society, The (Han), 88, 91
pandemic heresies, 86–92
pandemic queering, 79–86
pandemic thoughts, 76–78
paranoia, 82, 83
"Paranoid Reading and Reparative Reading, or, You're So Paranoid, You Probably Think This Essay Is about You" (Sedgwick), 78
patience, 92
"Pedagogy of Seeing, The" (Han), 90
Peduti, Douglas, 7, 175, 179
Pence, Mike, 63
Pentecostalism, 122–125
Perry, Samuel, 63
personal strength, 149–150
phármakon, 161
Piketty, Thomas, 66
police brutality, 118, 130, 135, 137, 140, 162, 180
polycrisis, 181
post-traumatic growth (PTG), 144
appreciation of life, 150
elements of, 148–149
facilitation of, 151
gratitude and, 151–152
new possibilities, 150
personal strength, 149–150
promotion of, 151
relating to others, 149
as restoration, 148
spiritual and existential change, 150–151
post-traumatic stress, 145–146
post-traumatic stress disorder (PTSD), 146–148
prejudice, 138
racial, 12
systemic, 11
Prideaux, Ed, 7
Proust, Marcel, 91
psychological harm, 27
psychopolitics, 88, 92
PTG. *See* post-traumatic growth (PTG)
PTSD. *See* post-traumatic stress disorder (PTSD)

QAnon theory, 64
queer performativity, 79, 81

race, 62, 100, 110, 116–117, 122, 125, 145, 159
racial superiority, 138
racial unrest, 53
racism, 13, 52, 64, 109, 112, 125, 130, 134, 136, 137
  institutionalized, 135
  societal, 180
  structural, 62, 174, 175
  systemic, 145, 173
Raffoul, François, 164
Rambo, Shelly, 167
Regeneration through Violence (Slotkin), 60
relational home, 163
religion, 20
  civil, 52–68
  competing, 59–62
religious practice (*sadhana dhāma*), 99
reorientation, 136–140
repair, 2, 26–28, 32, 53, 67, 81, 93, 111, 155–157, 160–169, 173, 181
  interpersonal, 47
  moral, 37, 47–48
  structural, 177
resilience, 7, 11, 25, 26, 29, 30, 77, 84, 178
restoration, 2, 5–16, 27, 30, 38, 47, 63, 121, 132, 173, 174
  post-traumatic growth as, 148
"Rethinking Humanity's Progress in Light of COVID-19," (Keenan), 136–137
retrenchment, theory of, 41
reverence, 29, 100, 106, 177
Rittenhouse, Kyle, 60
Rāmacaritamānasa (Tulasīdāsa), 106
Rogers, Robert, 18
Roman Empire, 37, 42
Roosevelt, Teddy: "Rough Rider" imperialism, 60
Rosenquist, Gary, 18
Rousseau, Jean-Jacques, 54
Roy, Arundhati, 10, 13, 27
Russell, Bertrand, 16

sacred scriptures, 131–132
sadism, 92
Sam's Club, 134
Sanders, Scott Russell, 28–29
saturated experience, 167
Scarsella, Hilary Jerome, 156
Schubert, Franz, 91
Second Amendment, 64
Sedgwick, Eve Kosofsky, 77–86, 89, 92, 93
self-affirmation, 100
self-degradation (*nātmānam avasādayet*), 100
self-determination, 12, 120
self-worth (*uddhared ātmanātmanaṁ*), 100
Shoop, Marcia Mount, 167
Sierra, M., 159
sin, 119
Slotkin, Richard, 59–60
social distancing, 118
Society of Jesus, 4
solitude, 11, 92
spiritual harm, 27
Sri Ramakrishna, 102
Star Wars, 60
Stewart, Katherine, 64–65
Stiegler, Bernard, 89
Stolorow, Robert, 163
Stop AAPI Hate, 133, 134
structural racism, 62, 174, 175
suffering to others (*hiṃsā*), 111
sukṛtám, 99
Swami Tyagananda, 101
Swanson, Frederick, 24

tadevānupraviśhat, 99
Taittirīya Upaniṣad, 99, 100, 102–103
Tea Party Movement, 64
Tedeschi, Richard, 149
Tendencies (Sedgwick), 79, 80, 82, 83
Tessler, Hannah, 134
thanatophobia, 88
theory for the sick and dying, 92–94
Thirteenth Amendment, 57
Thurman, Howard, 120
Toynbee, Arnold, 16
Tractatus (Wittgenstein), 163
transcendence, 20
  divine, 78
  self-transcendence, 78
trauma, 143–153
  definition of, 156
  generational, 144–145, 147, 148, 152
  personal, 162, 163
  as psychic therapy, 144–145
  social, 162, 163
  traumatic ontology, 155–169. See also *individual entries*
Trees of Goodness, 120
Trigg, Dylan, 156, 168
Trueblood, Elton, 69–70n25
Trump, Donald, 15, 62–64, 126n15, 134
Tulasīdāsa, 106
Twilight of the Idols (Nietzsche), 90

uncertainty: in pandemic age, 6–7, 15, 58, 132–137, 139, 140, 174
  socioeconomic, 130
United States (US): Capitol, 52, 62, 63
  civil religion, 52–68
  Congress, 56, 57
  Immigration and Nationality Act of 1965, 60
  "manifest destiny," 60
  National Rifle Association, 60
  policing system, 117
Upaniṣads, 99, 100, 102
US. *See* United States (US)

vaccination, 15, 160, 166
Valmiki, Omprakash, 97–98
Van Cleve, George, 56
Vette, Nathanael, 176
Vicini, Andrea, 133, 135
Vietnam War, 53, 58, 66, 175
Vivekacūḍāmaṇi, 98–99
Vogt, Tony, 24, 27

Wach, Joachim, 20
Warm Decembers, The (Sedgwick), 80–81
Washington, George, 53, 55
Weller, Francis, 180–181
Whitehead, Andrew, 63
whiteness, 116–117
white supremacy, 12, 64, 117, 119, 134
Willimon, William H., 6
Wittgenstein, Ludwig, 163
World Economic Forum, 181
World Health Organization, 1, 157, 173, 182n1
World War II, 41, 155

xenophobia, 109, 130, 134, 136, 137, 140, 173

yajña, 103–105
Yale School of Medicine, 159
Yancy, George, 165

Zen Buddhism, 84–85, 90
Zwinger, Ann, 29–31
Zwinger, Susan, 25